CentOS 8 Essentials

CentOS 8 Essentials

ISBN-13: 978-1-951442-09-5

Rev: 1.0

Contents

Table of Contents

1. Introduction 1

    1.1 Superuser Conventions.. 1

    1.2 Feedback 2

    1.3 Errata.. 2

    1.4 Download the eBook 2

2. A Brief History of CentOS Linux 3

    2.1 What exactly is Linux?... 3

    2.2 UNIX Origins 3

    2.3 Who Created Linux? 3

    2.4 The Early Days of Red Hat 4

    2.5 Red Hat Support... 4

    2.6 Open Source... 5

    2.7 The Fedora Project 5

    2.8 CentOS - The Free Alternative 5

    2.9 Summary 5

3. Installing CentOS 8 on a Clean Disk Drive 7

    3.1 Obtaining the CentOS Installation Media 7

    3.2 Writing the ISO Installation Image to a USB Drive.. 8

        3.2.1 Linux... 8

        3.2.2 macOS 9

        3.2.3 Windows 10

    3.3 Installing CentOS 8 11

    3.4 Partitioning a Disk for CentOS 8 15

    3.5 The Physical Installation 19

    3.6 Final Configuration Steps.. 20

    3.7 Installing Updates... 20

    3.8 Displaying Boot Messages... 20

    3.9 Summary 21

4. Dual Booting CentOS 8 with Windows 23

    4.1 Partition Resizing... 23

    4.2 Editing the CentOS 8 Boot Menu 25

    4.3 Changing the Default Boot Option... 26

    4.4 Accessing the Windows Partition from CentOS 8.. 28

    4.5 Summary 29

5. Allocating Windows Disk Partitions to CentOS 8 31

Table of Contents

5.1 Unmounting the Windows Partition 31
5.2 Deleting the Windows Partitions from the Disk 31
5.3 Formatting the Unallocated Disk Partition 34
5.4 Mounting the New Partition 34
5.5 Editing the Boot Menu 35
5.6 Summary 35

6. A Guided Tour of the GNOME 3 Desktop 37
6.1 Installing the GNOME Desktop 37
6.2 An Overview of the GNOME 3 Desktop 37
6.3 Launching Activities 38
6.4 Managing Windows 41
6.5 Using Workspaces 42
6.6 Calendar and Notifications 42
6.7 Desktop Settings 43
6.8 Summary 44

7. An Overview of the CentOS 8 Cockpit Web Interface 45
7.1 An Overview of Cockpit 45
7.2 Installing and Enabling Cockpit 46
7.3 Accessing Cockpit 46
7.4 System 47
7.5 Logs 47
7.6 Storage 48
7.7 Networking 48
7.8 Virtual Machines 49
7.9 Accounts 49
7.10 Services 50
7.11 Applications 50
7.12 Diagnostic Reports 50
7.13 Kernel Dump 51
7.14 SELinux 51
7.15 Software Updates 51
7.16 Terminal 52
7.17 Connecting to Multiple Servers 52
7.18 Enabling Stored Metrics 54
7.19 Summary 55

8. Using the Bash Shell on CentOS 8 57
8.1 What is a Shell? 57
8.2 Gaining Access to the Shell 57
8.3 Entering Commands at the Prompt 58
8.4 Getting Information about a Command 58

8.5 Bash Command-line Editing..58

8.6 Working with the Shell History...59

8.7 Filename Shorthand..60

8.8 Filename and Path Completion...60

8.9 Input and Output Redirection...60

8.10 Working with Pipes in the Bash Shell...61

8.11 Configuring Aliases 61

8.12 Environment Variables...62

8.13 Writing Shell Scripts 63

8.14 Summary...64

9. Managing CentOS 8 Users and Groups **65**

9.1 User Management from the Command-line 65

9.2 User Management with Cockpit..67

9.3 Summary...69

10. Understanding CentOS 8 Software Installation and Management...................**71**

10.1 Repositories..71

10.2 The BaseOS Repository 72

10.3 The AppStream Repository 73

10.4 Summary...76

11. Configuring CentOS 8 systemd Units..**77**

11.1 Understanding CentOS 8 systemd Targets...77

11.2 Understanding CentOS 8 systemd Services...77

11.3 CentOS 8 systemd Target Descriptions..77

11.4 Identifying and Configuring the Default Target 79

11.5 Understanding systemd Units and Unit Types.......................................80

11.6 Dynamically Changing the Current Target 80

11.7 Enabling, Disabling and Masking systemd Units 81

11.8 Working with systemd Units in Cockpit..82

11.9 Summary...84

12. CentOS 8 Network Management..**85**

12.1 An Introduction to NetworkManager...85

12.2 Installing and Enabling NetworkManager..86

12.3 Basic nmcli Commands..86

12.4 Working with Connection Profiles 90

12.5 Interactive Editing...92

12.6 Configuring NetworkManager Permissions..94

12.7 Summary...94

13. Basic CentOS 8 Firewall Configuration with firewalld **95**

13.1 An Introduction to firewalld..95

13.1.1 Zones 95

13.1.2 Interfaces..96

13.1.3 Services..97

13.1.4 Ports..97

13.2 Checking firewalld Status 97

13.3 Configuring Firewall Rules with firewall-cmd 97

13.3.1 Identifying and Changing the Default Zone 98

13.3.2 Displaying Zone Information 98

13.3.3 Adding and Removing Zone Services 99

13.3.4 Working with Port-based Rules 99

13.3.5 Creating a New Zone...100

13.3.6 Changing Zone/Interface Assignments 100

13.3.7 Masquerading 100

13.3.8 Adding ICMP Rules 100

13.3.9 Implementing Port Forwarding..101

13.4 Managing firewalld from the Cockpit Interface...102

13.5 Managing firewalld using firewall-config 102

13.6 Summary..104

14. Configuring SSH Key-based Authentication on CentOS 8 105

14.1 An Overview of Secure Shell (SSH)..105

14.2 SSH Key-based Authentication 105

14.3 Setting Up Key-based Authentication 106

14.4 SSH Key-based Authentication from Linux and macOS Clients....................106

14.5 Managing Multiple Keys 108

14.6 SSH Key-based Authentication from Windows 10 Clients 109

14.7 SSH Key-based Authentication using PuTTY 110

14.8 Generating a Private Key with PuTTYgen 112

14.9 Installing the Public Key for a Google Cloud Instance 113

14.10 Summary..114

15. CentOS 8 Remote Desktop Access with VNC...117

15.1 Secure and Insecure Remote Desktop Access 117

15.2 Installing the GNOME Desktop Environment 117

15.3 Installing VNC on CentOS 8 119

15.4 Configuring the VNC Server...119

15.5 Connecting to a VNC Server...120

15.6 Establishing a Secure Remote Desktop Session 121

15.7 Establishing a Secure Tunnel on Windows using PuTTY 123

15.8 Shutting Down a Desktop Session 124

15.9 Troubleshooting a VNC Connection 124

15.10 Summary..125

16. Displaying CentOS 8 Applications Remotely (X11 Forwarding)....................127

16.1 Requirements for Remotely Displaying CentOS 8 Applications 127
16.2 Remotely Displaying a CentOS 8 Application 128
16.3 Trusted X11 Forwarding 128
16.4 Compressed X11 Forwarding 128
16.5 Displaying Remote CentOS 8 Apps on Windows................................... 129
16.6 Summary 132

17. Using NFS to Share CentOS 8 Files with Remote Systems 133

17.1 Ensuring NFS Services are running on CentOS 8 133
17.2 Configuring the CentOS 8 Firewall to Allow NFS Traffic 134
17.3 Specifying the Folders to be Shared 134
17.4 Accessing Shared CentOS 8 Folders 135
17.5 Mounting an NFS Filesystem on System Startup 135
17.6 Unmounting an NFS Mount Point 135
17.7 Accessing NFS Filesystems in Cockpit 136
17.8 Summary 137

18. Sharing Files between CentOS 8 and Windows Systems with Samba........................... 139

18.1 Samba and Samba Client... 139
18.2 Installing Samba on a CentOS 8 System 139
18.3 Configuring the CentOS 8 Firewall to Enable Samba 140
18.4 Configuring the *smb.conf* File 140
    18.4.1 Configuring the [global] Section.. 140
    18.4.2 Configuring a Shared Resource 141
    18.4.3 Removing Unnecessary Shares 142
18.5 Configuring SELinux for Samba 142
18.6 Creating a Samba User 144
18.7 Testing the *smb.conf* File... 144
18.8 Starting the Samba and NetBIOS Name Services 146
18.9 Accessing Samba Shares 146
18.10 Accessing Windows Shares from CentOS 8 148
18.11 Summary 149

19. An Overview of Virtualization Techniques 151

19.1 Guest Operating System Virtualization 151
19.2 Hypervisor Virtualization 152
    19.2.1 Paravirtualization 153
    19.2.2 Full Virtualization.. 154
    19.2.3 Hardware Virtualization 154
19.3 Virtual Machine Networking... 155
19.4 Summary 155

20. Installing KVM Virtualization on CentOS 8 157

20.1 An Overview of KVM 157

20.2 KVM Hardware Requirements..157

20.3 Preparing CentOS 8 for KVM Virtualization 158

20.4 Verifying the KVM Installation..158

20.5 Summary 160

21. Creating KVM Virtual Machines using Cockpit and virt-manager......................161

21.1 Installing the Cockpit Virtual Machines Module 161

21.2 Creating a Virtual Machine in Cockpit 161

21.3 Starting the Installation 163

21.4 Creating a Virtual Machine using virt-manager..165

21.5 Starting the Virtual Machine Manager..165

21.6 Configuring the KVM Virtual System 166

21.7 Starting the KVM Virtual Machine 168

21.8 Summary 169

22. Creating KVM Virtual Machines with virt-install and virsh 171

22.1 Running virt-install to build a KVM Guest System 171

22.2 An Example CentOS 8 virt-install Command 172

22.3 Starting and Stopping a Virtual Machine from the Command-Line..............173

22.4 Creating a Virtual Machine from a Configuration File................................173

22.5 Summary 173

23. Creating a CentOS 8 KVM Networked Bridge Interface....................................175

23.1 Getting the Current Network Settings 175

23.2 Creating a Network Bridge from the Command-Line...................................177

23.3 Declaring the KVM Bridged Network 178

23.4 Using a Bridge Network in a Virtual Machine 179

23.5 Creating a Bridge Network using nm-connection-editor...............................180

23.6 Summary 183

24. Managing KVM using the virsh Command-Line Tool 185

24.1 The virsh Shell and Command-Line...185

24.2 Listing Guest System Status 186

24.3 Starting a Guest System 187

24.4 Shutting Down a Guest System 187

24.5 Suspending and Resuming a Guest System 187

24.6 Saving and Restoring Guest Systems 187

24.7 Rebooting a Guest System 188

24.8 Configuring the Memory Assigned to a Guest OS 188

24.9 Summary 188

25. An Introduction to Linux Containers...189

25.1 Linux Containers and Kernel Sharing..189

25.2 Container Uses and Advantages...190

25.3 CentOS 8 Container Tools 191
25.4 The Docker Registry 191
25.5 Container Networking.. 192
25.6 Summary 192

26. Working with Containers on CentOS 8 193

26.1 Pulling a Container Image 193
26.2 Running the Image in a Container 195
26.3 Managing a Container 196
26.4 Saving a Container to an Image 197
26.5 Removing an Image from Local Storage 197
26.6 Removing Containers.. 198
26.7 Building a Container with Buildah 198
26.8 Building a Container from Scratch 198
26.9 Container Bridge Networking 199
26.10 Summary 201

27. Setting Up a CentOS 8 Web Server 203

27.1 Requirements for Configuring a CentOS 8 Web Server 203
27.2 Installing the Apache Web Server Packages 203
27.3 Configuring the Firewall 204
27.4 Port Forwarding 204
27.5 Starting the Apache Web Server 204
27.6 Testing the Web Server 204
27.7 Configuring the Apache Web Server for Your Domain 205
27.8 The Basics of a Secure Web Site... 206
27.9 Configuring Apache for HTTPS 207
27.10 Obtaining an SSL Certificate 207
27.11 Summary.. 210

28. Configuring a CentOS 8 Postfix Email Server..211

28.1 The structure of the Email System 211
28.1.1 Mail User Agent 211
28.1.2 Mail Transfer Agent 211
28.1.3 Mail Delivery Agent 212
28.1.4 SMTP 212
28.1.5 SMTP Relay... 212
28.2 Configuring a CentOS 8 Email Server 212
28.3 Postfix Pre-Installation Steps 212
28.4 Firewall/Router Configuration.. 213
28.5 Installing Postfix on CentOS 8 213
28.6 Configuring Postfix 213
28.7 Configuring DNS MX Records 215

28.8 Starting Postfix on a CentOS 8 System..215
28.9 Testing Postfix..215
28.10 Sending Mail via an SMTP Relay Server..216
28.11 Summary...217

29. Adding a New Disk Drive to a CentOS 8 System 219

29.1 Mounted File Systems or Logical Volumes 219
29.2 Finding the New Hard Drive 219
29.3 Creating Linux Partitions 220
29.4 Creating a File System on a CentOS 8 Disk Partition 221
29.5 An Overview of Journaled File Systems...221
29.6 Mounting a File System 222
29.7 Configuring CentOS 8 to Automatically Mount a File System 223
29.8 Adding a Disk Using Cockpit 223
29.9 Summary...225

30. Adding a New Disk to a CentOS 8 Volume Group and Logical Volume..........227

30.1 An Overview of Logical Volume Management (LVM) 227
30.1.1 Volume Group (VG)...227
30.1.2 Physical Volume (PV) 227
30.1.3 Logical Volume (LV) 228
30.1.4 Physical Extent (PE) 228
30.1.5 Logical Extent (LE) 228
30.2 Getting Information about Logical Volumes 228
30.3 Adding Additional Space to a Volume Group from the Command-Line 230
30.4 Adding Additional Space to a Volume Group using Cockpit 232
30.5 Summary...234

31. Adding and Managing CentOS 8 Swap Space..235

31.1 What is Swap Space? 235
31.2 Recommended Swap Space for CentOS 8..235
31.3 Identifying Current Swap Space Usage 235
31.4 Adding a Swap File to a CentOS 8 System 236
31.5 Adding Swap as a Partition 237
31.6 Adding Space to a CentOS 8 LVM Swap Volume..237
31.7 Adding Swap Space to the Volume Group...238
31.8 Summary...240

Index...241

1. Introduction

CentOS 8 Essentials is designed to provide detailed information on the installation, use and administration of the distribution. For beginners, the book covers topics such as operating system installation, the basics of the GNOME desktop environment, configuring email and web servers and installing packages and system updates using App Streams. Additional installation topics such as dual booting with Microsoft Windows are also covered, together with all important security topics such as configuring a firewall and user and group administration.

For the experienced user, topics such as remote desktop access, the Cockpit web interface, logical volume management (LVM), disk partitioning, swap management, KVM virtualization, Secure Shell (SSH), Linux Containers and file sharing using both Samba and NFS are covered in detail to provide a thorough overview of this enterprise class operating system.

1.1 Superuser Conventions

CentOS 8, in common with Linux in general, has two types of user account, one being a standard user account with restricted access to many of the administrative files and features of the operating system, and the other a superuser (*root*) account with elevated privileges. Typically, a user can gain root access either by logging in as the root user, or using the *su* - command and entering the root password. In the following example, a user is gaining root access via the *su* - command:

```
[neil@centos8-demo ~]$ su -
Password:
[root@centos8-demo ~]#
```

Note that the command prompt for a regular user ends with a $ sign while the root user has a # character. When working with the command-line, this is a useful indication as to whether or not you are currently issuing commands as the root user.

Alternatively, a single command requiring root privileges may be executed by a non-root user via the *sudo* command. Consider the following attempt to update the operating system with the latest patches and packages:

```
[neil@centos8-demo ~]$ dnf update
Not root, Subscription Management repositories not updated
Error: This command has to be run under the root user.
```

Optionally, user accounts may be configured so that they have access to root level privileges. Instead of using the *su* - command to first gain root access, user accounts with administration privileges are able to run otherwise restricted commands using *sudo*.

```
[neil@centos8-demo]$ sudo dnf update

We trust you have received the usual lecture from the local System
Administrator. It usually boils down to these three things:
```

```
#1) Respect the privacy of others.
#2) Think before you type.
#3) With great power comes great responsibility.

[sudo] password for neil:
Updating Subscription Management repositories.
.

.
```

The reason for raising this issue so early in the book is that many of the command-line examples outlined in this book will require root privileges. Rather than repetitively preface every command-line example with directions to run the command as root, the command prompt at the start of the line will be used to indicate whether or not the command needs to be performed as root. If the command can be run as a regular user, the command will be prefixed with a $ command prompt as follows:

```
$ date
```

If, on the other hand, the command requires root privileges, the command will be preceded by a # command prompt:

```
# dnf install openssh
```

1.2 Feedback

We want you to be satisfied with your purchase of this book. If you find any errors in the book, or have any comments, questions or concerns please contact us at *feedback@ebookfrenzy.com*.

1.3 Errata

While we make every effort to ensure the accuracy of the content of this book, it is inevitable that a book covering a subject area of this size and complexity may include some errors and oversights. Any known issues with the book will be outlined, together with solutions, at the following URL:

https://www.ebookfrenzy.com/errata/centos8.html

In the event that you find an error not listed in the errata, please let us know by emailing our technical support team at *feedback@ebookfrenzy.com*. They are there to help you and will work to resolve any problems you may encounter.

1.4 Download the eBook

Thank you for purchasing the print edition of this book. If you would like to download the PDF version of this book, please email proof of purchase (for example a receipt, delivery notice or photo of the physical book) to *feedback@ebookfrenzy.com* and we will provide you with a download link for the book in PDF format.

2. A Brief History of CentOS Linux

CentOS is one of a number of variants (also referred to as *distributions*) of the Linux operating system. It is based on the source code of the Red Hat Enterprise Linux distribution, developed by a U.S. company named Red Hat, Inc., based in Raleigh, North Carolina. The company was founded in the mid-1990s through the merger of two companies owned at the time by Marc Ewing and Bob Young. The origins of Linux, however, go back even further. This chapter will outline the history of both the Linux operating system and Red Hat, Inc. before explaining how CentOS fits into this picture.

2.1 What exactly is Linux?

Linux is an operating system in much the same way that Windows is an operating system (and there any similarities between Linux and Windows end). The term operating system is used to describe the software that acts as a layer between the hardware in a computer and the applications that we all run on a daily basis. When programmers write applications, they interface with the operating system to perform such tasks as writing files to the hard disk drive and displaying information on the screen. Without an operating system, every programmer would have to write code to directly access the hardware of the system. In addition, the programmer would have to be able to support every single piece of hardware ever created to be sure the application would work on every possible hardware configuration. Because the operating system handles all of this hardware complexity, application development becomes a much easier task. Linux is just one of a number of different operating systems available today.

2.2 UNIX Origins

To understand the history of Linux, we first have to go back to AT&T Bell Laboratories in the late 1960s. During this time AT&T had discontinued involvement in the development of a new operating system named Multics. Two AT&T engineers, Ken Thompson and Dennis Ritchie, decided to take what they had learned from the Multics project and create a new operating system named UNIX which quickly gained popularity and wide adoption both with corporations and academic institutions.

A variety of proprietary UNIX implementations eventually came to market including those created by IBM (AIX), Hewlett-Packard (HP-UX) and Sun Microsystems (SunOS and Solaris). In addition, a UNIX-like operating system named MINIX was created by Andrew S. Tanenbaum designed for educational use with source code access provided to universities.

2.3 Who Created Linux?

The origins of Linux can be traced back to the work and philosophies of two people. At the heart of the Linux operating system is something called the kernel. This is the core set of features necessary for the operating system to function. The kernel manages the system's resources and handles communication between the hardware and the applications. The Linux kernel was developed by Linus Torvalds who, taking a dislike to MS-DOS, and impatient for the availability of MINIX for the new Intel 80386 microprocessor, decided to write his own UNIX-like kernel. When he had finished the first version of the kernel, he released it under an open source license that enabled anyone to download the source code and freely use and modify it without having to pay Linus any money.

Around the same time, Richard Stallman at the Free Software Foundation, a strong advocate of free and open source software, was working on an open source operating system of his own. Rather than focusing initially on the kernel, however, Stallman decided to begin by developing open source versions of all the UNIX tools, utilities and compilers necessary to use and maintain an operating system. By the time he had finished developing this infrastructure it seemed like the obvious solution was to combine his work with the kernel Linus had written to create a full operating system. This combination became known as GNU/Linux. Purists insist that Linux always be referred to as GNU/Linux (in fact, at one time, Richard Stallman refused to give press interviews to any publication which failed to refer to Linux as GNU/Linux). This is not unreasonable given that the GNU tools developed by the Free Software Foundation make up a significant and vital part of GNU/Linux. Unfortunately, most people and publications simply refer to Linux as Linux and this will probably always continue to be the case.

2.4 The Early Days of Red Hat

In 1993 Bob Young created a company named ACC Corporation which, according to Young, he ran from his "wife's sewing closet". The name ACC was intended to represent a catalog business but was also an abbreviation of a small business his wife ran called "Antiques and Collectibles of Connecticut". Among the items sold through the ACC catalog business were Linux CDs and related open source software.

Around the same time, Marc Ewing had created his own Linux distribution company which he named Red Hat Linux (after his propensity to wear a red baseball cap while at Carnegie Mellon University).

In 1995, ACC acquired Red Hat, adopted the name Red Hat, Inc. and experienced rapid and significant growth. Bob Young stepped down as CEO shortly after the company went public in August of 1999 and has since pursued a number of business and philanthropic efforts including a print-on-demand book publishing company named Lulu and ownership of two Canadian professional sports teams. In 2018, IBM announced plans to acquire Red Hat, Inc. in a deal valued at $34 billion.

2.5 Red Hat Support

Early releases of Red Hat Linux were shipped to customers on floppy disks and CDs (this, of course, predated the widespread availability of broadband internet connections). When users encountered problems with the software they were only able to contact Red Hat by email. In fact, Bob Young often jokes that this was effective in limiting support requests since, by the time a customer realized they needed help, their computer was usually inoperative and therefore unavailable to be used to send an email message seeking assistance from Red Hat's support team. In later years Red Hat provided better levels of support tied to paid subscriptions and now provides a variety of support levels ranging from "self help" (no support) up to premium support.

2.6 Open Source

Red Hat Enterprise Linux 8 is the current commercial offering from Red Hat and is primarily targeted at corporate, mission critical installations. It is also the cornerstone of an expanding ecosystem of products and services offered by Red Hat. RHEL is an open source product in that you can download the source code free of charge and build the software yourself if you wish to do so (a task not to be undertaken lightly). If, however, you wish to download a pre-built, ready to install binary version of the software (either with or without support), you have to pay for it.

2.7 The Fedora Project

Red Hat also sponsors the Fedora Project, the goal of which is to provide access to a free Linux operating system (in both source and binary distributions) in the form of Fedora Linux. Fedora Linux also serves as a proving ground for many of the new features that are eventually adopted into the Red Hat Enterprise Linux operating system family. CentOS 8.0, for example, was based to a large extent on Fedora 29.

2.8 CentOS - The Free Alternative

For users unable to afford a Red Hat Enterprise Linux subscription, another option is provided in the form of the CentOS operating system. The CentOS project, originally a community driven effort but now a collaboration with Red Hat, takes the Red Hat Enterprise Linux source code, removes the Red Hat branding and subscription requirements, compiles it and provides the distribution for download. Of course, while CentOS provides an operating system that is identical to RHEL in many ways, it does not include access to Red Hat technical support.

2.9 Summary

The origins of the Linux operating system can be traced back to the work of Linus Torvalds and Richard Stallman in the form of the Linux kernel combined with the tools and compilers built by the GNU project.

Over the years, the open source nature of Linux has resulted in the release of a wide range of different Linux distributions. One such distribution is Red Hat Enterprise Linux, created by Red Hat, Inc., a company founded by Bob Young and Mark Ewing. Red Hat specializes in providing enterprise level Linux software solutions combined with extensive technical support services. CentOS is essentially built from the same source code base as Red Hat Enterprise Linux, but with the Red Hat branding removed.

3. Installing CentOS 8 on a Clean Disk Drive

There are now two ways in which a CentOS 8 system can be deployed. One method is to either purchase new hardware or re-purpose an existing computer system on which to install and run the operating system. Another option is to create a cloud-based operating system instance using services such as Amazon AWS, Google Cloud or Microsoft Azure (to name but a few). Since cloud-based instances are typically created by selecting a pre-configured, ready to run operating system image that is already optimized for the cloud platform, and using that as the basis for the CentOS system, there is no need to perform a manual operating system installation in this situation.

If, on the other hand, you plan to install CentOS 8 on your own hardware, the first step on the path to learning about CentOS 8 involves installing the operating system.

CentOS can be installed either in a clean disk environment (where an entire disk is cleared of any existing partitions and dedicated entirely to CentOS) or in a dual boot environment where CentOS co-exists with another operating system on the disk (typically a member of the Microsoft Windows family of operating systems).

In this chapter we will be covering the clean disk approach to installation from local or remote installation media. Dual boot installation with a Windows 10 system will be covered in *"Dual Booting CentOS 8 with Windows"*.

3.1 Obtaining the CentOS Installation Media

The CentOS distribution can be downloaded from the CentOS Project website using the following URL:

https://www.centos.org/download/

The installation media is provided in the form of a DVD ISO image and is available in the following forms:

- **CentOS Linux DVD ISO** - Contains the installation image for the version of CentOS built from the RHEL 8 source code.

- **CentOS Stream DVD ISO** - Contains a continuously evolving version of CentOS that will eventually become the next versions of RHEL and CentOS.

For the purposes of this book, download the *CentOS Linux DVD ISO* image. The DVD ISO image is self-contained including all of the packages necessary to install a CentOS system and is named

Installing CentOS 8 on a Clean Disk Drive

using the following convention:

```
CentOS-<version>-<architecture>-dvd.iso
```

For example, the CentOS 8 DVD image for 64-bit Intel systems is named as follows:

```
CentOS-8-x86_64-1905-dvd1.iso
```

Having downloaded the image, either burn it to disk or use the steps in the next section to write the media to a USB drive, configure your virtualization environment to treat it as a DVD drive or use the steps outlined later in this chapter to access the installation image over a network connection.

3.2 Writing the ISO Installation Image to a USB Drive

These days it is more likely that an operating system installation will be performed from a USB drive than from a DVD. Having downloaded the ISO installation image for CentOS 8, the steps to write that image to a USB drive will differ depending on whether the drive is attached to a Linux, macOS or Windows system. The steps outlined in the remainder of this section assume that the USB drive is new, or has been reformatted to remove any existing data or partitions:

3.2.1 Linux

The first step in writing an ISO image to a USB drive on Linux is to identify the device name. Before inserting the USB drive, identify the storage devices already detected on the system by listing the devices in */dev* as follows:

```
# ls /dev/sd*
/dev/sda   /dev/sda1   /dev/sda2
```

Attach the USB drive to the Linux system and run the *dmesg* command to get a list of recent system messages, one of which will be a report that the USB drive was detected and will be similar to the following:

```
[445597.988045] sd 6:0:0:0: [sdb] Attached SCSI removable disk
```

This output tells us that we should expect the device name to include "sdb" which we can confirm by listing device names in */dev* again:

```
# ls /dev/sd*
/dev/sda    /dev/sda1    /dev/sda2    /dev/sdb
```

From this output we can tell that the USB drive has been assigned to /dev/sdb. The next step before writing the ISO image to the device is to run the *findmnt* command to make sure it has not been auto-mounted:

```
# findmnt /dev/sdb
TARGET                                            SOURCE    FSTYPE OPTIONS
/run/media/neil/d6bf9574-7e31-4f54-88b1           /dev/sdb  ext3   rw,nosuid,no
```

If the *findmnt* command indicates that the USB drive has been mounted, unmount it before continuing:

```
umount /run/media/neil/d6bf9574-7e31-4f54-88b1
```

Once the filesystem has been unmounted, use the *dd* command as follows to write the ISO image to the drive:

```
# dd if=/path/to/iso/image.iso of=/dev/sdb bs=512k
```

The writing process can take some time (as long as 10 - 15 minutes) to complete depending on the image size and speed of the system on which it is running. Once the image has been written, output similar to the following will appear and the USB drive is ready to be used to install CentOS 8:

```
5956+0 records in
5956+0 records out
3122659328 bytes (3.1 GB, 2.9 GiB) copied, 426.234 s, 7.3 MB/s
```

3.2.2 macOS

The first step in writing an ISO image to a USB drive attached to a macOS system is to identify the device using the *diskutil* tool. Before attaching the USB device, open a Terminal window and run the following command:

```
$ diskutil list
/dev/disk0 (internal, physical):
   #:                       TYPE NAME                    SIZE       IDENTIFIER
   0:      GUID_partition_scheme                        *1.0 TB     disk0
   1:                        EFI EFI                     209.7 MB   disk0s1
   2:                Apple_APFS Container disk2          1000.0 GB  disk0s2

/dev/disk1 (internal):
   #:                       TYPE NAME                    SIZE       IDENTIFIER
   0:      GUID_partition_scheme                         28.0 GB    disk1
   1:                        EFI EFI                     314.6 MB   disk1s1
   2:                Apple_APFS Container disk2           27.7 GB    disk1s2

/dev/disk2 (synthesized):
   #:                       TYPE NAME                    SIZE       IDENTIFIER
   0:      APFS Container Scheme -                       +1.0 TB     disk2
                                 Physical Stores disk1s2, disk0s2
   1:              APFS Volume Macintosh HD             473.6 GB    disk2s1
   2:              APFS Volume Preboot                   42.1 MB    disk2s2
   3:              APFS Volume Recovery                 517.0 MB    disk2s3
   4:              APFS Volume VM                         1.1 GB    disk2s4
```

Having established a baseline of detected devices, insert the USB drive into a port on the macOS system and run the command again. The same results should appear with one additional entry for the USB drive resembling the following:

```
/dev/disk3 (external, physical):
   #:                       TYPE NAME                    SIZE       IDENTIFIER
   0:                                                   *16.0 GB    disk3
```

Installing CentOS 8 on a Clean Disk Drive

In the above example, the USB drive has been assigned to /dev/disk3. Before proceeding, unmount the disk as follows:

```
$ diskutil unmountDisk /dev/disk3
Unmount of all volumes on disk3 was successful
```

Finally, use the *dd* command to write the ISO image to the device, taking care to reference the raw disk device (/dev/**r**disk3) and entering your user password when prompted:

```
$ sudo dd if=/path/to/iso/image.iso of=/dev/rdisk3 bs=1m
```

Once the image has been written, the USB drive is ready.

3.2.3 Windows

A number of free tools are available for Windows that will write an ISO image to a USB drive, but one written specifically for writing Linux ISO images is the Fedora Media Writer tool which can be downloaded from the following URL:

https://getfedora.org/en/workstation/download/

Once installed, launch the writer tool and select the *Custom image* option as highlighted in Figure 3-1:

Figure 3-1

In the resulting file selection dialog, navigate to and select the CentOS 8 installation ISO image and click on the *Open* button. After selecting the image, a dialog will appear within which the image can be written to the USB drive. Select the target USB drive from the device menu before clicking on the *Write to Disk* button:

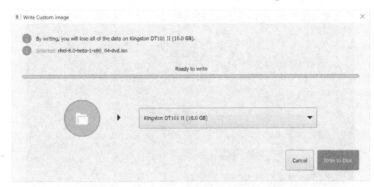

Figure 3-2

Once the image has been written to the device, the device is ready to be used to perform the installation.

3.3 Installing CentOS 8

Insert the CentOS 8 installation media into the appropriate drive and power on the system. If the system tries to boot from the hard disk drive you will need to enter the BIOS set up for your computer and change the boot order so that it boots from the installation media drive first. Once the system has booted you will be presented with the following screen:

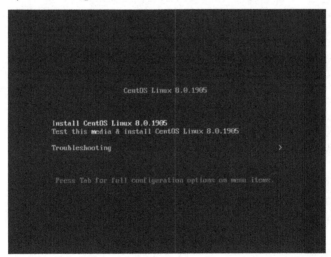

Figure 3-3

Use the arrow keys to navigate between the options and make a selection with the <Enter> key. If the *Troubleshooting* option is selected the screen shown in Figure 3-4 will appear including options to boot from the current operating system on the local drive (if one is installed), test the system memory, or rescue an installed CentOS 8 system. An option is also available to perform the installation in basic graphics mode for systems without a graphical console:

Installing CentOS 8 on a Clean Disk Drive

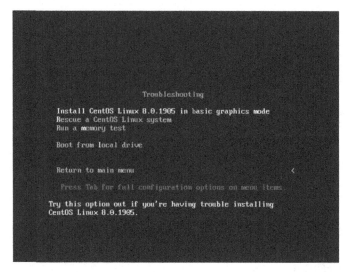

Figure 3-4

Select the option on the main screen to install CentOS and, after a short delay, the first screen of the graphical installer will appear:

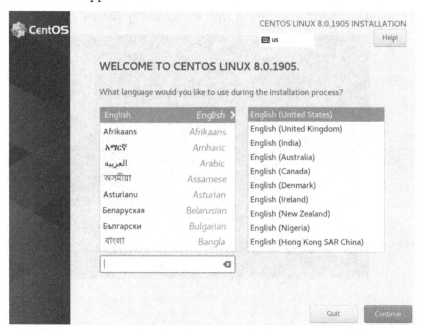

Figure 3-5

Select your preferred language on the first screen before clicking *Continue* to proceed to the main installation screen as shown in Figure 3-6:

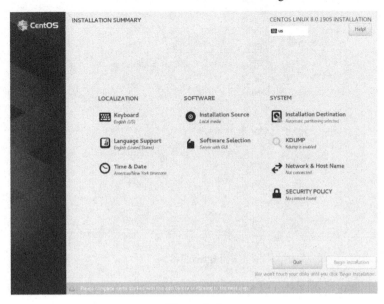

Figure 3-6

Begin by selecting the *Network & Host Name* option, enable a network device on your system and enter a host name before clicking the *Apply* button:

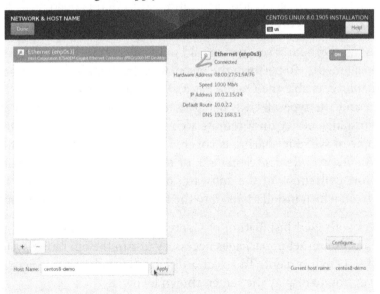

Figure 3-7

If your network connection requires additional settings, click on the *Configure...* button to access the advanced network settings screen illustrated in Figure 3-8:

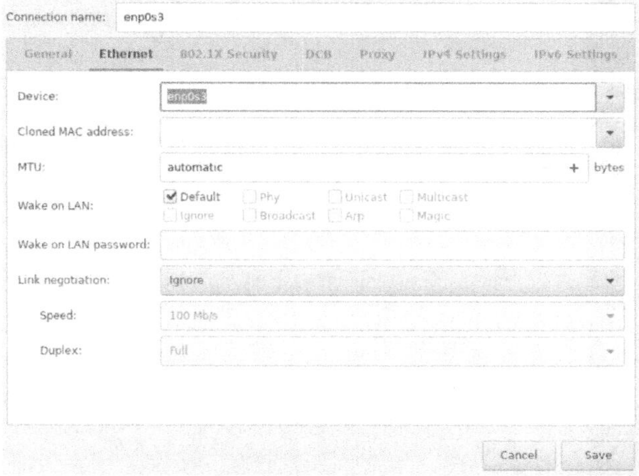

Figure 3-8

Once the host name has been defined and a network connection enabled, click *Done* to return to the main screen.

If you wish to change the keyboard, language or time and date settings, select the corresponding option from the Localization column of the main screen. On the *Time & Date* screen, make a selection corresponding to your geographical location. The option is also provided to use *Network Time* which automatically synchronizes the system with external Network Time Protocol servers.

Changes to the *Installation Source* settings should not be necessary since the installation is being performed from local media. To perform the installation from media located on a remote server, select *Installation Source*, enable the *On the network* option and then specify the location of the installation media and the type of URL being used. The installation media can, for example, be an ISO image installed either on a remote web server or on a system on the local network using NFS (the topic of NFS file sharing is covered in detail in the chapter entitled *"Using NFS to Share CentOS 8 Files with Remote Systems"*), or the URL of a remote repository (repositories are essentially online collections of the software, packages and applications that make up the operating system from which installations onto the local system can be performed).

By default, a Server with GUI installation of CentOS 8 will be performed by the installer. This will consist of the minimum set of packages necessary to run the operating system together with the graphical desktop environment. To select a different installation configuration, choose the *Software Selection* option to display the screen shown below:

Figure 3-9

Use the left-hand panel to select a basic configuration and the right-hand panel to add any additional packages you know you will need after the system starts up. If the CentOS 8 system is intended to be used with a graphical desktop environment, choose either the *Workstation* or *Server with GUI* option. Otherwise, it is generally recommended to start with a minimal system and install additional packages as needed once the system has booted. This avoids installing any packages that may never be needed.

The *Security Policy* option allows additional security packages to be installed on the system that allow security restrictions that comply with the Security Content Automation Protocol (SCAP) standards to be imposed on the system. While selecting a profile from the list installs the necessary packages, the policy restrictions are not enforced until they are enabled on the running system. Unless you work for a government entity or company that mandates this level of security, it is not necessary to select a policy on this screen.

The *Kdump* feature, when enabled, writes out the state of the operating system kernel in the event of a system crash. This dump file can be useful in identifying the cause of a crash but takes up system memory when enabled. Unless memory is limited on your system, this can be left in the enabled state.

Having configured the basic settings, the next step is to decide how the hard disk drive will be partitioned to accommodate the operating system.

3.4 Partitioning a Disk for CentOS 8

When the *Installation Destination* option is selected, the installer will present a screen similar to the one illustrated in Figure 3-10 below:

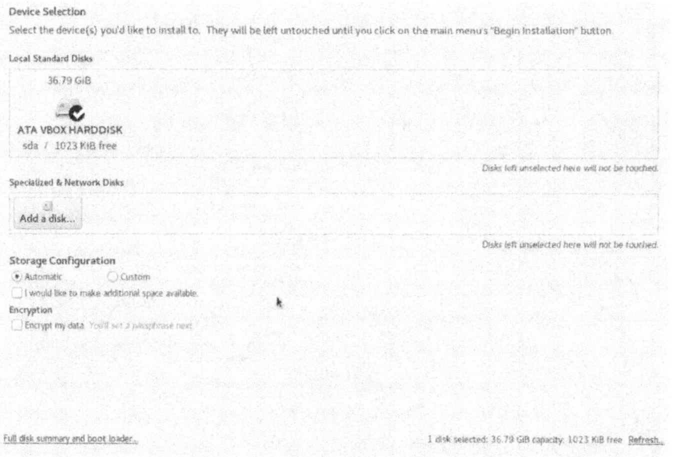

Installing CentOS 8 on a Clean Disk Drive

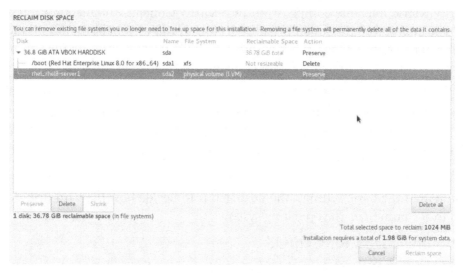

Figure 3-10

By default, the installer is configured to automatically install the operating system using the available space on the currently selected disk drive and to configure standard partition sizes. If the disk previously contained another operating system, these existing partitions will not be deleted, potentially leaving unused space on the drive after CentOS 8 has been installed. To remove any existing partitions so that they can be reclaimed and used by CentOS 8, enable the *I would like to make additional space available* option and click on the *Done* button to display the dialog shown in Figure 3-11.

Figure 3-11

To reclaim space, select a partition that is no longer needed and mark it for removal by clicking the *Delete* button. Once all the partitions that are to be removed have been selected, click on the *Reclaim Space* button to perform the deletion. The reclaimed space will now be used automatically by the CentOS 8 installer.

To manually configure the layout of the disk in terms of how the available space will be allocated, change the *Storage Allocation* setting from *Automatic* to *Custom* and click *Done* to display the Manual Partitioning screen (Figure 3-12):

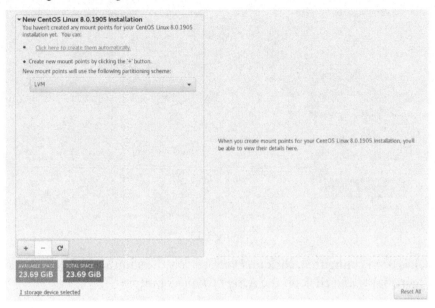

Figure 3-12

The manual partitioning screen provides the option to configure the disk using Logical Volume Management (LVM) or standard partitioning. LVM is the recommended option because it provides flexibility in terms of managing partition sizes once the system is up and running (LVM is covered in detail in the chapter entitled *"Adding a New Disk to a CentOS 8 Volume Group and Logical Volume"*).

Once a partitioning scheme has been selected, the last step is to decide on the sizes of the partitions and the corresponding filesystem mount points. In general, the default configuration provided by the *Click here to create them automatically* option will meet most system needs. To manually create partitions and allocate mount points, click on the + button to declare and assign each partition manually.

Another option is to select automatic partition creation, and then use the resulting screen to manually change the partition configuration as needed. Figure 3-13, for example, shows the partition configuration defined by selecting the automatic creation option and allows the settings for each partition to be modified before any changes are made to the disk:

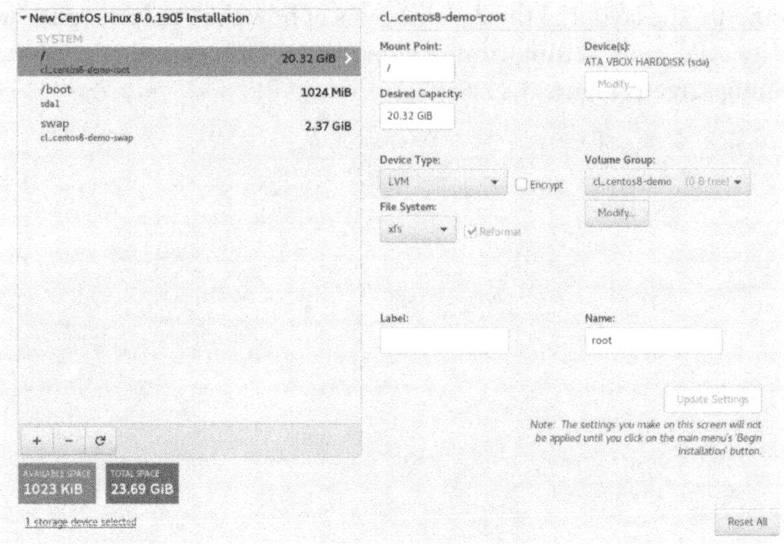

Figure 3-13

Once the disk has been configured, click on *Done*, review the summary of the changes to be made to the disk (Figure 3-14) and click on the *Accept Changes* button:

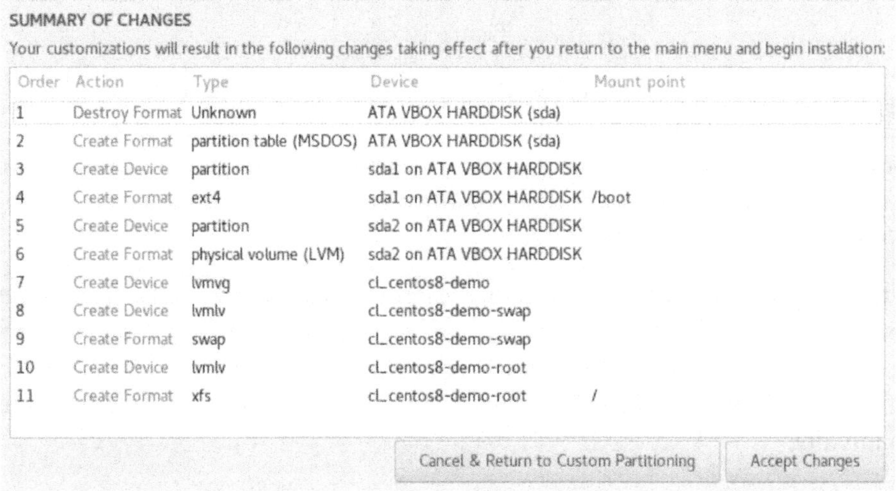

SUMMARY OF CHANGES

Your customizations will result in the following changes taking effect after you return to the main menu and begin installation:

Order	Action	Type	Device	Mount point
1	Destroy Format	Unknown	ATA VBOX HARDDISK (sda)	
2	Create Format	partition table (MSDOS)	ATA VBOX HARDDISK (sda)	
3	Create Device	partition	sda1 on ATA VBOX HARDDISK	
4	Create Format	ext4	sda1 on ATA VBOX HARDDISK	/boot
5	Create Device	partition	sda2 on ATA VBOX HARDDISK	
6	Create Format	physical volume (LVM)	sda2 on ATA VBOX HARDDISK	
7	Create Device	lvmvg	cl_centos8-demo	
8	Create Device	lvmlv	cl_centos8-demo-swap	
9	Create Format	swap	cl_centos8-demo-swap	
10	Create Device	lvmlv	cl_centos8-demo-root	
11	Create Format	xfs	cl_centos8-demo-root	/

Cancel & Return to Custom Partitioning | Accept Changes

Figure 3-14

CentOS 8 also allows the contents of the disk to be protected by encryption. This will require a passphrase to be entered each time the system boots. To enable encryption, select the *Encrypt my data* option on the main *Installation Destination* screen and, after clicking the *Done* button, enter the passphrase in the dialog shown in Figure 3-15:

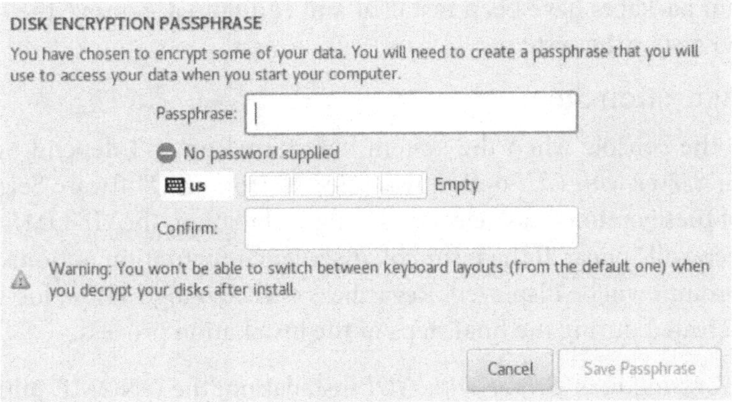

DISK ENCRYPTION PASSPHRASE
You have chosen to encrypt some of your data. You will need to create a passphrase that you will use to access your data when you start your computer.
Passphrase:
No password supplied
us
Empty
Confirm:
Warning: You won't be able to switch between keyboard layouts (from the default one) when you decrypt your disks after install.
Cancel
Save Passphrase

Figure 3-15

3.5 The Physical Installation

Having made the appropriate package selections, clicking *Begin Installation* will start the process of partitioning the disks and installing the packages that match the chosen installation settings. During this phase, a screen will appear (Figure 3-16) seeking the creation of a root password and an optional user account:

CentOS
CONFIGURATION
CENTOS LINUX 8.0.1905 INSTALLATION
us
Help!
USER SETTINGS
Root Password
Root password is not set
User Creation
No user will be created
Downloading packages

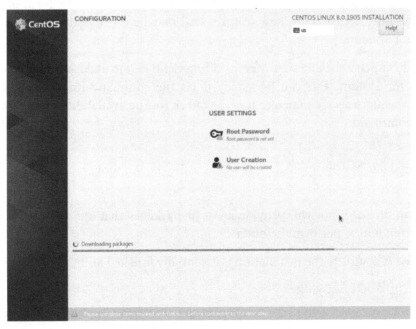

Figure 3-16

The root, or super-user account, is a special user that has administrative privileges on the system. While you will generally use your own account to log into the system, you will need to gain root privileges in order to configure the system and to perform other administrative tasks. Enter a root password, create a user account and wait for the installation to complete.

Once all the system packages have been installed and configured, remove the installation media and click *Reboot* to restart the system.

3.6 Final Configuration Steps

What appears on the console when the system has started up will depend on whether or not the *Workstation* or *Server with GUI* option was selected from the Software Selection installation screen. If either of these options was selected during installation, the GNOME Display Manager (GDM) login screen will appear. If the minimal or server configuration options were selected, the text based login prompt will be displayed. Regardless of the configuration, log into the system as the user that was created during the final steps of the installation process.

In the case of a *Workstation* or *Server with GUI* installation, the GNOME initial setup tool will launch providing configuration options such as language, keyboard layout, location services and connections to online accounts including Google and Facebook. After these settings have been configured (or skipped), the GNOME desktop welcome screen will appear containing links to tutorials on how to use the desktop environment.

3.7 Installing Updates

As with most operating systems today, each particular release of a CentOS distribution continues to evolve after it has been released to the public. This generally takes the form of bug fixes and security updates and, occasionally, new features that may be downloaded over the internet and installed on your system.

Best practices dictate that the first step after installing CentOS is to make sure any available updates are applied to the system. This can be achieved via the command-line prompt in a Terminal window using the *dnf* package manager tool. To check for the availability of updates, simply run the following command:

```
# dnf check-update
```

Any pending updates may be applied, once again using the *dnf* tool:

```
# dnf update
```

Upon execution, the *dnf* tool will provide a list of packages that are available for update and prompt for permission to perform the update.

Once the update is complete the installation is essentially finished and CentOS 8 is ready for use.

3.8 Displaying Boot Messages

During the boot process, CentOS 8 will display the Red Hat Graphical Boot (RHGB) screen which hides from view all of the boot messages generated by the system as it loads. To make these messages visible during the boot process (as shown in Figure 3-17), simply press the keyboard Esc key while the system is starting:

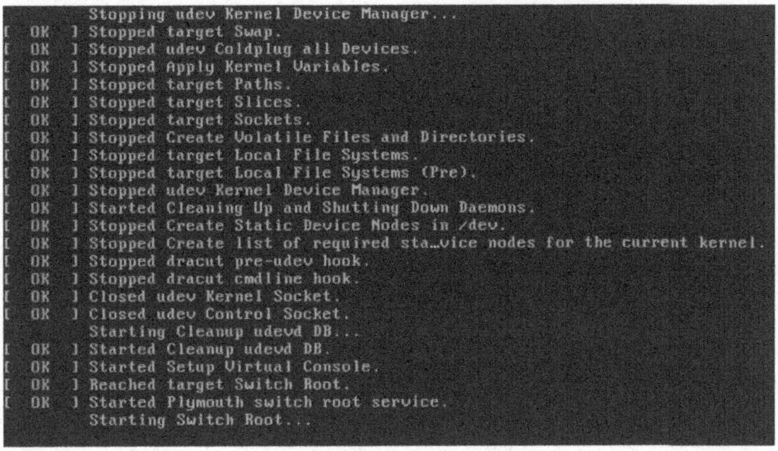

Figure 3-17

The default behavior can be changed so that messages are always displayed by default by editing the */etc/default/grub* file and changing the GRUB_CMDLINE_LINUX setting which, by default, will read as follows:

```
GRUB_CMDLINE_LINUX="crashkernel=auto rhgb quiet"
```

To remove the graphical boot screen so that messages are visible without pressing the Esc key, remove the "rhgb" option from the setting:

```
GRUB_CMDLINE_LINUX="crashkernel=auto rhgb quiet"
```

This change will cause the system to display only a subset of the boot messages generated by the system. To display all messages generated by the system, also remove the "quiet" option:

```
GRUB_CMDLINE_LINUX="crashkernel=auto quiet"
```

Once the changes have been made, run the following command to generate a new boot configuration to take effect next time the system starts:

```
# grub2-mkconfig --output=/boot/grub2/grub.cfg
```

3.9 Summary

The first step in working with CentOS 8 is to install the operating system. In the case of a cloud-based server, this task is typically performed automatically when an operating system image is selected for the system based on a range of options offered by the cloud service provider. Installation on your own hardware, however, involves downloading the installation media in the form of an ISO image, writing that image to suitable storage such as a DVD or USB drive and booting from it. Once running, the installation process allows a range of options to be configured ranging from networking, whether the installation should proceed from the local media or via a remote server or repository, the packages to be installed, and the partitioning of the disk. Once installation is complete, it is important to install any operating system updates that may have been released since the original installation image was created.

4. Dual Booting CentOS 8 with Windows

CentOS 8, just like most Linux distributions, will happily co-exist on a hard disk drive with just about any version of Windows up to and including Windows 10. This is a concept known as dual-booting. Essentially, when you power up the system, you will be presented with a menu providing the option to boot either your CentOS 8 installation or Windows. Obviously you can only run one operating system at a time, but it is worth noting that the files on the Windows partition of your disk drive will be available to you from CentOS 8 regardless of whether your Windows partition was formatted using NTFS, FAT16 or FAT32.

This installation method involves shrinking the size of the existing Windows partitions and then installing CentOS 8 into the reclaimed space. This chapter will assume that CentOS 8 is being installed on a system currently running Windows 10.

4.1 Partition Resizing

In order to accommodate CentOS on a disk drive that already contains a Windows installation, the first step involves shrinking the Windows partition to make some room. The recommended course of action is to use the Windows Disk Management interface to reduce the size of the partition before attempting to install CentOS 8.

To access Disk Management on Windows 10, right-click on the Start menu and select *Disk Management* from the resulting menu as highlighted in Figure 4-1:

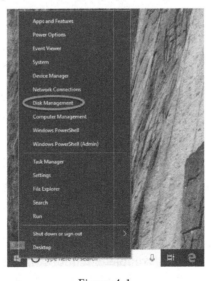

Figure 4-1

Dual Booting CentOS 8 with Windows

Once loaded, the Disk Management tool will display a graphical representation of the disk drives detected on the system:

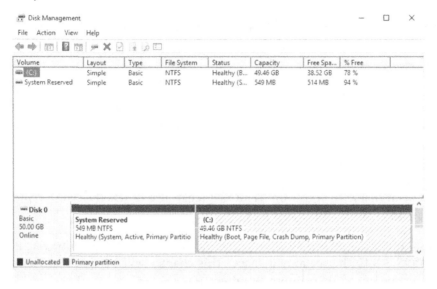

Figure 4-2

Right-click on the partition you wish to reduce in size and select *Shrink Volume...* from the popup menu. The tool will calculate the maximum amount by which the volume size can be reduced without data loss (a process that can take several minutes depending on the overall size of the partition). Once this analysis is complete, a dialog similar to the one in Figure 4-3 below will appear:

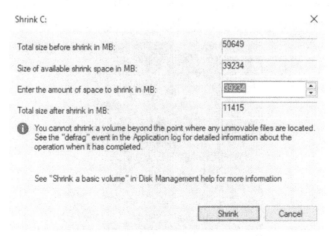

Figure 4-3

Specify a value in the *Enter amount of space to shrink in MB* field and click on the *Shrink* button to proceed. Once the resizing operation is complete, reboot using the CentOS 8 installation media (as outlined in *"Installing CentOS 8 on a Clean Disk Drive"*) and proceed with the installation making use of the new free space.

4.2 Editing the CentOS 8 Boot Menu

Once installation of CentOS onto the disk is complete and the system has restarted, the standard CentOS boot menu will appear:

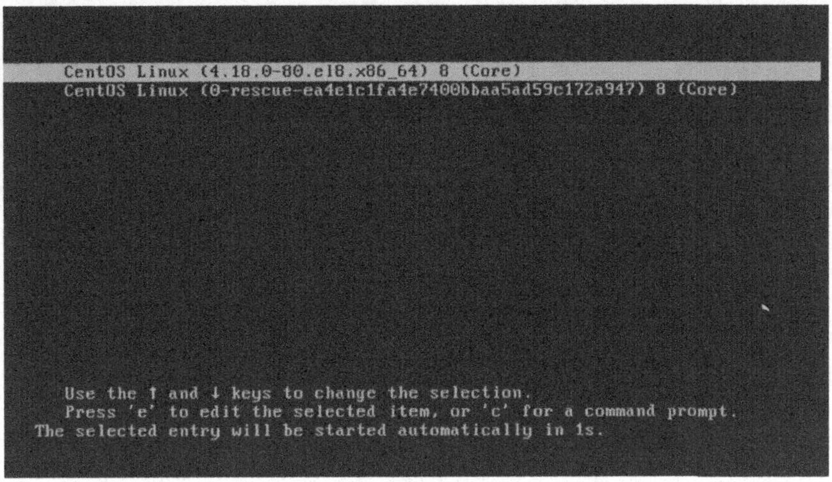

Figure 4-4

At this point, the boot menu only provides the option to boot the CentOS 8 system. Clearly an option also needs to be added so that the Windows system is still accessible. These steps will need to be taken from within the CentOS 8 system, so start the system and log in as root.

The first step is to identify the Windows boot partition on the disk drive using the *fdisk* command as follows:

```
# fdisk -l
.
.
.
Device      Boot    Start        End   Sectors   Size  Id  Type
/dev/sda1   *        2048    1126399   1124352   549M   7  HPFS/NTFS/exFAT
/dev/sda2         1126400   53655551  52529152    25G   7  HPFS/NTFS/exFAT
/dev/sda3        53655552   55752703   2097152     1G  83  Linux
/dev/sda4        55752704  104857599  49104896  23.4G   5  Extended
/dev/sda5        55754752  104857599  49102848  23.4G  8e  Linux LVM
```

In the above output */dev/sda3* through to */dev/sda5* are clearly the CentOS 8 partitions. The smaller */dev/sda1* partition is the Windows system partition, leaving */dev/sda2* as the Windows boot partition.

The CentOS 8 boot system works using partition indexes where the first partition is partition 0, the second is partition 1 and so on. As such, the Windows boot partition from the point of view of the boot menu is located on hard disk 0 at partition index location 1 and is defined in the boot configuration as "hd0,1".

Dual Booting CentOS 8 with Windows

The boot menu configuration settings are stored in the */boot/grub2/grub.cfg* file which is generated using the *grub2-mkconfig* tool based on the content of the configuration files located in the */etc/grub.d* directory. To add the Windows boot option to the configuration, edit the */etc/grub.d/40_custom* file which should read as follows:

```
#!/bin/sh
exec tail -n +3 $0
# This file provides an easy way to add custom menu entries.  Simply type the
# menu entries you want to add after this comment.  Be careful not to change
# the 'exec tail' line above.
```

Edit the file to add the following entry to the end of the *40_custom* file:

```
menuentry "Windows 10" {
        set root=(hd0,1)
        chainloader +1
        }
```

Save the file and generate the boot menu as follows:

```
# grub2-mkconfig --output=/boot/grub2/grub.cfg
Generating grub configuration file ...
done
```

On the next reboot, Windows will now be included as a boot option as shown in Figure 4-5:

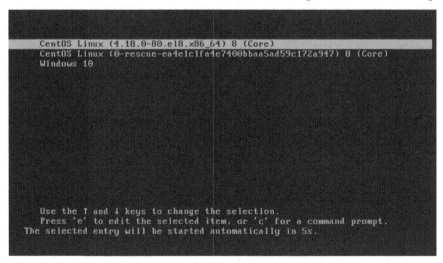

Figure 4-5

4.3 Changing the Default Boot Option

When the system starts, the boot options screen will appear and wait 5 seconds for the user to make an operating system choice. If no selection has been made before the timeout elapses, the default operating system will be started. On a newly configured system, the default operating system will be the standard (non-rescue) CentOS 8 image. This default can, however, be changed from within CentOS.

A range of boot configuration options (including the 5 second timeout and the boot RHGB settings outlined in *"Installing CentOS 8 on a Clean Disk Drive"*) are declared in the */etc/default/ grub* file which reads as follows on a new installation:

```
GRUB_TIMEOUT=5
GRUB_DISTRIBUTOR="$(sed 's, release .*$,,g' /etc/system-release)"
GRUB_DEFAULT=saved
GRUB_DISABLE_SUBMENU=true
GRUB_TERMINAL_OUTPUT="console"
GRUB_CMDLINE_LINUX="crashkernel=auto resume=/dev/mapper/cl-swap rd.lvm.lv=cl/root
rd.lvm.lv=cl/swap rhgb quiet"
GRUB_DISABLE_RECOVERY="true"
GRUB_ENABLE_BLSCFG=true
```

The first step in changing the default boot system is to declare the GRUB_SAVEDEFAULT setting within this file:

```
GRUB_TIMEOUT=5
GRUB_DISTRIBUTOR="$(sed 's, release .*$,,g' /etc/system-release)"
GRUB_DEFAULT=saved
GRUB_SAVEDEFAULT=true
.


.
```

This setting allows a new default value to be saved within the boot configuration. Next, run the *grub2-set-default* command to change the default setting using a numbering system that counts the first option as 0. For the boot options shown in Figure 4-5 above, for example, the first CentOS entry is position 0 while the Windows 10 option is position 2. The command to make Windows 10 the default boot option, therefore, would read as follows:

```
# grub2-set-default 2
```

Check that the new setting has taken effect by running the following command:

```
# grub2-editenv list
saved_entry=2
kernelopts=root=/dev/mapper/cl-root ro crashkernel=auto resume=/dev/mapper/cl-
swap rd.lvm.lv=cl/root rd.lvm.lv=cl/swap rhgb quiet
boot_success=0
boot_indeterminate=0
```

Note that the *saved_entry* value is now set to 2. After changing the default, regenerate the boot configuration file as follows:

```
# grub2-mkconfig --output=/boot/grub2/grub.cfg
```

Reboot the system and verify that the boot menu defaults to the Windows 10 option and that Windows loads after the timeout expires.

4.4 Accessing the Windows Partition from CentOS 8

When running CentOS in a dual boot configuration it is still possible to access files located on the Windows partition. This can be achieved by manually mounting the partition from the command-line. Before doing so, however, some additional packages need to be installed on the system. First the *fuse* kernel module needs to be downloaded and installed:

```
# dnf install fuse
# modprobe fuse
```

Next, the Fuse NTFS driver needs to be installed. Unfortunately, this package is not included in the standard CentOS 8 repositories so the Extra Packages for Enterprise Linux (EPEL) repository needs to be added to the system as follows:

```
# dnf install wget
# wget http://dl.fedoraproject.org/pub/epel/epel-release-latest-8.noarch.rpm
# rpm -ivh epel-release-latest-8.noarch.rpm
```

With the EPEL repository added, the driver can now be installed:

```
# dnf install fuse-ntfs-3g
```

Once the requisite packages are installed, the next step is to create a directory to use as the mount point for our Windows partition. In this example we will create a directory named */mnt/windows*:

```
# mkdir /mnt/windows
```

In order to identify the device name that has been assigned to the Windows partition, use the *fdisk* command as follows:

```
# fdisk -l
.
.
.
```

Device Boot		Start	End	Blocks	Id	System
/dev/sda1	*	1	13	102400	7	HPFS/NTFS
/dev/sda2		13	1400	11141120	7	HPFS/NTFS
/dev/sda3		1400	1464	512000	83	Linux
/dev/sda4		1464	2611	9214976	5	Extended
/dev/sda5		1464	2611	9213952	8e	Linux LVM

In the above output, the main Windows partition containing the files we need access to is represented by */dev/sda2*. Next, we need to run the *mount* command (assuming the Windows partition is /dev/sda2 and NTFS format) as follows:

```
# mount /dev/sda2 /mnt/windows
```

Check that the mount was successful by listing the contents of the top level directory of the mount point:

```
# ls /mnt/windows
'$Recycle.Bin'            ProgramData              swapfile.sys
'Documents and Settings'  'Program Files'          'System Volume Information'
 pagefile.sys             'Program Files (x86)'    Users
```

```
PerfLogs                    Recovery                    Windows
```

To automate the mount each time the system is booted, simply add the appropriate mount line to the *etc/fstab* file:

```
/dev/sda2 /mnt/windows ntfs defaults 0 0
```

To unmount the Windows file system at any time:

```
umount /mnt/windows
```

4.5 Summary

CentOS 8 can safely co-exist on the same disk drive as a Windows operating system by creating a dual boot environment. This involves shrinking the amount of space occupied by the Windows system to make room for CentOS 8 before performing the installation. Once CentOS has been installed, the boot menu configuration must be modified to include the option to boot from Windows. To access the Windows filesystem from within CentOS, the Fuse NTFS driver needs to be installed and used to mount the Windows partitions.

5. Allocating Windows Disk Partitions to CentOS 8

In the previous chapter we looked at how to install CentOS 8 on the same disk as Windows. This so called "dual boot" configuration allows the user to have both operating systems installed on a single disk drive with the option to boot one or the other when the system is powered on.

This chapter is intended for users who have decided they like CentOS 8 enough to delete Windows entirely from the disk, and use the resulting space for Linux. In the following sections we will work through this process step by step.

5.1 Unmounting the Windows Partition

If the steps in the *"Dual Booting CentOS 8 with Windows"* chapter were followed to mount the Windows partition from within CentOS 8, steps should be taken to unmount the partition before continuing with this chapter. Assuming that the Windows partition was mounted as */mnt/windows*, it can be unmounted as follows:

```
# umount /mnt/windows
```

The */etc/fstab* file should also be edited to remove the */mnt/windows* auto-mount if it was previously added.

5.2 Deleting the Windows Partitions from the Disk

The first step in freeing up the Windows partition for use by CentOS is to delete that partition. Before doing so, however, it is imperative that any data you need to keep is backed up from both the Windows and CentOS partitions. Having done that, it is safe to proceed with this chapter.

In order to remove the Windows partitions we first need to identify the disk on which they reside using the *fdisk* tool:

```
# fdisk -l
Disk /dev/sda: 50 GiB, 53687091200 bytes, 104857600 sectors
Units: sectors of 1 * 512 = 512 bytes
Sector size (logical/physical): 512 bytes / 512 bytes
I/O size (minimum/optimal): 512 bytes / 512 bytes
Disklabel type: dos
Disk identifier: 0xe3673009


Device     Boot    Start       End   Sectors  Size Id Type
/dev/sda1  *        2048   1126399   1124352  549M  7 HPFS/NTFS/exFAT
/dev/sda2         1126400  53655551  52529152   25G  7 HPFS/NTFS/exFAT
/dev/sda3        53655552  55752703   2097152    1G 83 Linux
```

```
/dev/sda4        55752704 104857599 49104896 23.4G  5 Extended
/dev/sda5        55754752 104857599 49102848 23.4G 8e Linux LVM
```

In the above example output the system contains one physical disk drive referenced by device name */dev/sda*. On that disk drive are five partitions accessed via the device names */dev/sda1* through */dev/sda5* respectively. Based on the values in the System column, there are two NTFS partitions. The first is the Windows system partition while the second, much larger, NTFS partition is the Windows boot partition containing the Windows operating system and user data.

To remove the partitions, start the *fdisk* tool using the device name of the disk containing the partition (*/dev/sda* in this instance) and follow the instructions to once again display the partition and sector information:

```
# fdisk /dev/sda

Welcome to fdisk (util-linux 2.32.1).
Changes will remain in memory only, until you decide to write them.
Be careful before using the write command.

Command (m for help): p
Disk /dev/sda: 50 GiB, 53687091200 bytes, 104857600 sectors
Units: sectors of 1 * 512 = 512 bytes
Sector size (logical/physical): 512 bytes / 512 bytes
I/O size (minimum/optimal): 512 bytes / 512 bytes
Disklabel type: dos
Disk identifier: 0xe3673009

Device     Boot    Start       End   Sectors  Size Id Type
/dev/sda1  *        2048   1126399   1124352  549M  7 HPFS/NTFS/exFAT
/dev/sda2         1126400  53655551 52529152   25G  7 HPFS/NTFS/exFAT
/dev/sda3        53655552  55752703  2097152    1G 83 Linux
/dev/sda4        55752704 104857599 49104896 23.4G  5 Extended
/dev/sda5        55754752 104857599 49102848 23.4G 8e Linux LVM

Command (m for help):
```

Currently, the Windows system partition is listed as being the bootable partition. Since we will be deleting this partition, the Linux boot partition needs to be marked as bootable. In the above configuration, this is represented by */dev/sda3*. Remaining within the *fdisk* tool, make this the bootable partition as follows:

```
Command (m for help): a
Partition number (1,3-5, default 5): 3
The bootable flag on partition 3 is enabled now.
```

Before proceeding, make a note of the start and end addresses of the partitions we will be deleting (in other words the start of */dev/sda1* and the end of */dev/sda2*).

At the command prompt, delete the Windows partitions (these being partitions 1 and 2 on our example system):

```
Command (m for help): d
Partition number (1-5, default 5): 1

Partition 1 has been deleted.

Command (m for help): d
Partition number (2-5, default 5): 2

Partition 2 has been deleted.
```

Now that we have deleted the Windows partitions we need to create the new CentOS partition in the vacated disk space. The partition number must match the number of the partition removed (in this case 1) and is going to be a primary partition. It will also be necessary to enter the Start and End sectors of the partition exactly as reported for the old partition (*fdisk* will typically offer the correct values by default, though it is wise to double check). If you are prompted to remove the NTFS signature, enter Y:

```
Command (m for help): n
Partition type
   p    primary (1 primary, 1 extended, 2 free)
   l    logical (numbered from 5)
Select (default p): p
Partition number (1,2, default 1): 1
First sector (2048-104857599, default 2048):
Last sector, +sectors or +size{K,M,G,T,P} (2048-53655551, default 53655551):

Created a new partition 1 of type 'Linux' and of size 25.6 GiB.
Partition #1 contains a ntfs signature.

Do you want to remove the signature? [Y]es/[N]o: y

The signature will be removed by a write command.
```

Having made these changes the next step is to check that the settings are correct (taking this opportunity to double check that the Linux boot partition is bootable):

```
Command (m for help): p
Disk /dev/sda: 50 GiB, 53687091200 bytes, 104857600 sectors
Units: sectors of 1 * 512 = 512 bytes
Sector size (logical/physical): 512 bytes / 512 bytes
I/O size (minimum/optimal): 512 bytes / 512 bytes
Disklabel type: dos
Disk identifier: 0xe3673009
```

Allocating Windows Disk Partitions to CentOS 8

```
Device     Boot    Start      End  Sectors  Size Id Type
/dev/sda1           2048  53655551 53653504 25.6G 83 Linux
/dev/sda3    *  53655552  55752703  2097152   1G 83 Linux
/dev/sda4       55752704 104857599 49104896 23.4G  5 Extended
/dev/sda5       55754752 104857599 49102848 23.4G 8e Linux LVM

Filesystem/RAID signature on partition 1 will be wiped.
```

To commit the changes we now need to write the new partition information to disk and quit from the *fdisk* tool:

```
Command (m for help): w
The partition table has been altered.
Syncing disks.
```

5.3 Formatting the Unallocated Disk Partition

In order to make the new partition suitable for use by CentOS 8, it needs to have a file system created on it. The default file system type for the current release of CentOS is XFS and will be covered in greater detail in the chapter entitled *"Adding a New Disk Drive to a CentOS 8 System"*. Creation of the file system is performed using the *mkfs.xfs* command as follows:

```
# mkfs.xfs -f /dev/sda1
meta-data=/dev/sda1              isize=512    agcount=4, agsize=1676672 blks
         =                       sectsz=512   attr=2, projid32bit=1
         =                       crc=1        finobt=1, sparse=1, rmapbt=0
         =                       reflink=1
data     =                       bsize=4096   blocks=6706688, imaxpct=25
         =                       sunit=0      swidth=0 blks
naming   =version 2             bsize=4096   ascii-ci=0, ftype=1
log      =internal log          bsize=4096   blocks=3274, version=2
         =                       sectsz=512   sunit=0 blks, lazy-count=1
realtime =none                   extsz=4096   blocks=0, rtextents=0
```

5.4 Mounting the New Partition

Next, we need to mount the new partition. In this example we will mount it in a directory named /*data*. You are free, however, to mount the new partition using any valid mount point you desire or to use it as part of a logical volume (details of which are covered in the chapter entitled *"Adding a New Disk to a CentOS 8 Volume Group and Logical Volume"*). First we need to create the directory to act as the mount point:

```
# mkdir /data
```

Secondly, we need to edit the mount table in */etc/fstab* so that the partition is automatically mounted each time the system starts. At the bottom of the */etc/fstab* file, add the following line to mount the new partition (modifying the */dev/sda1* device to match your environment):

```
/dev/sda1 /data xfs  defaults 0 0
```

Finally, we can manually mount the new partition (note that on subsequent reboots this will not be necessary as the partition will automount as a result of the setting we added to the *letc/fstab* file above).

```
# mount /data
```

To check the partition, run the following command to display the available space:

```
# df -h /data
Filesystem     Size  Used Avail Use% Mounted on
/dev/sda1      26G   215M   26G   1% /data
```

5.5 Editing the Boot Menu

The next step is to modify the CentOS boot menu. Since this was originally a dual boot system, the menu is configured to provide the option of booting either Windows or CentOS. Now that the Windows partition is gone, we need to remove this boot option. Start by editing the *letc/ grub.d/40_custom* file and removing the Windows menu entry:

```
#!/bin/sh
exec tail -n +3 $0
# This file provides an easy way to add custom menu entries.  Simply type the
# menu entries you want to add after this comment.  Be careful not to change
# the 'exec tail' line above.
menuentry "Windows 10" {
            set root=(hd0,1)
            chainloader +1
            }
```

Save the file and use the *grub2-mkconfig* tool to generate the */boot/grub2/grub.cfg* file as follows:

```
# grub2-mkconfig --output=/boot/grub2/grub.cfg
Generating grub configuration file ...
done
```

Next time the system restarts, the Windows 10 option will no longer be provided by the boot menu.

5.6 Summary

The Windows partitions in a dual boot configuration can be removed at any time to free up space for a CentOS system by identifying which partitions belong to Windows and then deleting them using the *fdisk* tool. Once deleted, the unallocated space can be used to create a new filesystem and mounted to make it available to the CentOS system. The final task is to remove the Windows option from the boot menu configuration.

6. A Guided Tour of the GNOME 3 Desktop

CentOS 8 includes the GNOME 3 desktop environment. Although lacking the complexity of Windows and macOS desktops, GNOME 3 provides an uncluttered and intuitive desktop environment that provides all of the essential features of a windowing environment with the added advantage that it can be learned quickly.

In this chapter, the main features of the GNOME desktop will be covered together with an outline of how basic tasks are performed.

6.1 Installing the GNOME Desktop

If either the Workstation or Server with GUI software configuration was selected during the CentOS 8 installation process, the GNOME desktop will already be installed and will automatically launch each time the system starts.

If any other software configuration was selected during the CentOS 8 installation process, the GNOME desktop will not have been included in the packages installed on the system. On server-based systems without a display attached, the idea of installing a graphical desktop environment may seem redundant. It is worth noting, however, that remote access to the GNOME desktop is also possible so, even on so called *headless servers* (i.e. servers lacking a monitor, keyboard and mouse) it may still be beneficial to install the GNOME desktop packages. The topic of establishing remote desktop access will be covered in detail in the *"CentOS 8 Remote Desktop Access with VNC"* chapter of this book.

If the installation configuration did not include the GNOME desktop, it may be installed at any time using the following command:

```
# dnf groupinstall "Workstation"
```

Once the installation is complete, the desktop environment may be launched from the command prompt on a monitor as follows:

```
$ startx
```

6.2 An Overview of the GNOME 3 Desktop

The screen shown in Figure 6-1 below shows the appearance of a typical, newly launched GNOME desktop session before any other programs have been launched or configuration changes made.

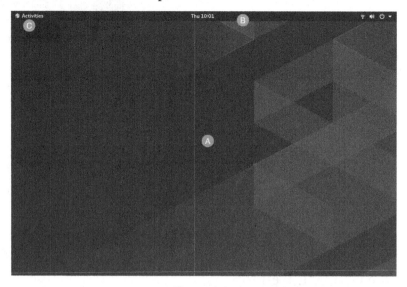

Figure 6-1

The main desktop area (marked A) is where windows will appear when applications and utilities are launched. Unlike other desktop environments, it is not possible to drag and drop files or applications onto the desktop, providing a clean and uncluttered workspace.

The bar at the top of the screen (B) is called the *top bar* and includes the Activities menu (C), the day and time and a collection of buttons and icons including network status, audio volume, battery power and other status and account settings. The application menu for the currently active application running on the desktop will also appear in the top bar. Figure 6-2, for example, shows the application menu for the Terminal program:

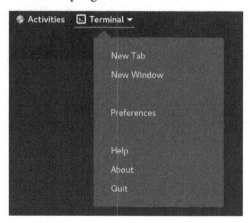

Figure 6-2

6.3 Launching Activities

Applications and utilities are launched using the Activities overview dashboard (referred to as the *dash*) which may be displayed either by clicking on the Activities button in the top bar or pressing the *special key* on the keyboard. On Windows systems this is the Windows key, on macOS the Command key and on Chromebooks the key displaying a magnifying glass.

When displayed, the dash will appear as shown in Figure 6-3 below:

Figure 6-3

By default the dash will display an icon for a predefined set of commonly used applications and will also include an icon for any applications that are currently running. If the application is currently running it will appear with a bar marker beneath the icon.

To launch an application, simply click on the icon in the dash.

To find an application not included on the dash, one option is to select the bottom most icon (the square comprising nine dots) to display a browsable list of applications as shown in Figure 6-4:

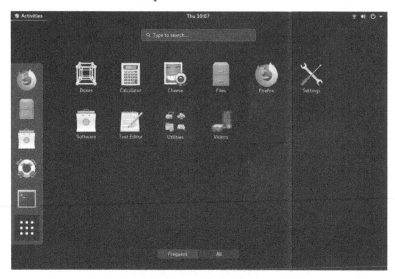

Figure 6-4

Note that the list can be filtered to display all applications or only those used frequently by selecting the buttons at the bottom center of the screen. It is also important to be aware that some entries in the list are actually folders holding addtional applications. In the above screenshot, for example, the *Utilities* entry provides access to a collection of other tools such as the system monitor and disk management tools and the Terminal window application.

An alternative to browsing the applications is to perform a search using the search bar which appears when the dash is displayed as shown in Figure 6-5:

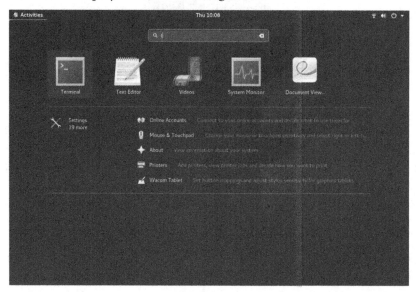

Figure 6-5

As text is typed into the search box, the list of possible matches will be refined.

To add an application to the dash for more convenient access, locate the icon for the application, right-click on it and select the *Add to Favorites* menu option:

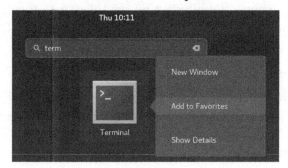

Figure 6-6

To remove an app from the dash, repeat these steps, this time selecting *Remove from Favorites*.

6.4 Managing Windows

As with other desktop environments, applications run on GNOME in windows. When multiple application windows are open, the Super + Tab keyboard shortcut will display the switcher panel (Figure 6-7) allowing a different window to be chosen as the currently active window (the Super key is either the Windows key or, in the case of a Mac keyboard, the Cmd key):

Figure 6-7

If a single application has more than one window open, the switcher will display those windows in a second panel so that a specific window can be selected:

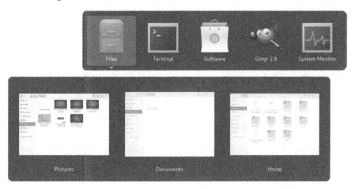

Figure 6-8

To cycle backwards through the icons in the switcher, use the Shift + Tab keyboard shortcut.

To maximize a window so that it fills the entire screen click the title bar and drag the window to the top of the screen. To return the window to its original size, click on the title bar and drag downwards. Alternatively, simply double-click on the title bar to toggle between window sizes. Similarly, dragging a window to the left or right side of the screen will cause the window to fill that half of the screen.

6.5 Using Workspaces

The area of the screen where the application windows appear is referred to as the *workspace* and GNOME 3 allows multiple workspaces to be configured. To create a new workspace, display the Activities overview and move the mouse pointer to the far right of the screen to display the workspaces panel (Figure 6-9):

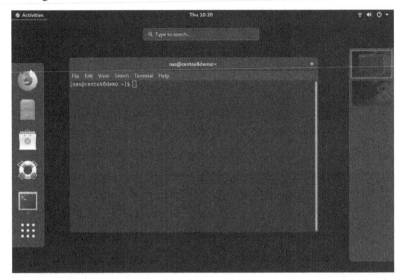

Figure 6-9

To switch to a different panel, simply select it from the list. To move a window from one workspace to another, display the workspaces panel and drag and drop the application window (either the actual window from the current workspace or the thumbnail window in the workspaces panel) onto the destination workspace. When a window is added to a blank workspace, another blank workspace is added to the workspace panel, allowing multiple workspaces to be created.

To remove a workspace either close all the windows on that workspace, or move them to another workspace.

6.6 Calendar and Notifications

When the system needs to notify you of an event (such as the availability of system or application updates), a popup panel will appear at the top of the workspace. Access to the calendar and any previous notifications is available by clicking on the day and time in the top bar as shown in Figure 6-10:

Figure 6-10

6.7 Desktop Settings

To access the Settings application, click on the down arrow on the far right of the top bar and select the button with the tools icon as highlighted in Figure 6-11:

Figure 6-11

The Settings application provides a wide range of options such as Ethernet and Wi-Fi connections, screen background customization options, screen locking and power management controls and language preferences. To explore the settings available in each category, simply select an option from the left-hand panel in the Settings window:

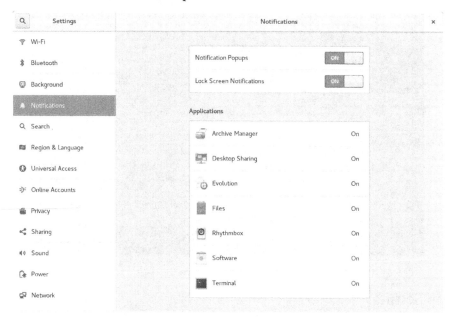

Figure 6-12

The menu shown in Figure 6-11 above also includes options to switch user, adjust audio volume, change to a different Wi-Fi network and to log out, restart or power off the system.

6.8 Summary

CentOS 8 includes the GNOME 3 desktop environment which may either be included during the initial installation or installed later using the *dnf* group package installation feature. Unlike most other desktop environments, GNOME 3 is intended to provide a clean and easy to use windowing user interface. Key areas of the GNOME 3 desktop include the top bar, Activities overview and dash. In addition, GNOME 3 supports multiple workspaces keeping running applications organized and the screen uncluttered. A variety of configuration options is also available within the Settings app including desktop background settings, audio, network configuration and Wi-Fi network selection.

7. An Overview of the CentOS 8 Cockpit Web Interface

Although it comes equipped with the latest in Linux desktop environments, CentOS 8 is very much a server operating system and, as such, the majority of CentOS deployments will either be to remote physical servers or as cloud-based virtual machine instances. Invariably, these systems run without a keyboard, mouse or monitor, with direct access only available via the command-prompt over a network connection. This presents a challenge in terms of administering the system from remote locations. While much can certainly be achieved via remote access to the command-line and desktop environments, this is far from a consistent and cohesive solution to the administrative and monitoring tasks that need to be performed on a daily basis on an enterprise level operating system such as CentOS 8.

This issue has been addressed with the introduction of the Cockpit web-based administration interface. This chapter will explain how to install, configure and access the Cockpit interface while also providing an overview of the key features of Cockpit, many of which will be covered in greater detail in later chapters.

7.1 An Overview of Cockpit

Cockpit is a light-weight, web-based interface that allows general system administrative tasks to be performed remotely. When installed and configured, the system administrator simply opens a local browser window and navigates to the Cockpit port on the remote server. After loading the Cockpit interface into the browser and logging in, a wide range of tasks can be performed visually using administration and monitoring tools.

Behind the scenes, Cockpit uses the same tools to perform tasks as would normally be used when working at the command-line, and updates automatically to reflect changes occurring elsewhere on the system. This allows Cockpit to be used in conjunction with other administration tools and techniques without the risk of one approach overriding another. Cockpit can also be configured to access more than one server, allowing multiple servers to be administered and monitored simultaneously through a single browser session.

Cockpit is installed by default with a wide range of tools already bundled. Cockpit also, however, allows additional extension plugins to be installed as needed. Cockpit is also designed so that you can create your own extensions using a combination of HTML and JavaScript to add missing or custom functionality.

Cockpit's modular design also allows many features to be embedded into other web-based applications.

7.2 Installing and Enabling Cockpit

Cockpit is generally not installed on CentOS 8 by default, but can be set up and enabled in a few simple steps. The first step is to install the Cockpit package as follows:

```
# dnf install cockpit
```

Next, the Cockpit socket service needs to be enabled:

```
# systemctl enable --now cockpit.socket
```

Finally, the necessary ports need to be opened on the firewall to allow remote browser connections to reach Cockpit:

```
# firewall-cmd --add-service=cockpit --permanent
# firewall-cmd --reload
```

7.3 Accessing Cockpit

If you have access to the desktop environment of the server on which Cockpit has been installed, open a browser window and navigate to *https://localhost:9090* to access the Cockpit sign in screen. If, on the other hand, the server is remote, simply navigate to the server using the domain name or IP address (for example *https://myserver.com*:9090).

When the connection is established, the browser may issue a warning that the connection is not secure. This is because the Cockpit service is using a self-signed certificate. Either select the option to proceed to the web site or, to avoid this message in the future, select the advanced option and add an exception for the server address.

Once connected, the browser will load the log in page shown in Figure 7-1 below:

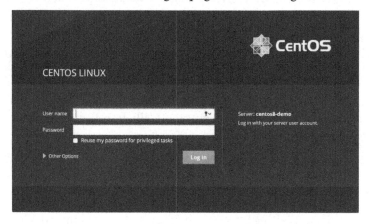

Figure 7-1

Sign in to the Cockpit interface either as root or with your a user account credentials. Note that when signed in as a user some tasks will be restricted within the Cockpit interface due to permission constraints. After signing in, Cockpit will display the System screen.

7.4 System

The System screen provides an overview of the current system including realtime performance metrics for CPU, memory, disk I/O and network usage. This screen also includes information about the system including the underlying hardware, host name, system time and whether the system software is up to date. Options are also provided to restart or shutdown the system.

Figure 7-2, for example, shows the system monitoring page of the Cockpit interface:

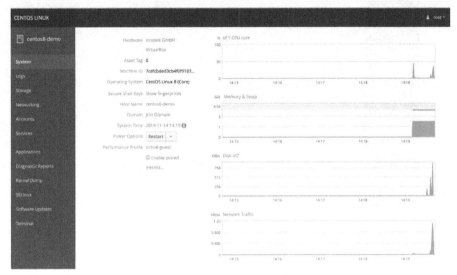

Figure 7-2

7.5 Logs

When the Logs category is selected, Cockpit displays the contents of the *systemd* journal logs. Selecting a log entry will display the entire log message. The log entries are ordered with the most recent at the top and menus are included to filter the logs for different time durations and based on message severity.

Figure 7-3

7.6 Storage

Select the Storage option to review and manage the storage on the system including disks, partitions and volume groups, Network File System (NFS) mounts and RAID storage. This screen also allows disk I/O activity to be monitored in realtime and lists log output from the system *udisksd* service used to query and manage storage devices.

Figure 7-4

7.7 Networking

The Network screen provides information on a wide range of network related configurations and services including network interfaces and firewall settings and allows configuration changes to be made such as creating network bridges or setting up virtual networks.

Figure 7-5

7.8 Virtual Machines

Virtualization allows multiple operating system instances to run simultaneously on a single computer system, with each system running inside its own *virtual machine*. The Virtual Machines Cockpit extension provides a way to create and manage the virtual machine guests installed on the server.

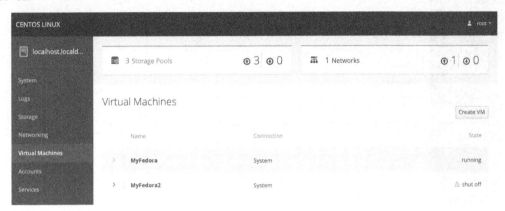

Figure 7-6

The Virtual Machines extension is not installed by default but can be added to Cockpit by running the following command:

```
# dnf install cockpit-machines
```

The use of virtualization with CentOS 8 is covered starting with the chapter entitled *"Installing KVM Virtualization on CentOS 8"*

7.9 Accounts

Select this option to view the current user accounts configured on the system, and create accounts for additional users. The topic of user management will be covered later in the chapter entitled *"Managing CentOS 8 Users and Groups"*.

Figure 7-7

Click on an existing account to view details and make changes. The user account details page may also be used to review and add Public SSH keys to the user's account for remote access to the server as outlined in the chapter entitled *"Configuring SSH Key-based Authentication on CentOS 8"*.

An Overview of the CentOS 8 Cockpit Web Interface

7.10 Services

This screen displays a list of the system services running on the server and allows those services to be added, removed, stopped and started.

Figure 7-8

The topic of services will be covered in detail in the chapter entitled *"Configuring CentOS 8 systemd Units"*.

7.11 Applications

As previously mentioned, additional functionality can be added to Cockpit in the form of extensions. These can either be self-developed extensions, or those provided by third parties. The Applications screen lists installed extensions and allows extensions to be added or deleted.

Figure 7-9

7.12 Diagnostic Reports

When selected, this option allows a diagnostic report to be generated and downloaded to the local system for analysis. The generated report is provided in the form of a compressed archive file containing a collection of all the log files on the server system.

Figure 7-10

7.13 Kernel Dump

This screen simply displays the current KDump service status and indicates where the kernel dump file will be located in the event of a kernel crash on the system. This dump file can then be used to identify the cause of the crash. A button is provided to test the Kernel dump by triggering a kernel crash, though use of this option is not recommended on a production server system:

Figure 7-11

7.14 SELinux

When selected, the SELinux category indicates whether SELinux policy is currently being enforced and displays any alerts generated by this security system.

Figure 7-12

7.15 Software Updates

If any software updates are available for the system they will be listed on this screen. If updates are available, they can be installed from this screen.

An Overview of the CentOS 8 Cockpit Web Interface

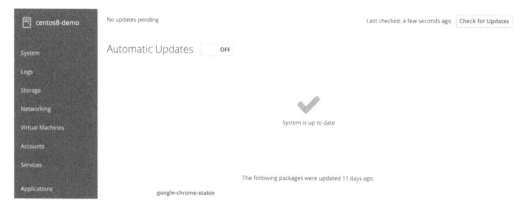

Figure 7-13

7.16 Terminal

As the name suggests, the Terminal screen provides access to the command-line prompt.

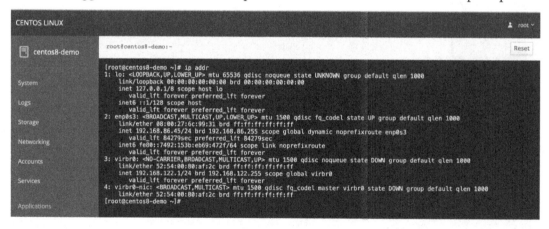

Figure 7-14

7.17 Connecting to Multiple Servers

Cockpit can be configured to administer multiple servers from within a single session. This requires that the Cockpit dashboard be installed on the primary system (in other words the system to which the initial Cockpit session will be established) To install the Cockpit dashboard package, run the following command:

```
# dnf install cockpit-dashboard
```

Once the dashboard has been installed, sign out of Cockpit and then sign in again. The dashboard will now appear in the Cockpit interface as highlighted in Figure 7-15:

Figure 7-15

When selected, the dashboard page will display performance graphs for the current system and provide a list of currently connected systems:

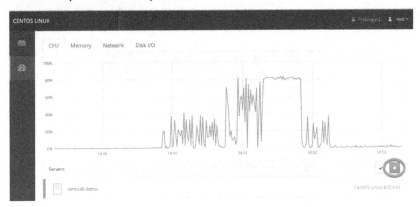

Figure 7-16

To add another system, click on the + button highlighted in Figure 7-16 above, enter the IP address or host name of the other system and select a color by which to distinguish this server from any others added to Cockpit before clicking on the Add button:

Figure 7-17

Enter the user name and password to be used when connecting to the other system, then click on the log in button. The newly added server will now be listed in the Cockpit dashboard and will appear in graphs represented by the previously selected color:

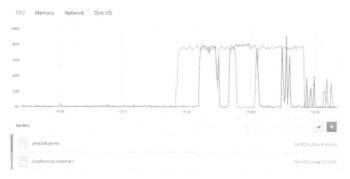

Figure 7-18

To switch between systems when using Cockpit, simply use the drop down menu shown in Figure 7-19 below:

Figure 7-19

7.18 Enabling Stored Metrics

In a standard installation Cockpit does not retain any of the performance metric data beyond what is displayed in the short time window covered by the graphs. To retain the data collected by Cockpit, the stored metrics feature needs to be installed. Begin by installing the *cockpit-pcp* package as follows:

```
# dnf install cockpit-pcp
```

To enable metric persistence, display the System screen and click on the *Enable stored metrics...* link highlighted in Figure 7-20:

Figure 7-20

Once this option has been selected, Cockpit will request permission to install the *cockpit-pcp*, *pcp-libs* and *pcp-selinux* packages. Once these packages have been installed, the *Enable persistent metrics* link will have been replaced by a control labeled *Store Metrics*. When this option is enabled, the performance graphs will include additional controls allowing you to move back and forth in time to view historical data and to change the data time frame ranging from 1 hour up to 1 week:

Figure 7-21

7.19 Summary

The Cockpit web interface allows remote system administration tasks to be performed visually from within a web browser without the need to rely on the command-prompt and command-line tools. Once installed and enabled, the system administrator simply opens a web browser, connects to the remote server and signs into the Cockpit interface. Behind the scenes, Cockpit uses the same command-line tools as those available via the command prompt, thereby allowing both options to be used without the risk of configuration conflicts. Cockpit uses a modular framework allowing additional extensions to be added, and for custom extensions to be developed and integrated. A Cockpit session can be used to administer a single server, or configured to access multiple servers simultaneously.

8. Using the Bash Shell on CentOS 8

An important part of learning to work with CentOS 8, and Linux distributions in general, involves gaining proficiency in working in the shell environment. While the graphical desktop environments such as GNOME included with Linux provide a user friendly interface to the operating system, in practice the shell environment provides far greater capabilities, flexibility and automation than can ever be achieved using graphical desktop tools. The shell environment also provides a means for interacting with the operating system when a desktop environment is not available; a common occurrence when working with a server-based operating system such as CentOS 8 or a damaged system that will not fully boot.

The goal of this chapter, therefore, is to provide an overview of the default shell environment on CentOS 8 (specifically the Bash shell).

8.1 What is a Shell?

The shell is an interactive command interpreter environment within which commands may be typed at a prompt or entered into a file in the form of a script and executed. The origins of the shell can be traced back to the early days of the UNIX operating system. In fact, in the early days of Linux before the introduction of graphical desktops the shell was the only way for a user to interact with the operating system.

A variety of shell environments have been developed over the years. The first widely used shell was the Bourne shell, written by Stephen Bourne at Bell Labs.

Yet another early creation was the C shell which shared some syntax similarities with the C Programming Language and introduced usability enhancements such as command-line editing and history.

The Korn shell (developed by David Korn at Bell Labs) is based on features provided by both the Bourne shell and the C shell.

The default shell on CentOS 8 is the Bash shell (shorthand for Bourne Again SHell). This shell, which began life as an open source version of the Bourne shell, was developed for the GNU Project by Brian Fox and is based on features provided by both the Bourne shell and the C shell.

8.2 Gaining Access to the Shell

From within the GNOME desktop environment, the shell prompt may be accessed from a Terminal window by selecting the Activities option in the top bar, entering Terminal into the search bar and clicking on the Terminal icon.

When remotely logging into a CentOS 8 server, for example using SSH, the user is also presented with a shell prompt. Details on accessing a remote server using SSH will be covered in the chapter entitled *"Configuring SSH Key-based Authentication on CentOS 8"*. When booting a server-based system in which a desktop environment has not been installed, the shell is entered immediately after the user completes the login procedure at the physical console terminal or remote login session.

8.3 Entering Commands at the Prompt

Commands are entered at the shell command prompt simply by typing the command and pressing the Enter key. While some commands perform tasks silently, most will display some form of output before returning to the prompt. For example, the *ls* command can be used to display the files and directories in the current working directory:

```
$ ls
Desktop  Documents  Downloads  Music  Pictures  Public  Templates  Videos
```

The available commands are either built into the shell itself, or reside on the physical file system. The location on the file system of a command may be identified using the *which* command. For example, to find out where the *ls* executable resides on the file system:

```
$ which ls
alias ls='ls --color=auto'
       /usr/bin/ls
```

Clearly the *ls* command resides in the */usr/bin* directory. Note also that an alias is configured, a topic which will be covered later in this chapter. Using the *which* command to locate the path to commands that are built into the shell will result in a message indicating the executable cannot be found. For example, attempting to find the location of the *history* command (which is actually built into the shell rather than existing as an executable on the file system) will result in output similar to the following:

```
$ which history
/usr/bin/which: no history in (/home/demo/.local/bin:/home/demo/bin:/usr/share/
Modules/bin:/usr/local/bin:/usr/bin:/usr/local/sbin:/usr/sbin)
```

8.4 Getting Information about a Command

Many of the commands available to the Linux shell can seem cryptic to begin with. To find out detailed information about what a command does and how to use it, use the *man* command specifying the name of the command as an argument. For example, to learn more about the *pwd* command:

```
$ man pwd
```

When the above command is executed, a detailed description of the *pwd* command will be displayed. Many commands will also provide additional information when run with the *--help* command-line option:

```
$ wc --help
```

8.5 Bash Command-line Editing

Early shell environments did not provide any form of line editing capabilities. This meant that if you spotted an error at the beginning of a long command-line you were typing, you had to delete all the following characters, correct the error and then re-enter the remainder of the command. Fortunately Bash provides a wide range of command-line editing options as outlined in the following table:

Key Sequence	Action
Ctrl-b or Left Arrow	Move cursor back one position
Ctrl-f or Right Arrow	Move cursor forward one position
Delete	Delete character currently beneath the cursor
Backspace	Delete character to the left of the cursor
Ctrl-_	Undo previous change (can be repeated to undo all previous changes)
Ctrl-a	Move cursor to the start of the line
Ctrl-e	Move cursor to the end of the line
Meta-f or Esc then f	Move cursor forward one word
Meta-b or Esc then b	Move cursor back one word
Ctrl-l	Clear the screen of everything except current command
Ctrl-k	Delete to end of line from current cursor position
Meta-d or Esc then d	Delete to end of current word
Meta-DEL or Esc then DEL	Delete beginning to current word
Ctrl-w	Delete from current cursor position to previous white space

Table 8-1

8.6 Working with the Shell History

In addition to command-line editing features, the Bash shell also provides command-line history support. A list of previously executed commands may be viewed using the *history* command:

```
$ history
    1  ps
    2  ls
    3  ls -l /
    4  ls
    5  man pwd
    6  man apropos
```

In addition, Ctrl-p (or up arrow) and Ctrl-n (or down arrow) may be used to scroll back and forth through previously entered commands. When the desired command from the history is displayed, press the Enter key to execute it.

Another option is to enter the '!' character followed by the first few characters of the command to be repeated followed by the Enter key.

8.7 Filename Shorthand

Many shell commands take one or more filenames as arguments. For example, to display the content of a text file named *list.txt*, the *cat* command would be used as follows:

```
$ cat list.txt
```

Similarly, the content of multiple text files could be displayed by specifying all the file names as arguments:

```
$ cat list.txt list2.txt list3.txt list4.txt
```

Instead of typing in each name, pattern matching can be used to specify all files with names matching certain criteria. For example, the '*' wildcard character can be used to simplify the above example:

```
$ cat *.txt
```

The above command will display the content of all files ending with a *.txt* extension. This could be further restricted to any file names beginning with *list* and ending in *.txt*:

```
$ cat list*.txt
```

Single character matches may be specified using the '?' character:

```
$ cat list?.txt
```

8.8 Filename and Path Completion

Rather than typing in an entire file name or path, or using pattern matching to reduce the amount of typing, the shell provides the *filename completion* feature. In order to use filename completion, simply enter the first few characters of the file or path name and then press the Esc key twice. The shell will then complete the filename for you with the first file or path name in the directory that matches the characters you entered. To obtain a list of possible matches, press Esc = after entering the first few characters.

8.9 Input and Output Redirection

As previously mentioned, many shell commands output information when executed. By default this output goes to a device file called *stdout* which is essentially the terminal window or console in which the shell is running. Conversely, the shell takes input from a device file named *stdin*, which by default is the keyboard.

Output from a command can be redirected from stdout to a physical file on the file system using the '>' character. For example, to redirect the output from an *ls* command to a file named *files.txt*, the following command would be required:

```
$ ls *.txt > files.txt
```

Upon completion, *files.txt* will contain the list of files in the current directory. Similarly, the contents of a file may be fed into a command in place of stdin. For example, to redirect the contents of a file as input to a command:

```
$ wc -l < files.txt
```

The above command will display the number of lines contained in the *files.txt* file.

It is important to note that the '>' redirection operator creates a new file, or truncates an existing file when used. In order to append to an existing file, use the '>>' operator:

```
$ ls *.dat >> files.txt
```

In addition to standard output, the shell also provides standard error output using *stderr*. While output from a command is directed to stdout, any error messages generated by the command are directed to stderr. This means that if stdout is directed to a file, error messages will still appear in the terminal. This is generally the desired behavior, though stderr may also be redirected if desired using the '2>' operator:

```
$ ls dkjfnvkjdnf 2> errormsg
```

On completion of the command, an error reporting the fact that the file named *dkjfnvkjdnf* could not be found will be contained in the *errormsg* file.

Both stderr and stdout may be redirected to the same file using the &> operator:

```
$ ls /etc dkjfnvkjdnf &> alloutput
```

On completion of execution, the *alloutput* file will contain both a listing of the contents of the */etc* directory, and the error message associated with the attempt to list a non-existent file.

8.10 Working with Pipes in the Bash Shell

In addition to I/O redirection, the shell also allows output from one command to be piped directly as input to another command. A pipe operation is achieved by placing the '|' character between two or more commands on a command-line. For example, to count the number of processes running on a system, the output from the *ps* command can be piped through to the *wc* command:

```
$ ps -ef | wc -l
```

There is no limit to the number of pipe operations that can be performed on a command-line. For example, to find the number of lines in a file which contain the name Smith:

```
$ cat namesfile | grep Smith | wc -l
```

8.11 Configuring Aliases

As you gain proficiency with the shell environment it is likely that you will find yourself frequently issuing commands with the same arguments. For example, you may often use the *ls* command with the *l* and *t* options:

```
$ ls -lt
```

To reduce the amount of typing involved in issuing a command, it is possible to create an alias that maps to the command and arguments. For example, to create an alias such that entering the letter *l* will cause the *ls -lt* command to be executed, the following statement would be used:

```
$ alias l="ls -lt"
```

Entering *l* at the command prompt will now execute the original statement.

8.12 Environment Variables

Shell environment variables provide temporary storage of data and configuration settings. The shell itself sets up a number of environment variables that may be changed by the user to modify the behavior of the shell. A listing of currently defined variables may be obtained using the *env* command:

```
$ env
SSH_CONNECTION=192.168.0.19 61231 192.168.0.28 22
MODULES_RUN_QUARANTINE=LD_LIBRARY_PATH
LANG=en_US.UTF-8
HISTCONTROL=ignoredups
HOSTNAME=-pc.ebookfrenzy.com
XDG_SESSION_ID=15
MODULES_CMD=/usr/share/Modules/libexec/modulecmd.tcl
USER=demo
ENV=/usr/share/Modules/init/profile.sh
SELINUX_ROLE_REQUESTED=
PWD=/home/demo
HOME=/home/demo
SSH_CLIENT=192.168.0.19 61231 22
SELINUX_LEVEL_REQUESTED=
.
.
.
```

Perhaps the most useful environment variable is PATH. This defines the directories in which the shell will search for commands entered at the command prompt, and the order in which it will do so. The PATH environment variable for a user account on a newly installed CentOS 8 system will likely be configured as follows:

```
$ echo $PATH
/home/demo/.local/bin:/home/demo/bin:/usr/share/Modules/bin:/usr/local/bin:/usr/
bin:/usr/local/sbin:/usr/sbin
```

Another useful variable is HOME which specifies the home directory of the current user. If, for example, you wanted the shell to also look for commands in the scripts directory located in your home directory, you would modify the PATH variable as follows:

```
$ export PATH=$PATH:$HOME/scripts
```

The current value of an existing environment variable may be displayed using the echo command:

```
$ echo $PATH
```

You can create your own environment variables using the *export* command. For example:

```
$ export DATAPATH=/data/files
```

A useful trick to assign the output from a command to an environment variable involves the use of back quotes (`) around the command. For example, to assign the current date and time to an environment variable called NOW:

```
$ export NOW=`date`
$ echo $NOW
Tue Apr 2 13:48:40 EDT 2019
```

If there are environment variable or alias settings that you need to be configured each time you enter the shell environment, they may be added to a file in your home directory named *.bashrc*. For example, the following example *.bashrc* file is configured to set up the DATAPATH environment variable and an alias:

```
# .bashrc

# Source global definitions
if [ -f /etc/bashrc ]; then
        . /etc/bashrc
fi

# User specific environment
PATH="$HOME/.local/bin:$HOME/bin:$PATH"
export PATH

# Uncomment the following line if you don't like systemctl's auto-paging feature:
# export SYSTEMD_PAGER=

# User specific aliases and functions
export DATAPATH=/data/files
alias l="ls -lt"
```

8.13 Writing Shell Scripts

So far we have focused exclusively on the interactive nature of the Bash shell. By interactive we mean manually entering commands at the prompt one by one and executing them. In fact, this is only a small part of what the shell is capable of. Arguably one of the most powerful aspects of the shell involves the ability to create shell scripts. Shell scripts are essentially text files containing sequences of statements that can be executed within the shell environment to perform tasks. In addition to the ability to execute commands, the shell provides many of the programming constructs such as *for* and *do* loops and *if* statements that you might reasonably expect to find in a scripting language.

Unfortunately a detailed overview of shell scripting is beyond the scope of this chapter. There are, however, many books and web resources dedicated to shell scripting that do the subject much more justice than we could ever hope to achieve here. In this section, therefore, we will only be providing a very small taste of shell scripting.

The first step in creating a shell script is to create a file (for the purposes of this example we name it *simple.sh*) and add the following as the first line:

```
#!/bin/sh
```

The #! is called the "shebang" and is a special sequence of characters indicating that the path to the interpreter needed to execute the script is the next item on the line (in this case the *sh* executable located in /bin). This could equally be, for example, */bin/csh* or */bin/ksh* if either were the interpreter you wanted to use.

The next step is to write a simple script:

```
#!/bin/sh
for i in *
do
    echo $i
done
```

All this script does is iterate through all the files in the current directory and display the name of each file. This may be executed by passing the name of the script through as an argument to *sh*:

```
$ sh simple.sh
```

In order to make the file executable (thereby negating the need to pass it through to the *sh* command) the *chmod* command can be used:

```
$ chmod +x simple.sh
```

Once the execute bit has been set on the file's permissions, it may be executed directly. For example:

```
$ ./simple.sh
```

8.14 Summary

In this chapter of CentOS 8 Essentials we have taken a brief tour of the Bash shell environment. In the world of graphical desktop environments it is easy to forget that the true power and flexibility of an operating system can often only be utilized by dropping down below the user friendly desktop interface and using a shell environment. Moreover, familiarity with the shell is a necessity when required to administer and maintain server-based systems that do not have the desktop installed or when attempting to repair a system that is damaged to the point that the desktop or Cockpit interface will no longer launch.

The capabilities of the shell go far beyond the areas covered in this chapter. If you are new to the shell then we strongly encourage you to seek out additional resources. Once familiar with the concepts you will quickly find that it is quicker to perform many tasks using the shell in a terminal window than it is to wade through menus and dialogs on the desktop.

9. Managing CentOS 8 Users and Groups

During the installation of CentOS 8, the installer created a root, or superuser account, and required that a password be configured. The installer also provided the opportunity to create a user account for the system. We should not lose sight of the fact that CentOS 8 is actually an enterprise class, multi-user and multi-tasking operating system. In order to use the full power of CentOS 8, therefore, it is likely that more than one user will need to be given access to the system. Each user should have his or her own user account login, password, home directory and privileges.

Users are further divided into groups for the purposes of easier administration and those groups can have different levels of privileges. For example, you may have a group of users who work in the Accounting department. In such an environment you may wish to create an accounts group and assign all the Accounting department users to that group.

In this chapter we will cover the steps to add, remove and manage users and groups on a CentOS 8 system. There are a number of ways to manage users and groups on a CentOS 8 system, the most common options being command-line tools and the Cockpit web interface. In this chapter we will look at both approaches.

9.1 User Management from the Command-line

New users may be added to a CentOS 8 system via the command-line using the *useradd* utility. To create a new user account, enter a command similar to the following:

```
# useradd john
```

By default, this will create a home directory for the user in the */home* directory (in this case /home/john). To specify a different home directory, use the -d command-line option when creating the account:

```
# useradd -d /users/johnsmith john
```

Once the account has been created, a password needs to be assigned using the *passwd* tool before the user will be able to log into the system:

```
# passwd john
Changing password for user john.
New password:
Retype new password:
passwd: all authentication tokens updated successfully.
```

An existing user may be deleted via the command-line using the *userdel* utility:

```
# userdel john
```

It is also possible to remove the user's home directory and mail spool as part of the deletion process:

```
# userdel --remove john
```

All users on a CentOS 8 system are members of one or more groups. By default, new users are added to a private group with the same name as the user (in the above example, the account created for user john was a member of a private group also named john). As an administrator, it makes sense to organize users into more logical groups. For example all sales people might belong to a sales group, while accounting staff might belong to the accounts group and so on. New groups are added from the command-line using the *groupadd* command-line tool, for example:

```
# groupadd accounts
```

Use the *usermod* tool to add an existing user to an existing group from the command-line:

```
# usermod -G accounts john
```

To add an existing user to multiple existing groups, run the *usermod* command with the -G option:

```
# usermod -G accounts,sales,support john
```

Note that the above commands remove the user from any supplementary groups which are not listed after the -G, but to which the user is currently a member. To retain any current group memberships, use the -a flag to append the new group memberships:

```
# usermod -aG accounts,sales,support john
```

An existing group may be deleted from a system using the *groupdel* utility:

```
# groupdel accounts
```

Note that if the group to be deleted is the primary or initial group for any user it cannot be deleted. The user must first be deleted, or assigned a new primary group using the *usermod* command before the group can be removed. A user can be assigned to a new primary group using the *usermod* -g option:

```
# usermod -g sales john
# groupdel accounts
```

To find out the groups to which a user belongs, simply run the *groups* command. For example:

```
$ groups john
john : john accounts support
```

By default, a user account will not be able to perform tasks that require superuser (root) privileges unless they know the root password. It is, however, possible to configure a user account so that privileged tasks can be performed using the *sudo* command. This involves adding the user account as a member of the *wheel* group, for example:

```
# usermod -aG wheel john
```

Once added to the wheel group, the user will be able to perform otherwise restricted tasks using *sudo* as follows:

```
$ sudo dnf update
[sudo] password for demo:
Updating Subscription Management repositories.
.
.
```

The sudo capabilities of the wheel group may be modified by editing the */etc/sudoers* file and locating the following section:

```
## Allows people in group wheel to run all commands
%wheel   ALL=(ALL)        ALL


## Same thing without a password
# %wheel         ALL=(ALL)       NOPASSWD: ALL
```

To disable sudo for all wheel group members, comment out the second line as follows:

```
## Allows people in group wheel to run all commands
# %wheel   ALL=(ALL)        ALL
```

To allow wheel group members to use sudo without entering a password (for security reasons this is not recommended), uncomment the corresponding line in the sudoers file:

```
## Same thing without a password
%wheel         ALL=(ALL)       NOPASSWD: ALL
```

It is worth noting here that behind the scenes, all of these commands are simply making changes to the */etc/passwd*, */etc/group* and */etc/shadow* files on the system.

9.2 User Management with Cockpit

If the Cockpit web interface is installed and enabled on the system (a topic covered in the chapter entitled *"An Overview of the CentOS 8 Cockpit Web Interface"*), a number of user management tasks can be performed within the Accounts screen shown in Figure 9-1 below:

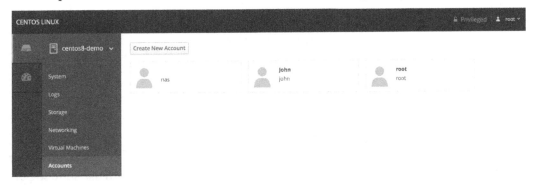

Figure 9-1

The screen will display any existing user accounts on the system and provides a button to add additional accounts. To create a new account, click on the *Create New Account* button and enter the requested information in the resulting dialog (Figure 9-2). Note that the option is also available to create the account but to lock it until later:

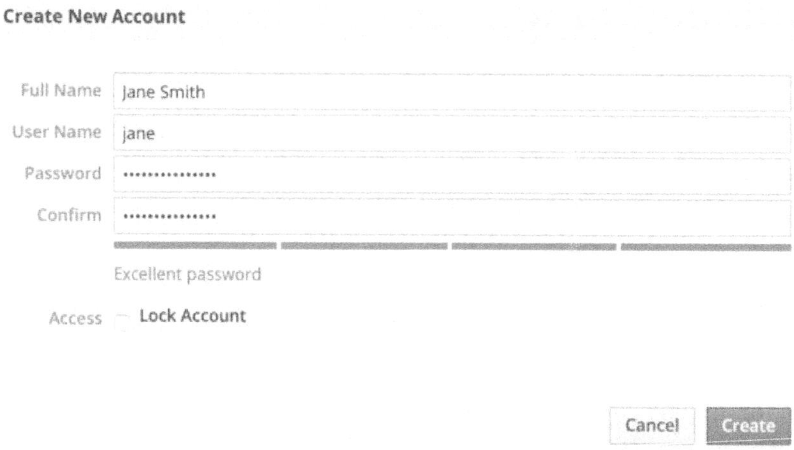

Figure 9-2

To modify a user account, select it from the main screen and make any modifications to the account details:

Figure 9-3

This screen allows a variety of tasks to be performed including locking or unlocking the account, changing the password or forcing the user to configure a new password. If the Server Administrator option is selected, the user will be added to the wheel group and permitted to use sudo to perform administrative tasks. A button is also provided to delete the user from the system.

If the user will be accessing the system remotely using an SSH connection with key encryption, the user's public key may be added within this screen. SSH access and authentication will be covered later in *"Configuring SSH Key-based Authentication on CentOS 8"*.

9.3 Summary

As a multi-user operating system, CentOS 8 has been designed to support controlled access for multiple users. During installation, the root user account was created and assigned a password and the option to create a user account was also provided. Additional user accounts may be added to the system using a set of command-line tools or via the Cockpit web interface. In addition to user accounts, Linux also implements the concept of groups. New groups can be added and users assigned to those groups using command-line tools and each user must belong to at least one group. By default a standard, non-root user does not have permission to perform privileged tasks. Users that are members of the special wheel group, however, may perform privileged tasks by making use of the *sudo* command.

10. Understanding CentOS 8 Software Installation and Management

It is highly unlikely that a newly installed CentOS 8 system will contain all of the software packages to perform the tasks for which it is intended. Even once all the required software has been installed, it is almost certain that newer versions of many of those packages will be released during the lifespan of the system. In some cases, you will need to ensure that these latest package releases are installed on the system to ensure that any bugs are fixed. In other cases, however, an older version of a particular software package may need to be kept on the system for compatibility with other software.

This chapter introduces the basic concepts of software management on CentOS 8, explains how these issues are addressed, introduces the concepts of repositories, software packages and the CentOS Application Stream (AppStream) and explores how to list, install and remove the software packages that make up a functioning CentOS 8 system.

10.1 Repositories

Linux is essentially comprised of a set of base packages that provide the core functionality of the operating system together with a range of other packages and modules that add functionality and features on top of the base operating system.

When CentOS 8 is first installed, a number of different packages will be installed depending on the software options selected during the installation phase. Once the system is up and running, however, additional software can be installed as needed. Typically, all software that is part of CentOS 8 (in other words software that is not provided by a third party vendor) is downloaded and installed on the system using the *dnf* command. As we have seen in earlier chapters, this typically consists of a command similar to the following being issued at the command prompt:

```
# dnf install httpd
```

When such a command is issued, the requested software is downloaded from a remote *repository* and installed on the local system. By default, CentOS 8 is configured to download software from two repositories named BaseOS and AppStream. Running the following command will provide a list of the repositories the system is currently configured to use when downloading software:

```
# dnf repolist
Last metadata expiration check: 0:01:02 ago on Thu 14 Nov 2019 03:43:07 PM EST.
repo id              repo name                                    status
AppStream            CentOS-8 - AppStream                         5,089
BaseOS               CentOS-8 - Base                              2,843
extras               CentOS-8 - Extras                                3
google-chrome        google-chrome                                   3
```

The above example shows that repositories for both AppStream and BaseOS are enabled on the system. Note also that repositories may also be added for third party software, as is the case for the Google Chrome repository listed above.

Additional repositories may be added to the system by placing entries in the */etc/dnf/dnf.conf* file, or by adding *.repo* files to the */etc/yum.repos.d/* directory. Alternatively, the repository may be added using the *dnf config-manager* tool, passing the URL of the *.repo* file for the repository as a command-line argument:

```
# dnf config-manager --add-repo https://url/of/repo/file
```

10.2 The BaseOS Repository

The BaseOS repository contains the packages that make up the core functionality of the operating system. These software elements are downloaded in the form of Red Hat Package Manager (RPM) package files and then installed on the system. A typical CentOS 8 system will have around 1500 RPM packages installed. To see a list of all the RPM packages currently installed on the system simply run the *rpm* command as follows:

```
# rpm -qa | more
qemu-kvm-block-rbd-2.12.0-41.el8+2104+3e32e6f8.x86_64
kyotocabinet-libs-1.2.76-17.el8.x86_64
cyrus-sasl-scram-2.1.27-0.3rc7.el8.x86_64
curl-7.61.1-5.el8.x86_64
.
.
```

A list of packages available for installation from the BaseOS repository is available by running the *dnf* command as follows:

```
# dnf list
```

To obtain a list of packages that match a search string use *dnf* as follows:

```
# dnf search "search string"
```

It is also possible to identify which package contains a specific file:

```
# dnf provides filename
```

For example:

```
# dnf provides /etc/httpd/conf/httpd.conf
Last metadata expiration check: 0:03:03 ago on Thu 14 Nov 2019 03:43:07 PM EST.
httpd-2.4.37-12.module_el8.0.0+185+5908b0db.x86_64 : Apache HTTP Server
Repo        : AppStream
Matched from:
Filename    : /etc/httpd/conf/httpd.conf
```

To install a package, run the following command:

```
# dnf install packagename
```

Similarly, to delete a package:

```
# dnf delete packagename
```

When a newer version of a BaseOS package is made available it will be downloaded and installed when the system is next updated, typically via the *dnf* command:

```
# dnf update
```

Any updated packages will replace the older version currently installed on the system. While this is generally the ideal situation when working with base operating system packages, this is not necessarily the desired behavior when dealing with other packages such as programming environments or development libraries where upgrading to a new version may cause compatibility issues with other packages installed in the system. This issue is addressed by the AppStream repository.

10.3 The AppStream Repository

The AppStream repository manages software in terms of *packages, modules, streams* and *profiles*. AppStream packages are, once again, RPM packages as outlined in the previous section describing BaseOS. AppStream modules, on the other hand, are groups of packages that belong together or for which dependencies exist (for example the group of packages that would need to be installed together when building a web server). Each module can have multiple streams, where each *module stream* represents a different version of the software module.

Consider, for example, a CentOS 8 system hosting a web site which depends on version 7.1 of the PHP scripting language. The server still needs to receive any updates to PHP 7.1 to benefit from patches and bug fixes, but is not compatible with the latest version of PHP (version 7.2). Before the introduction of AppStream, it would have been difficult to continue receiving version 7.1 updates when newer versions have been released.

To address this issue, the CentOS software management tools can use the AppStream repository to subscribe only to a specific stream for a specific module (in this case the version 7.1 stream of the PHP module).

In addition to streams, modules may also be sub-classed by *module profile*. Module profiles provide different configurations of packages that make up a module to be installed dependent on the requirements of the system. The nodejs JavaScript runtime environment module, for example, is available for installation using either the *development* or *minimal* profiles. On a system where development is taking place using nodejs, the development profile would most likely be used. When the software developed using nodejs is deployed, the minimal system containing just the runtime might be installed instead.

To view the list of modules available for installation use the *dnf* command as follows:

```
# dnf module list
CentOS-8 - AppStream
Name                 Stream         Profiles       Summary
389-ds               1.4            default         389 Directory Server (base)
App-cpanminus        1.7044 [d]     default [d]    Get, unpack, build and install
```

```
CPAN modules
DBD-MySQL            4.046 [d]     default [d]   A MySQL interface for Perl
DBD-Pg               3.7 [d]       default [d]   A PostgreSQL interface for Perl
DBD-SQLite           1.58 [d]      default [d]   SQLite DBI driver
DBI                  1.641 [d]     default [d]   A database access API for Perl
YAML                 1.24 [d]      default [d]   Perl parser for YAML
.
.
.

Hint: [d]efault, [e]nabled, [x]disabled, [i]nstalled
```

The first column in the list is the name of the module, the second the stream name (which is typically the version of the module). The letter after the stream name indicates whether the stream is the default (i.e. this is the stream that will be used for installation if no specific stream is referenced) or if it has been enabled for use when performing installations. The third column lists the profiles available for the corresponding package together with an indication of whether the profile is the default, has been installed or is disabled.

The *dnf* command to list information about a specific module is structured as follows:

```
# dnf module list modulename
```

The following output, for example, lists information about the PHP modules available for installation:

```
# dnf module list php
.
.
Name        Stream        Profiles                    Summary
php         7.1           devel, minimal, default [d]  PHP scripting language
php         7.2 [d]       devel, minimal, default [d]  PHP scripting language
```

Clearly version 7.2 will be installed on the system by default, and the module is available in development, default and minimal profile configurations.

To install a module using the default stream and profile, the *dnf* command can be used with the following syntax:

```
# dnf install @modulename
```

For example:

```
# dnf install @php
```

Alternatively, a stream may be specified from which to perform the installation:

```
# dnf install @modulename:stream
```

For example:

```
# dnf install @php:7.2
```

Finally, a profile may also be declared as follows:

```
# dnf install @modulename:stream/profile
```

For example, to install the minimal set of packages for PHP 7.2:

```
# dnf install @php:7.2/minimal
```

After executing the above command, the PHP modules will now be listed as follows:

```
php      7.1 [e]    devel, minimal [i], default [d]    PHP scripting language
php      7.2 [d][e] common [d], devel, minimal [i]     PHP scripting language
```

The "[e]" indicator in the stream column tells us that the 7.2 stream has been enabled while the "[i]" in the profile column shows that the module has been installed using the minimal profile.

To enable a stream without installing a module, use *dnf* as follows:

```
# dnf module enable modulename
```

Similarly, a stream may be disabled as follows:

```
# dnf module disable modulename
```

To uninstall a module, use the following syntax:

```
# dnf module remove modulename
```

Additional information about a module may be identified using the following *dnf* command:

```
# dnf module info modulename
```

To find out which RPM packages make up the different profiles of a specific module and stream combination, use *dnf* as follows:

```
# dnf module info --profile modulename:stream
```

For example:

```
# dnf module info --profile php:7.2
Last metadata expiration check: 0:02:11 ago on Thu 14 Nov 2019 04:31:25 PM EST.
Name     : php:7.2:8000020190628155007:ad195792:x86_64
common   : php-cli
         : php-common
         : php-fpm
         : php-json
         : php-mbstring
         : php-xml
devel    : libzip
         : php-cli
         : php-common
         : php-devel
         : php-fpm
         : php-json
         : php-mbstring
         : php-pear
         : php-pecl-zip
```

```
            : php-process
            : php-xml
minimal : php-cli
            : php-common
```

Finally, to switch from one module stream to another, simply run the installation command referencing the new stream as follows:

```
# dnf install @modulename:otherstream
```

This command will download the packages for the new stream and either upgrade or downgrade the existing packages to the specified version. Once this process is complete, resynchronize module packages for the new stream:

```
# dnf distro-sync
```

10.4 Summary

The CentOS 8 system is comprised of RPM format software packages that are downloaded and installed from the CentOS BaseOS and AppStream repositories. Additional repositories can be added to the system for installation packages as needed.

The BaseOS repository contains the packages that implement the base core functionality of the operating system. The AppStream packages, on the other hand, provide additional features and functionality that will be installed selectively depending on the purpose for which the system is being configured. In a complex system of this nature, there can be a significant amount of package interdependency where part of the system may require a specific version of another software package to function correctly. AppStreams allow modules and profiles to be created that contain all of the dependent packages necessary to install a particular feature together at the correct version level. AppStreams also allow installed packages to receive updates to the current version without having to download the next major version, thereby avoiding disrupting the dependencies of other packages.

11. Configuring CentOS 8 systemd Units

In order to gain proficiency in CentOS 8 system administration it is important to understand the concepts of systemd units with a particular emphasis on two specific types known as targets and services. The goal of this chapter, therefore, is to provide a basic overview of the different systemd units supported by CentOS 8 combined with an overview of how to configure the many services that run in the background of a running Linux system.

11.1 Understanding CentOS 8 systemd Targets

CentOS 8 can be configured to boot into one of a number of states (referred to as *targets*), each of which is designed to provide a specific level of operating system functionality. The target to which a system will boot by default is configured by the system administrator based on the purpose for which the system is being used. A desktop system, for example, will most likely be configured to boot using the graphical user interface target, while a cloud-based server system would be more likely to boot to the multi-user target level.

During the boot sequence, a process named *systemd* looks in the */etc/systemd/system* folder to find the default target setting. Having identified the default target, it proceeds to start the systemd units associated with that target so that the system boots with all the necessary processes running.

For those familiar with previous CentOS versions, systemd targets are the replacement for the older *runlevel* system.

11.2 Understanding CentOS 8 systemd Services

A service is essentially a process, typically running in the background, that provides specific functionality. The sshd service, for example, is the background process (also referred to as a daemon) that provides secure shell access to the system. Different systemd targets are configured to automatically launch different collections of services, depending on the functionality that is to be provided by that target.

Targets and services are types of *systemd unit*, a topic which will be covered later in this chapter.

11.3 CentOS 8 systemd Target Descriptions

As previously outlined, CentOS 8 can be booted into one of a number of target levels. The default target to which the system is configured to boot will, in turn, dictate which systemd units are started. The targets that relate specifically to system startup and shutdown can be summarized as follows:

• **poweroff.target** - This is the target in which the system shuts down. For obvious reasons it is unlikely you would want this as your default target.

• **rescue.target** – Causes the system to start up in a single user mode under which only the root user can log in. In this mode the system does not start any networking, graphical user interface or multi-user services. This run level is ideal for system administrators to perform system maintenance or repair activities.

• **multi-user.target** - Boots the system into a multi-user mode with text based console login capability.

• **graphical.target** - Boots the system into a networked, multi-user state with X Window System capability. By default the graphical desktop environment will start at the end of the boot process. This is the most common run level for desktop or workstation use.

• **reboot.target** - Reboots the system. Another target that, for obvious reasons, you are unlikely to want as your default.

In addition to the above targets, the system also includes about 70 other targets, many of which are essentially sub-targets used by the above main targets. Behind the scenes, for example, *multi-user.target* will also start a target named *basic.target* which will, in turn, start the *sockets.target* unit which is required for communication between different processes. This ensures that all of the services on which the multi-user target is dependent are also started during the boot process.

A list of the targets and services on which a specified target is dependent can be viewed by running the following command in a terminal window:

```
# systemctl list-dependencies <target>
```

Figure 11-1, for example, shows a partial listing of the systemd unit dependencies for the multi-user target (the full listing contains over 120 targets and services required for a fully functional multi-user system):

```
[root@rhel80desktop system]# systemctl list-dependencies multi-user.target
multi-user.target
● ├─atd.service
● ├─auditd.service
● ├─avahi-daemon.service
● ├─chronyd.service
● ├─crond.service
● ├─dbus.service
● ├─dnf-makecache.timer
● ├─firewalld.service
● ├─irqbalance.service
● ├─kdump.service
● ├─ksm.service
● ├─ksmtuned.service
● ├─libstoragemgmt.service
```

Figure 11-1

The listing is presented as a hierarchical tree illustrating how some dependencies have sub-dependencies of their own. Scrolling to the bottom of the list, for example, would reveal that the multi-user target depends on two network filesystem related targets (namely *nfs-client.target* and *remote-fs.target*), each with its own service and target sub-dependencies:

```
  ●   ┌nfs-client.target
  ●   │├auth-rpcgss-module.service
  ●   │├rpc-statd-notify.service
  ●   │└remote-fs-pre.target
  ●   │  └lvm2-activation-net.service
  ●   └remote-fs.target
  ●   ├var-lib-machines.mount
  ●   └nfs-client.target
  ●      ├auth-rpcgss-module.service
  ●      ├rpc-statd-notify.service
  ●      └remote-fs-pre.target
  ●         └lvm2-activation-net.service
```

Figure 11-2

The colored dots to the left of each entry in the list indicate the current status of that service or target as follows:

- **Green** - The service or target is active and running.

- **White** - The service or target is inactive (dead). Typically because the service or target has not yet been enabled, has been stopped for some reason, or a condition on which the service or target depends has not been met.

- **Red** - The service or target failed to start due to a fatal error.

To find out more details about the status of a systemd unit, use the *systemctl* command followed by the unit name as follows:

```
# systemctl status systemd-machine-id-commit.service
● systemd-machine-id-commit.service - Commit a transient machine-id on disk
   Loaded: loaded (/usr/lib/systemd/system/systemd-machine-id-commit.service;
static; vendor preset: disabled)
   Active: inactive (dead)
Condition: start condition failed at Thu 2019-02-14 15:27:47 EST; 1h 14min ago
           ConditionPathIsMountPoint=/etc/machine-id was not met
     Docs: man:systemd-machine-id-commit.service(8)
```

11.4 Identifying and Configuring the Default Target

The current default target for a CentOS 8 system can be identified using the *systemctl* command as follows:

```
# systemctl get-default
multi-user.target
```

In the above case, the system is configured to boot using the multi-user target by default. The default setting can be changed at any time using the *systemctl* command with the *set-default* option. The following example changes the default target to start the graphical user interface the next time the system boots:

```
# systemctl set-default graphical.target
Removed /etc/systemd/system/default.target.
Created symlink /etc/systemd/system/default.target → /usr/lib/systemd/system/
graphical.target.
```

The output from the default change operation reveals the steps performed in the background by the *systemctl* command to implement the change. The current default is configured by establishing a symbolic link from the *default.target* file located in */etc/systemd/system* to point to the corresponding target file located in the */usr/lib/systemd/system* folder (in this case the *graphical.target* file).

11.5 Understanding systemd Units and Unit Types

As previously mentioned, targets and services are both types of *systemd unit*. All of the files within the */usr/lib/systemd/system* folder are referred to as *systemd unit configuration files*, each of which represents a systemd unit. Each unit is, in turn, categorized as being of a particular *unit type*. CentOS 8 supports 12 different unit types including the target and service unit types already covered in this chapter.

The type of a unit file is represented by the filename extension as outlined in Table 11-1 below:

Unit Type	Filename Extension	Type Description
Service	.service	System service.
Target	.target	Group of systemd units.
Automount	.automount	File system auto-mount point.
Device	.device	Device file recognized by the kernel.
Mount	.mount	File system mount point.
Path	.path	File or directory in a file system.
Scope	.scope	Externally created process.
Slice	.slice	Group of hierarchically organized units that manage system processes.
Snapshot	.snapshot	Saved state of the systemd manager.
Socket	.socket	Inter-process communication socket.
Swap	.swap	Swap device or a swap file.
Timer	.timer	Systemd timer.

Table 11-1

Note that the target unit type differs from other types in that it is essentially comprised of a group of systemd units such as services or other targets.

11.6 Dynamically Changing the Current Target

The above step specifies the target that will be used the next time the system starts, but does not change the state of the currently running system. To change to a different target dynamically, use the *systemctl* command once again, this time using the *isolate* option followed by the destination target. To switch the current system to the graphical target without rebooting, for example, the following command would be used:

```
# systemctl isolate graphical.target
```

Once executed, the system will start the graphical desktop environment.

11.7 Enabling, Disabling and Masking systemd Units

A newly installed CentOS 8 system will include the base systemd service units but is unlikely to include all of the services that will eventually be needed by the system once it goes into a production environment. A basic CentOS 8 installation, for example, will typically not include the packages necessary to run an Apache web server, a key element of which is the *httpd.service* unit.

The system administrator will resolve this problem by installing the necessary httpd packages using the following command:

```
# dnf install httpd
```

Having configured the web server, the next task will be to check the status of the httpd service unit to identify whether it was activated as part of the installation process:

```
# systemctl status httpd.service
 httpd.service - The Apache HTTP Server
   Loaded: loaded (/usr/lib/systemd/system/httpd.service; disabled; vendor
preset: disabled)
   Active: inactive (dead)
     Docs: man:httpd.service(8)
```

Note that the service has loaded but is inactive because it is preset by the vendor to be disabled when first installed. To start the service, the following command can be used:

```
# systemctl start httpd.service
```

A status check will now indicate that the service is active:

```
 httpd.service - The Apache HTTP Server
   Loaded: loaded (/usr/lib/systemd/system/httpd.service; disabled; vendor
preset: disabled)
   Active: active (running) since Fri 2019-02-15 11:13:26 EST; 8s ago
     Docs: man:httpd.service(8)
 Main PID: 10721 (httpd)
   Status: "Started, listening on: port 80"
    Tasks: 213 (limit: 13923)
   Memory: 24.1M
   .
   .
   .
```

Note, however that the status indicates that the service is still disabled. This means that next time the system reboots, the httpd service will not start automatically and will need to be started manually by the system administrator.

To configure the httpd service to start automatically each time the system starts, it must be enabled as follows:

```
# systemctl enable httpd.service
```

Once the service has been enabled, the Loaded section of the status output will read as follows:

```
Loaded: loaded (/usr/lib/systemd/system/httpd.service; enabled; vendor preset:
disabled)
```

Now that it has been enabled, the next time the system reboots to the current target, the httpd service will start automatically. Assuming, for example, that the service was enabled while the system was running the multi-user target, the httpd service will have been added as another dependency to the *multi-user.target* systemd unit.

Behind the scenes, *systemctl* adds dependencies to targets by creating symbolic links in the *.wants* folder for the target within the */etc/systemd/system* folder. The *multi-user.target* unit, for example, has a folder named *multi-user.target.wants* in */etc/systemd/system* containing symbolic links to all of the systemd units located in */usr/lib/systemd/system* on which it is dependent. A review of this folder will show a correlation with the dependencies listed by the *systemctl list-dependencies* command outlined earlier in the chapter.

To disable a service so that it no longer starts automatically as a target dependency, simply disable it as follows:

```
# systemctl disable httpd.service
```

This command will remove the symbolic link to the *httpd.service* unit file from the *.wants* directory so that it is no longer a dependency and, as such, will not be started the next time the system boots.

The *.wants* folder contains dependencies which, if not available, will not prevent the unit from starting and functioning. Mandatory dependencies (in other words dependencies that will cause the unit to fail if not available) should be placed in the *.requires* folder (for example *multi-user. target.requires*).

In addition to enabling and disabling, it is also possible to mask a systemd unit as follows:

```
# systemctl mask httpd.service
```

A masked systemd unit cannot be enabled, disabled or started under any circumstances even if it is listed as a dependency for another unit. In fact, as far has the system is concerned, it is as though a masked systemd unit no longer exists. This can be useful for ensuring that a unit is never started regardless of the system conditions. The only way to regain access to the service is to unmask it:

```
# systemctl unmask httpd.service
```

11.8 Working with systemd Units in Cockpit

In addition to the command-line techniques outlined so far in this chapter, it is also possible to review and manage systemd units from within the Cockpit web-based interface. Assuming that Cockpit has been installed and set up as outlined in the chapter entitled *"An Overview of the CentOS 8 Cockpit Web Interface"*, access to the list of systemd units on the system can be accessed by logging into Cockpit and selecting the Services option in the left-hand navigation panel marked A in Figure 11-3:

Figure 11-3

The button marked B displays units of specific types in the main area marked C where the current status of each unit is listed in the State column.

Selecting a unit from the list will display detailed information. Figure 11-4, for example, shows the detail screen for an *httpd.service* instance including service logs (A) and menu options (B) for performing tasks such as starting, stopping, enabling/disabling and masking/unmasking the unit.

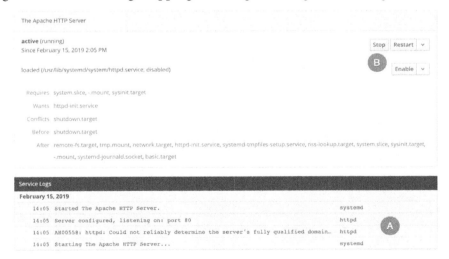

Figure 11-4

11.9 Summary

A newly installed CentOS 8 system includes a base set of systemd units many of which run in the background to provide much of the functionality of the system. These units are categorized by type, the most common of which being targets and services. A target unit is simply a group of other units that are to be started collectively. The system has a default target unit which defines the other units which are to be started up each time the system boots. The most common targets are those which boot the system to either multi-user or graphical mode. The *systemctl* command-line tool provides a range of options for performing systemd unit configuration tasks, many of which are also available through the Cockpit web-based interface.

12. CentOS 8 Network Management

It is difficult to envisage a CentOS 8 system that does not have at least one network connection, and harder still to imagine how such an isolated system could be of much practical use. The simple fact is that CentOS 8 is designed to provide enterprise level services over network and internet connections. A key part of learning how to administer a CentOS 8 system involves learning how to configure and manage the network interfaces installed on the system.

This chapter is intended to provide an overview of network management on CentOS 8 including the NetworkManager service and tools together with some other useful utilities.

12.1 An Introduction to NetworkManager

NetworkManager is a service and set of tools designed specifically to make it easier to manage the networking configuration on Linux systems and is the default network management service on CentOS 8.

In addition to a service that runs in the background, NetworkManager also includes the following tools:

- **nmcli** - A tool for working with NetworkManager via the command-line. This tool is useful when access to a graphical environment is not available and can also be used within scripts to make network configuration changes.

- **nmtui** - A basic text-based user interface for managing NetworkManager. This tool can be run within any terminal window and allows changes to be made by making menu selections and entering data. While useful for performing basic tasks, *nmtui* lacks many of the features provided by the *nmcli* tool.

- **nm-connection-editor** - A full graphical management tool providing access to most of the NetworkManager configuration options.

- **GNOME Settings** - The Network screen of the GNOME desktop Settings application allows basic network management tasks to be performed.

- **Cockpit Network Settings** - The Network screen of the Cockpit web interface allows a range of network management tasks to be performed.

Although there a number of different ways to manage the network environment on a CentOS 8 system, for the purposes of this chapter we will focus on the *nmcli* command. While the graphical tools are certainly useful when you have access to a desktop environment or Cockpit has been enabled, understanding the command-line interface is essential for situations where a command prompt is all that is available. Also, the graphical tools (Cockpit included) do not include all of the capabilities of the *nmcli* tool. Finally, once you have gained some familiarity with NetworkManager and *nmcli*, those skills will translate easily when using the more intuitive tool options. The same cannot be said of the graphical tool options. It is harder to use *nmcli* if, for example, you have only ever used *nm-connection-editor*.

12.2 Installing and Enabling NetworkManager

NetworkManager should be installed by default for most CentOS 8 installations. Use the *rpm* command to find out if it needs to be installed:

```
# rpm -q NetworkManager
NetworkManager-1.14.0-14.el8.x86_64
```

If necessary, install the package as follows:

```
# dnf install NetworkManager
```

Once the package is installed, the NetworkManager daemon will need to be enabled so that it starts each time the system boots:

```
# systemctl enable NetworkManager
```

Finally, start the service running and check the status to verify that the launch was successful:

```
# systemctl start NetworkManager
# systemctl status NetworkManager
● NetworkManager.service - Network Manager
   Loaded: loaded (/usr/lib/systemd/system/NetworkManager.service; enabled;
vendor >
   Drop-In: /usr/lib/systemd/system/NetworkManager.service.d
            └─NetworkManager-ovs.conf
   Active: active (running) since Tue 2019-04-09 10:07:22 EDT; 2h 48min ago
 .
 .
```

12.3 Basic nmcli Commands

The *nmcli* command will have been installed as part of the Networkmanager package and can be executed from the command-line using the following syntax:

```
# nmcli [Options] Object {Command | help}
```

In the above syntax, *Object* will be one of *general*, *networking*, *radio*, *connection*, *monitor*, *device* or *agent*, all of which can be abbreviated to a few letters of the word (for example *con*, or even just the letter *c*, for *connection*). For example, all of the following commands will output help information relating to the *device* object:

```
# nmcli device help
# nmcli dev help
# nmcli d help
```

To check the overall status of NetworkManager on the system, use the following command:

```
# nmcli general status
STATE        CONNECTIVITY  WIFI-HW  WIFI     WWAN-HW  WWAN
connected    full          enabled  enabled  enabled  enabled
```

To check the status of the devices installed on a system, the following command can be used:

```
# nmcli dev status
DEVICE          TYPE        STATE         CONNECTION
eno1            ethernet    connected     eno1
wlp0s26u1u2     wifi        connected     zoneone
virbr0          bridge      connected     virbr0
lo              loopback    unmanaged     --
virbr0-nic      tun         unmanaged     --
```

The output may also be modified by using the -p (pretty) option to make the output more human friendly:

```
# nmcli -p dev status
=====================
  Status of devices
=====================
DEVICE          TYPE        STATE         CONNECTION
-----------------------------------------------------------------
eno1            ethernet    connected     eno1
wlp0s26u1u2     wifi        connected     zoneone
virbr0          bridge      connected     virbr0
lo              loopback    unmanaged     --
virbr0-nic      tun         unmanaged     --
```

Conversely, the -t option may be used to make the output more terse and suitable for automated processing:

```
# nmcli -t dev status
eno1:ethernet:connected:eno1
wlp0s26u1u2:wifi:connected:emilyzone
virbr0:bridge:connected:virbr0
lo:loopback:unmanaged:
virbr0-nic:tun:unmanaged:
```

From the status output, we can see that the system has two physical devices installed, one Ethernet and the other a Wi-Fi device.

The bridge (virbr) entries are virtual devices used to provide networking for virtual machines (the topic of virtualization will be covered starting with the chapter entitled *"An Overview of Virtualization Techniques"*). The loopback interface is a special virtual device that allows the system to communicate with itself and is typically used to perform network diagnostics.

When working with NetworkManager, it is important to understand the difference between a device and a connection. As described above, a device is either a physical or virtual network device while a connection is a network configuration that the device connects to.

The following command displays information about the connections configured on the system:

```
# nmcli con show
```

CentOS 8 Network Management

```
NAME            UUID                                    TYPE        DEVICE
zoneone         2abecafa-4ea2-47f6-b20f-4fb0c0fd5e94    wifi        wlp0s26u1u2
eno1            99d40009-6bb1-4182-baad-a103941c90ff    ethernet    eno1
virbr0          e13e9552-1765-42d1-b739-ff981668fbee    bridge      virbr0
zonetwo         f940a2d1-8c18-4a9e-bf29-817702429b8a    wifi        --
zonethree       fd65c5e5-3e92-4e9e-b924-1b0b07b70032    wifi        --
```

From the above output, we can see that the Wi-Fi device (*wlp0s26u1u2*) is connected to a wireless network named *zoneone* while the Ethernet device (*eno1*) is connected to a connection named *eno1*. In addition to zoneone, NetworkManager has also listed two other Wi-Fi connections named *zonetwo* and *zonethree*, neither of which currently have a device connected.

To find out the IP address allocated to a connection, the *ip* tool can be used with the *address* option:

```
# ip address
```

This can also be abbreviated:

```
# ip a
.
.
.
3: wlp0s26u1u2: <BROADCAST,MULTICAST,UP,LOWER_UP> mtu 1500 qdisc mq state UP
group default qlen 1000
    link/ether 74:da:38:ee:be:50 brd ff:ff:ff:ff:ff:ff
    inet 192.168.1.121/24 brd 192.168.1.255 scope global dynamic noprefixroute
wlp0s26u1u2
        valid_lft 57584sec preferred_lft 57584sec
.
.
.
```

The ip command will output information for all of the devices detected on the system. The above output shows that the Wi-Fi device has been assigned an IP address of 192.168.1.121.

If we only wanted to list active connections, the *nmcli* command could have been used with the -a option:

```
# nmcli con show -a
NAME         UUID                                    TYPE        DEVICE
emilyzone    2abecafa-4ea2-47f6-b20f-4fb0c0fd5e94    wifi        wlp0s26u1u2
eno1         99d40009-6bb1-4182-baad-a103941c90ff    ethernet    eno1
virbr0       e13e9552-1765-42d1-b739-ff981668fbee    bridge      virbr0
```

To switch the Wi-Fi device connection from zoneone to zonetwo, we can run the following command:

```
# nmcli device wifi connect zonetwo -ask
Password:
```

The -*ask* flag causes *nmcli* to prompt the user to enter the password for the Wi-Fi network. To include the Wi-Fi password on the command-line (particularly useful if the command is being executed in a script), use the *password* option:

```
# nmcli device wifi connect zonetwo password <password here>
```

The *nmcli* tool may also be used to scan for available Wi-Fi networks as follows:

```
# nmcli device wifi list
IN-USE  SSID        MODE   CHAN  RATE        SIGNAL  BARS  SECURITY
        zoneone     Infra  6     195 Mbit/s  80            WPA2
*       zonetwo     Infra  11    130 Mbit/s  74            WPA1 WPA2
```

A currently active connection can be deactivated as follows:

```
# nmcli con down <connection name>
```

Similarly, an inactive connection can be brought back up at any time:

```
# nmcli con up <connection name>
```

When a connection is brought down, NetworkManager automatically searches for another connection, activates it and assigns it to the device to which the previous connection was established. To prevent a connection from being used in this situation, disable the autoconnect option as follows:

```
# nmcli con mod <connection name> connection.autoconnect no
```

The following command may be used to obtain additional information about a specific connection. This includes the current values for all the connection properties:

```
# nmcli con show eno1
connection.id:                      eno1
connection.uuid:                    99d40009-6bb1-4182-baad-a103941c90ff
connection.stable-id:               --
connection.type:                    802-3-ethernet
connection.interface-name:          eno1
connection.autoconnect:             yes
connection.autoconnect-priority:    0
connection.autoconnect-retries:     -1 (default)
connection.multi-connect:           0 (default)
connection.auth-retries:            -1
connection.timestamp:               1554833695
connection.read-only:               no
connection.permissions:             --
connection.zone:                    --
connection.master:                  --
connection.slave-type:              --
connection.autoconnect-slaves:      -1 (default)
.
.
.
```

All of these properties can be modified using *nmcli* with the modify option using the following syntax:

```
# nmcli con mod <connection name> connection.<property name> <setting>
```

12.4 Working with Connection Profiles

So far we have explored the use of connections without explaining how a connection is configured. The configuration of a connection is referred to as a *connection profile* and is stored in a file located in the */etc/sysconfig/network-scripts* directory, the contents of which might read as follows:

```
# ls /etc/sysconfig/network-scripts
ifcfg-zoneone      ifcfg-eno1         ifdown-ppp
ifcfg-zonethree    ifcfg-zonetwo      ifup-ppp           keys-zonethree
keys-zoneone       keys-zonetwo
```

Each of the files prefixed with *ifcg-* is an interface configuration file containing the connection profile for the corresponding connection while the *key-* files contain the passwords for the Wi-Fi connections.

Consider, for example, the contents of the *ifcfg-eno1* file:

```
TYPE=Ethernet
PROXY_METHOD=none
BROWSER_ONLY=no
DEFROUTE=yes
IPV4_FAILURE_FATAL=no
NAME=eno1
UUID=99d40009-6bb1-4182-baad-a103941c90ff
DEVICE=eno1
ONBOOT=yes
BOOTPROTO=dhcp
IPV6INIT=yes
IPV6_AUTOCONF=yes
IPV6_DEFROUTE=yes
IPV6_FAILURE_FATAL=no
IPV6_ADDR_GEN_MODE=stable-privacy
```

The file contains basic information about the connection, including the type (Ethernet) of the device to which it is currently assigned (eno1) and the fact that the connection is to be automatically activated on system boot with an IP address obtained using DHCP. Changes to the connection profile can be implemented by modifying this file and instructing *nmcli* to reload the connection configuration files:

```
# nmcli con reload
```

New connection profiles can also be created manually or generated automatically by *nmcli*. As an example, assume that a new network device has been installed on the system. When this happens, the NetworkManager service will detect the new hardware and create a device for it. In the example below, the new device has been assigned the name *eno2*:

```
# nmcli dev status
```

```
DEVICE        TYPE        STATE        CONNECTION
en01          ethernet    connected    eno1
eno2          ethernet    connected    Wired connection 1
```

NetworkManager automatically detected the device, activated it and assigned it to a connection named "Wired connection 1". This is a default connection over which we have no configuration control because there is no interface configuration file for it in */etc/sysconfig/network-scripts*. The next steps are to delete the "Wired connection 1" connection and use *nmcli* to create a new connection and assign it to the device. The command to delete a connection is as follows:

```
# nmcli con delete "Wired connection 1"
```

Next, *nmcli* can be used to create a new connection profile configured either with a static IP address, or a dynamic IP address obtained from a DHCP server. To create a dynamic connection profile named *dyn_ip*, the following command would be used:

```
# nmcli connection add type ethernet con-name dyn_ip ifname eno2
Connection 'dyn_ip' (160d9e10-bbc8-439a-9c47-a2ec52990472) successfully added.
```

To create a new connection profile without locking it to a specific device, simply omit the *ifname* option in the command:

```
# nmcli connection add type ethernet con-name dyn_ip
```

After the connection has been created, a file named *ifcg-dyn_ip* will have been added to the */etc/sysconfig/network-scripts* directory.

Alternatively, to create a connection named *static_ip* assigned a static IP address (in this case 192.168.1.200) the following command would be used:

```
# nmcli con add type ethernet con-name static_ip ifname eno0 ip4 192.168.1.200/24
gw4 192.168.1.1
Connection 'static_ip' (3fccafb3-e761-4271-b310-ad0f28ee8606) successfully added.
```

The corresponding *ifcg-static_ip* file will read as follows:

```
TYPE=Ethernet
PROXY_METHOD=none
BROWSER_ONLY=no
BOOTPROTO=none
IPADDR=192.168.1.200
PREFIX=24
GATEWAY=192.168.1.1
DEFROUTE=yes
IPV4_FAILURE_FATAL=no
IPV6INIT=yes
IPV6_AUTOCONF=yes
IPV6_DEFROUTE=yes
IPV6_FAILURE_FATAL=no
IPV6_ADDR_GEN_MODE=stable-privacy
NAME=static_ip
```

```
UUID=3fccafb3-e761-4271-b310-ad0f28ee8606
DEVICE=eno2
ONBOOT=yes
```

The command to add a new connection may be altered slightly to also assign both IPv4 and IPv6 static addresses:

```
# nmcli con add type ethernet con-name static_ip ifname eno0 ip4 192.168.1.200/24
gw4 192.168.1.1  gw4 192.168.1.1 ip6 cabf::4532 gw6 2010:dfa::1
```

12.5 Interactive Editing

In addition to using *nmcli* with command-line options, the tool also includes an interactive mode that can be used to create and modify connection profiles. The following transcript, for example, shows interactive mode being used to create a new Ethernet connection named *demo_con*:

```
# nmcli con edit
Valid connection types: 6lowpan, 802-11-olpc-mesh (olpc-mesh), 802-11-wireless
(wifi), 802-3-ethernet (ethernet), adsl, bluetooth, bond, bridge, cdma, dummy,
generic, gsm, infiniband, ip-tunnel, macsec, macvlan, ovs-bridge, ovs-interface,
ovs-port, pppoe, team, tun, vlan, vpn, vxlan, wimax, wpan, bond-slave, bridge-
slave, team-slave
Enter connection type: ethernet


===| nmcli interactive connection editor |===


Adding a new '802-3-ethernet' connection


Type 'help' or '?' for available commands.
Type 'print' to show all the connection properties.
Type 'describe [<setting>.<prop>]' for detailed property description.


You may edit the following settings: connection, 802-3-ethernet (ethernet), 802-
1x, dcb, sriov, ethtool, match, ipv4, ipv6, tc, proxy
nmcli> set connection.id demo_con
nmcli> set connection.interface eno1
nmcli> set connection.autoconnect yes
nmcli> set ipv4.method auto
nmcli> set 802-3-ethernet.mtu auto
nmcli> set ipv6.method auto
nmcli> save
Saving the connection with 'autoconnect=yes'. That might result in an immediate
activation of the connection.
Do you still want to save? (yes/no) [yes] yes
Connection 'demo_con' (cb837408-6c6f-4572-9548-4932f88b9275) successfully saved.
nmcli> quit
```

The following transcript, on the other hand, modifies the previously created *static_ip* connection profile to use a different static IP address to the one originally specified:

```
# nmcli con edit static_ip

===| nmcli interactive connection editor |===

Editing existing '802-3-ethernet' connection: 'static_ip'

Type 'help' or '?' for available commands.
Type 'print' to show all the connection properties.
Type 'describe [<setting>.<prop>]' for detailed property description.

You may edit the following settings: connection, 802-3-ethernet (ethernet), 802-
1x, dcb, sriov, ethtool, match, ipv4, ipv6, tc, proxy
nmcli> print ipv4.addresses
ipv4.addresses: 192.168.1.200/24
nmcli> set ipv4.addresses 192.168.1.201/24
nmcli> save
Connection 'static_ip' (3fccafb3-e761-4271-b310-ad0f28ee8606) successfully
updated.
nmcli> quit
```

After modifying an existing connection, remember to instruct NetworkManager to reload the configuration profiles:

```
# nmcli con reload
```

When using interactive mode, it is useful to know that there is an extensive built-in help system available to learn how to use the tool. The help topics can be accessed by typing **help** or *?* at the *nmcli* > prompt:

```
nmcli> ?
------------------------------------------------------------------------------
---[ Main menu ]---
goto     [<setting> | <prop>]          :: go to a setting or property
remove   <setting>[.<prop>] | <prop>  :: remove setting or reset property value
set      [<setting>.<prop> <value>]    :: set property value
describe [<setting>.<prop>]            :: describe property
print    [all | <setting>[.<prop>]]   :: print the connection
verify   [all | fix]                  :: verify the connection
save     [persistent|temporary]        :: save the connection
activate [<ifname>] [/<ap>|<nsp>]     :: activate the connection
back                                   :: go one level up (back)
help/?   [<command>]                   :: print this help
nmcli    <conf-option> <value>         :: nmcli configuration
quit                                   :: exit nmcli
------------------------------------------------------------------------------
```

12.6 Configuring NetworkManager Permissions

In addition to making it easier to manage networks on CentOS 8, NetworkManager also allows permissions to be specified for connections. The following command, for example, restricts a connection profile to root and user accounts named john and caitlyn:

```
# nmcli con mod static_ip connection.permissions user:root,john,caitlyn
```

Once the connection profiles have been reloaded by NetworkManager, the *static_ip* connection will only be active and accessible to other users when at least one of the designated users is logged in to an active session on the system. As soon as the last of these users logs out, the connection will go down and remain inactive until one of the users signs back in.

In addition, only users with permission are able to make changes to the connection status or configuration.

12.7 Summary

Network management on CentOS 8 is handled by the NetworkManager service. NetworkManager views a network as consisting of network interface devices and connections. A network device can be a physical Ethernet or Wi-Fi device or a virtual device used by a virtual machine guest. Connections represent the network to which the devices connect and are configured by connection profiles. A configuration profile will, among other settings, define whether the connection has a static or dynamic IP address, the IP address of any gateway used by the network and whether or not the connection should be established automatically each time the system starts up.

NetworkManager can be administered using a number of different tools including the *nmcli* and *nmtui* command-line tools, the *nm-connection-editor* graphical tool and the network settings section of the Cockpit web interface. In general, the *nmcli* command-line tool provides the most features and flexibility.

13. Basic CentOS 8 Firewall Configuration with firewalld

A firewall is a vital component in protecting a computer system or network of computers from external attack (typically from an external source via an internet connection). Any computer connected directly to an internet connection must run a firewall to protect against malicious activity. Similarly, any internal network must have some form of firewall between it and an external internet connection.

All Linux distributions are provided with a firewall solution of some form. In the case of CentOS 8 this takes the form of a service named *firewalld*.

While the subject of firewall configuration can be complex, fortunately CentOS 8 provides command-line, web-based and graphical tools that ease the firewall configuration process. This chapter will introduce the basic concepts of firewalld and cover the steps necessary to configure a firewall using the tools provided with the operating system.

13.1 An Introduction to firewalld

The firewalld service uses a set a rules to control incoming network traffic and define which traffic is to be blocked and which is to be allowed to pass through to the system and is built on top of a more complex firewall tool named *iptables*.

The firewalld system provides a flexible way to manage incoming traffic. The firewall could, for example, be configured to block traffic arriving from a specific external IP address, or to prevent all traffic arriving on a particular TCP/IP port. Rules may also be defined to forward incoming traffic to different systems or to act as an internet gateway to protect other computers on a network.

In keeping with common security practices, a default firewalld installation is configured to block all access with the exception of SSH remote login and the DHCP service used by the system to obtain a dynamic IP address (both of which are essential if the system administrator is to be able to gain access to the system after completing the installation).

The key elements of firewall configuration on CentOS 8 are *zones*, *interfaces*, *services* and *ports*.

13.1.1 Zones

By default, firewalld is installed with a range of pre-configured *zones*. A zone is a preconfigured set of rules which can be applied to the system at any time to quickly implement firewall configurations for specific scenarios. The *block* zone, for example, blocks all incoming traffic, while the *home* zone imposes less strict rules on the assumption that the system is running in a safer environment where a greater level of trust is expected. New zones may be added to the system, and existing zones modified to add or remove rules. Zones may also be deleted entirely from the system. Table 13-1 lists the set of zones available by default on a CentOS 8 system:

Zone	Description
drop	The most secure zone. Only outgoing connections are permitted and all incoming connections are dropped without any notification to the connecting client.
block	Similar to the drop zone with the exception that incoming connections are rejected with an icmp-host-prohibited or icmp6-adm-prohibited notification.
public	Intended for use when connected to public networks or the internet where other computers are not known to be trustworthy. Allows select incoming connections.
external	When a system is acting as the internet gateway for a network of computers, the external zone is applied to the interface that is connected to the internet. This zone is used in conjunction with the *internal* zone when implementing masquerading or network address translation (NAT) as outlined later in this chapter. Allows select incoming connections
internal	Used with the *external* zone and applied to the interface that is connected to the internal network. Assumes that the computers on the internal network are trusted. Allows select incoming connections.
dmz	For use when the system is running in the demilitarized zone (DMZ). These are generally computers that are publicly accessible but isolated from other parts of your internal network. Allows select incoming connections.
work	For use when running a system on a network in a work environment where other computers are trusted. Allows select incoming connections.
home	For use when running a system on a home network where other computers are trusted. Allows select incoming connections.
trusted	The least secure zone. All incoming connections are accepted.

Table 13-1

13.1.2 Interfaces

Any CentOS 8 system connected to the internet or a network (or both) will contain at least one *interface* in the form of either a physical or virtual network device. When firewalld is active, each of these interfaces is assigned to a zone allowing different levels of firewall security to be assigned to different interfaces. Consider a server containing two interfaces, one connected externally to the internet and the other to an internal network. In such a scenario, the external facing interface would most likely be assigned to the more restrictive *external* zone while the internal interface might use the *internal* zone.

13.1.3 Services

TCP/IP defines a set of services that communicate on standard ports. Secure HTTPS web connections, for example, use port 443, while the SMTP email service uses port 25. To selectively enable incoming traffic for specific services, firewalld rules can be added to zones. The *home* zone, for example, does not permit incoming HTTPS connections by default. This traffic can be enabled by adding rules to a zone to allow incoming HTTPS connections without having to reference the specific port number.

13.1.4 Ports

Although common TCP/IP services can be referenced when adding firewalld rules, situations will arise where incoming connections need to be allowed on a specific port that is not allocated to a service. This can be achieved by adding rules that reference specific ports instead of services. This technique was used in the chapter entitled *"An Overview of the CentOS 8 Cockpit Web Interface"* when port 9090 was opened to allow access to the Cockpit web interface.

13.2 Checking firewalld Status

The firewalld service is installed and enabled by default on all CentOS 8 installations. The status of the service can be checked via the following command:

```
# systemctl status firewalld
 firewalld.service - firewalld - dynamic firewall daemon
   Loaded: loaded (/usr/lib/systemd/system/firewalld.service; enabled; vendor
preset: enabled)
   Active: active (running) since Thu 2019-02-14 14:24:31 EST; 3 days ago
     Docs: man:firewalld(1)
 Main PID: 816 (firewalld)
    Tasks: 2 (limit: 25026)
   Memory: 30.6M
   CGroup: /system.slice/firewalld.service
           816 /usr/libexec/platform-python -s /usr/sbin/firewalld --nofork
--nopid
```

If necessary, the firewalld service may be installed as follows:

```
# dnf install firewalld
```

The firewalld service is enabled by default so will start automatically both after installation is complete and each time the system boots.

13.3 Configuring Firewall Rules with firewall-cmd

The *firewall-cmd* command-line utility allows information about the firewalld configuration to be viewed and changes to be made to zones and rules from within a terminal window.

When making changes to the firewall settings, it is important to be aware of the concepts of *runtime* and *permanent* configurations. By default, any rule changes are considered to be runtime configuration changes. This means that while the changes will take effect immediately, they will be lost next time the system restarts or the firewalld service reloads, for example by issuing the

Basic CentOS 8 Firewall Configuration with firewalld

following command:

```
# firewall-cmd --reload
```

To make a change permanent, the *--permanent* command-line option must be used. Permanent changes do not take effect until the firewalld service reloads but will remain in place until manually changed.

13.3.1 Identifying and Changing the Default Zone

To identify the default zone (in other words the zone to which all interfaces will be assigned unless a different zone is specifically selected) use the *firewall-cmd* tool as follows:

```
# firewall-cmd --get-default-zone
public
```

To change the default to a different zone:

```
# firewall-cmd --set-default-zone=home
success
```

13.3.2 Displaying Zone Information

To list all of the zones available on the system:

```
# firewall-cmd --get-zones
block dmz drop external home internal libvirt public trusted work
```

Obtain a list of zones currently active together with the interfaces to which they are assigned as follows:

```
# firewall-cmd --get-active-zones
external
  interfaces: eth0
internal
 interfaces: eth1
```

All of the rules currently configured for a specific zone may be listed as follows:

```
# firewall-cmd --zone=home --list-all
home (active)
  target: default
  icmp-block-inversion: no
  interfaces: eth0
  sources:
  services: cockpit dhcpv6-client http mdns samba-client ssh
  ports:
  protocols:
  masquerade: no
  forward-ports:
  source-ports:
  icmp-blocks:
  rich rules:
```

Use the following command to list the services currently available for inclusion in a firewalld rule:

```
# firewall-cmd --get-services
RH-Satellite-6 amanda-client amanda-k5-client amqp amqps apcupsd audit bacula
bacula-client bgp bitcoin bitcoin-rpc bitcoin-testnet bitcoin-testnet-rpc ceph
ceph-mon cfengine cockpit ...
```

To list the services currently enabled for a zone:

```
# firewall-cmd --zone=public --list-services
cockpit dhcpv6-client ssh
```

A list of port rules can be obtained as follows:

```
# firewall-cmd --zone=public --list-ports
9090/tcp
```

13.3.3 Adding and Removing Zone Services

To add a service to a zone, in this case adding HTTPS to the public zone, the following command would be used:

```
# firewall-cmd --zone=public --add-service=https
success
```

By default this is a *runtime* change, so the added rule will be lost after a system reboot. To add a service permanently so that it remains in effect next time the system restarts, use the *--permanent* flag:

```
# firewall-cmd --zone=public --permanent --add-service=https
success
```

To verify that a service has been added permanently, be sure to include the *--permanent* flag when requesting the service list:

```
# firewall-cmd --zone=public --permanent --list-services
cockpit dhcpv6-client http https ssh
```

Note that as a permanent change, this new rule will not take effect until the system restarts or firewalld reloads:

```
# firewall-cmd --reload
```

Remove a service from a zone using the *--remove-service* option. Since this is a runtime change, the rule will be re-instated the next time the system restarts:

```
# firewall-cmd --zone=public --remove-service=https
```

To remove a service permanently use the *--permanent* flag, remembering to reload firewalld if the change is required to take immediate effect.:

```
# firewall-cmd --zone=public --permanent --remove-service=https
```

13.3.4 Working with Port-based Rules

To enable a specific port, use the *--add-port* option. Note that when manually defining the port, both the port number and protocol (TCP or UDP) will need to be provided:

```
# firewall-cmd --zone=public --permanent --add-port=5000/tcp
```

It is also possible to specify a range of ports when adding a rule to a zone:

```
# firewall-cmd --zone=public --permanent --add-port=5900-5999/udp
```

13.3.5 Creating a New Zone

An entirely new zone may be created by running the following command. Once created, the zone may be managed in the same way as any of the predefined zones:

```
# firewall-cmd --permanent --new-zone=myoffice
success
```

After adding a new zone, firewalld will need to be restarted before the zone becomes available:

```
# firewall-cmd --reload
success
```

13.3.6 Changing Zone/Interface Assignments

As previously discussed, each interface on the system must be assigned to a zone. The zone to which an interface is assigned can also be changed using the *firewall-cmd* tool. In the following example, the eth0 interface is assigned to the *public* zone:

```
# firewall-cmd --zone=public --change-interface=eth0
success
```

13.3.7 Masquerading

Masquerading is better known in networking administration circles as Network Address Translation (NAT). When using a CentOS 8 system as a gateway to the internet for a network of computers, masquerading allows all of the internal systems to use the IP address of that CentOS 8 system when communicating over the internet. This has the advantage of hiding the internal IP addresses of any systems from malicious external entities and also avoids the necessity to allocate a public IP address to every computer on the network.

Use the following command to check whether masquerading is already enabled on the firewall:

```
# firewall-cmd --zone=external --query-masquerade
```

Use the following command to enable masquerading (remembering to use the *--permanent* flag if the change is to be permanent):

```
firewall-cmd --zone=external --add-masquerade
```

13.3.8 Adding ICMP Rules

The Internet Control Message Protocol (ICMP) is used by client systems on networks to send information such as error messages to each other. It is also the foundation of the *ping* command which is used by network administrators and users alike to detect whether a particular client is alive on a network. The ICMP category allows for the blocking of specific ICMP message types. For example, an administrator might choose to block incoming ping (Echo Request) ICMP messages to prevent the possibility of a ping based denial of service (DoS) attack (where a server is maliciously bombarded with so many ping messages that it becomes unable to respond to legitimate requests).

To view the ICMP types available for inclusion in firewalld rules, run the following command:

```
# firewall-cmd --get-icmptypes
address-unreachable bad-header beyond-scope communication-prohibited destination-
unreachable echo-reply ...
```

The following command, for example, permanently adds a rule to block echo-reply (ping request) messages for the public zone:

```
# firewall-cmd --zone=public --permanent --add-icmp-block=echo-reply
```

13.3.9 Implementing Port Forwarding

Port forwarding is used in conjunction with masquerading when the CentOS 8 system is acting as a gateway to the internet for an internal network of computer systems. Port forwarding allows traffic arriving at the firewall via the internet on a specific port to be forwarded to a particular system on the internal network. This is perhaps best described by way of an example.

Suppose that a CentOS 8 system is acting as the firewall for an internal network of computers and one of the systems on the network is configured as a web server. Let's assume the web server system has an IP address of 192.168.2.20. The domain record for the web site hosted on this system is configured with the public IP address behind which the CentOS 8 firewall system sits. When an HTTP web page request arrives on port 80 the CentOS 8 system acting as the firewall needs to know what to do with it. By configuring port forwarding it is possible to direct all web traffic to the internal system hosting the web server (in this case, IP address 192.168.2.20), either continuing to use port 80 or diverting the traffic to a different port on the destination server. In fact, port forwarding can even be configured to forward the traffic to a different port on the same system as the firewall (a concept known as local forwarding).

To use port forwarding, begin by enabling masquerading as follows (in this case the assumption is made that the interface connected to the internet has been assigned to the *external* zone):

```
# firewall-cmd --zone=external --add-masquerade
```

To forward from a port to a different local port, a command similar to the following would be used:

```
# firewall-cmd --zone=external --add-forward-port=port=22:proto=tcp:toport=2750
```

In the above example, any TCP traffic arriving on port 22 will be forwarded to port 2750 on the local system. The following command, on the other hand, forwards port 20 on the local system to port 22 on the system with the IP address of 192.168.0.19:

```
# firewall-cmd --zone=external \
        --add-forward-port=port=20:proto=tcp:toport=22:toaddr=192.168.0.19
```

Similarly, the following command forwards local port 20 to port 2750 on the system with IP address 192.168.0.18:

```
# firewall-cmd --zone=external --add-forward-port=port=20:proto=tcp:toport=2750:to
addr=192.168.0.18
```

13.4 Managing firewalld from the Cockpit Interface

So far this chapter has provided an overview of firewalld and explored the use of the *firewall-cmd* command-line tool to manage firewall zones and interfaces. While *firewall-cmd* provides the most flexible way to manage the firewalld configuration, it is also possible to view and manage the services for the default zone within the Cockpit web console.

To access the firewalld settings, sign into the Cockpit interface and select *Networking* from the navigation panel. On the networking page, select the *Firewall* option as highlighted in Figure 13-1 below:

Figure 13-1

The Firewall page displays the current service rules configured for the default zone (and allows services to be removed using the trash can buttons), new services to be added to the zone and for the firewall to be turned on and off:

Figure 13-2

13.5 Managing firewalld using firewall-config

If you have access to the graphical desktop environment, the firewall may also be configured using the *firewall-config* tool. Though not installed by default, *firewall-config* may be installed as follows:

```
# dnf install firewall-config
```

When launched, the main *firewall-config* screen appears as illustrated in Figure 13-3:

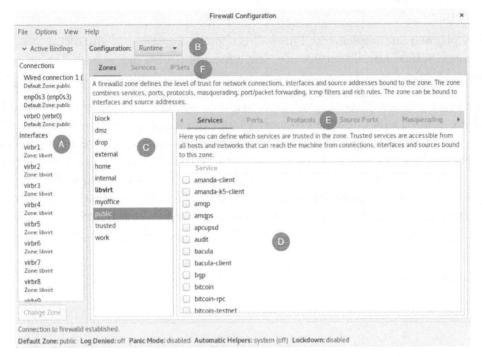

Figure 13-3

The key areas of the tool can be summarized as follows:

A - Displays all of the currently active interfaces and the zones to which they are assigned. To assign an interface to a different zone, select it from this panel, click on the *Change Zone* button and select the required zone from the resulting dialog.

B - Controls whether the information displayed and any changes made within the tool apply to the runtime or permanent rules.

C - The list of zones, services or IPSets configured on the system. The information listed in this panel depends on the selection made from toolbar F. Selecting an item from the list in this panel updates the main panel marked D.

D - The main panel containing information about the current category selection in toolbar E. In this example, the panel is displaying services for the *public* zone. The checkboxes next to each service control whether the service is enabled or not within the firewall. It is within these category panels that new rules can be added or existing rules configured or removed.

E - Controls the content displayed in panel D. Selecting items from this bar displays the current rule for the chosen category.

F - Controls the list displayed in panel C.

The *firewall-config* tool is straightforward and intuitive to use and allows many of the tasks available with *firewall-cmd* to be performed in a visual environment.

13.6 Summary

A carefully planned and implemented firewall is a vital component of any secure system. In the case of CentOS 8, the firewalld service provides a firewall system that is both flexible and easy to administer.

The firewalld service uses the concept of zones to group together sets of firewall rules and includes a suite of pre-defined zones designed to meet a range of firewall protection requirements. These zones may be modified to add or remove rules, or entirely new zones created and configured. The network devices on the system that connect to networks or the internet are referred to as interfaces. Each interface, in turn, is assigned to a zone. The primary tools for working with firewalld are the *firewall-cmd* command-line tool and the *firewall-config* graphical utility. Minimal firewall management options are also available via the Cockpit web interface.

14. Configuring SSH Key-based Authentication on CentOS 8

When a CentOS 8 system is first installed, it is configured by default to allow remote command-line access via Secure Shell (SSH) connections. This provides password protected and encrypted access to the system for the root account and any other users added during the installation phase. This level of security is far from adequate and should be upgraded to SSH key-based authentication as soon as possible.

This chapter will outline the steps to increase the security of a CentOS 8 system by implementing key-based SSH authentication.

14.1 An Overview of Secure Shell (SSH)

SSH is designed to allow secure remote access to systems for the purposes of gaining shell access and transferring files and data. As will be covered in *"CentOS 8 Remote Desktop Access with VNC"*, SSH can also be used to provide a secure *tunnel* through which remote access to the GNOME desktop can be achieved over a network connection.

A basic SSH configuration consists of a client (used on the computer establishing the connection) and a server (running on the system to which the connection is to be established). A user might, for example, use an SSH client running on a Linux, Windows or macOS system to connect to the SSH server running on a CentOS 8 system to gain access to a shell command-line prompt or to perform file transfers. All of the communications between client and server, including the password entered to gain access, are encrypted preventing outside parties from intercepting the data.

The inherent weakness in a basic SSH implementation is that it depends entirely on the strength of the passwords assigned to the accounts on the system. If a malicious party is able to identify the password for an account (either through guess work, subterfuge or a brute force attack) the system becomes vulnerable. This weakness can be addressed by implementing SSH key-based authentication.

14.2 SSH Key-based Authentication

SSH key-based authentication makes use of asymmetric *public key encryption* to add an extra layer of security to remote system access. The concept of public key encryption was devised in 1975 by Whitfield Diffie and Martin Hellman and is based on the concept of using a pair of keys, one private and one public.

In a public key encryption system, the public key is used to encrypt data that can only be decrypted by the owner of the private key.

In the case of SSH key-based authentication, the private key is held by the host on which the SSH client is located while the corresponding public key resides on the system on which the SSH server is running. It is important to protect the private key, since ownership of the key will allow anyone to log into the remote system. As an added layer of protection, therefore, the private key may also be encrypted and protected by a password which must be entered each time a connection is established to the server.

14.3 Setting Up Key-based Authentication

There are four steps to setting up key-based SSH authentication which can be summarized as follows:

1. Generate the public and private keys.

2. Install the public key on the server.

3. Test authentication.

4. Disable password-based authentication on the server.

The remainder of this chapter will outline these steps in greater detail for Linux, macOS and Windows-based client operating systems.

14.4 SSH Key-based Authentication from Linux and macOS Clients

The first step in setting up SSH key-based authentication is to generate the key pairs on the client system. If the client system is running Linux or macOS, this is achieved using the *ssh-keygen* utility:

```
# ssh-keygen
```

This will result in output similar to the following:

```
Generating public/private rsa key pair.
Enter file in which to save the key (/home/<username>/.ssh/id_rsa):
```

Press the Enter key to accept the default location for the key files. This will place two files in the *.ssh* sub-directory of the current user's home directory. The private key will be stored in a file named *id_rsa* while the public key will reside in the file named *id_rsa.pub*.

Next, *ssh-keygen* will prompt for a passphrase with which to protect the private key. If a passphrase is provided, the private key will be encrypted on the local disk and the passphrase required in order to gain access to the remote system. For better security, use of a passphrase is recommended.

```
Enter passphrase (empty for no passphrase):
```

Finally, the *ssh-keygen* tool will generate the following output indicating that the keys have been generated:

```
Your identification has been saved in /home/neil/.ssh/id_rsa.
Your public key has been saved in /home/neil/.ssh/id_rsa.pub.
The key fingerprint is:
SHA256:FOLGWEEGFIjWnCT5wtTOv5VK4hdimzWghZizUEMYbfo <username>@<hostname>
```

```
The key's randomart image is:
+---[RSA 2048]----+
|.BB+=+*..        |
|o+B= *  . .      |
|===.. + .        |
|*+ *  . .        |
|.++ o    S       |
|..E+ * o         |
| o B *           |
|   + +           |
|    .            |
+----[SHA256]-----+
```

The next step is to install the public key onto the remote server system. This can be achieved using the *ssh-copy-id* utility as follows:

```
$ ssh-copy-id username@remote_hostname
```

For example:

```
$ ssh-copy-id neil@192.168.1.100
/usr/bin/ssh-copy-id: INFO: Source of key(s) to be installed: "/home/neil/.ssh/
id_rsa.pub"
/usr/bin/ssh-copy-id: INFO: attempting to log in with the new key(s), to filter
out any that are already installed
/usr/bin/ssh-copy-id: INFO: 1 key(s) remain to be installed -- if you are
prompted now it is to install the new keys
neil@192.168.1.100's password:

Number of key(s) added: 1

Now try logging into the machine, with:   "ssh 'neil@192.168.1.100'"
and check to make sure that only the key(s) you wanted were added.
```

Once the key is installed, test that the authentication works by attempting a remote login using the *ssh* client:

```
$ ssh -l <username> <hostname>
```

If the private key is encrypted and protected with a passphrase, enter the phrase when prompted to complete the authentication and establish remote access to the CentOS 8 system:

```
Enter passphrase for key '/home/neil/.ssh/id_rsa':
Last login: Thu Feb 21 13:41:23 2019 from 192.168.1.101
[neil@demosystem02 ~]$
```

Repeat these steps for any other accounts on the server for which remote access is required. If access is also required from other client systems, simply copy the *id_rsa* private key file to the *.ssh* sub-directory of your home folder of the other systems.

As currently configured, access to the remote system can still be achieved using the less secure password authentication. Once you have verified that key-based authentication works, log into the remote system, edit the */etc/ssh/ssh_config* file and change the *PasswordAuthentication* setting to *no*:

```
PasswordAuthentication no
```

Save the file and restart the *sshd* service to implement the change:

```
# systemctl restart sshd.service
```

From this point on, it will only be possible to remotely access the system using SSH key-based authentication.

14.5 Managing Multiple Keys

It is not uncommon for multiple private keys to reside on a client system, each providing access to a different server. There are a number of options for selecting a specific key when establishing a connection. It is possible, for example, to specify the private key file to be used when launching the *ssh* client as follows:

```
$ ssh -l neilsmyth -i ~/.ssh/id_work 35.194.18.119
```

Alternatively, the SSH client user configuration file may be used to associate key files with servers. The configuration file is named *config*, must reside in the *.ssh* directory of the user's home directory and can be used to configure a wide range of options including the private key file, the default port to use when connecting, the default user name, and an abbreviated nickname via which to reference the server. The following example *config* file defines different key files for two servers and allows them to be referenced by the nicknames *home* and *work*. In the case of the work system, the file also specifies the user name to be used when authenticating:

```
Host work
    HostName 35.194.18.119
    IdentityFile ~/.ssh/id_work
    User neilsmyth

Host home
    HostName 192.168.0.21
    IdentityFile ~/.ssh/id_home
```

Prior to setting up the configuration file, the user would have used the following command to connect to the work system:

```
$ ssh -l neilsmyth -i ~/.ssh/id_work 35.194.18.119
```

Now, however, the command can be shortened as follows:

```
$ ssh work
```

A full listing of configuration file options can be found by running the following command:

```
$ man ssh_config
```

14.6 SSH Key-based Authentication from Windows 10 Clients

Recent releases of Windows 10 include a subset of the OpenSSH implementation that is used by most Linux and macOS systems as part of Windows PowerShell. This allows SSH key-based authentication to be set up from a Windows 10 client using similar steps to those outlined above for Linux and macOS.

To open Windows PowerShell on a Windows 10 system press the Win+X keyboard combination and select it from the menu, or locate and select it from the Start menu. Once running, the PowerShell window will appear as shown in Figure 14-1:

Figure 14-1

If you already have a private key from another client system, simply copy the *id_rsa* file to a folder named *.ssh* on the Windows 10 system. Once the file is in place, test the authentication within the PowerShell window as follows:

```
$ ssh -l <username>@<hostname>
```

For example:

```
PS C:\Users\neil> ssh -l neil 192.168.1.101
Enter passphrase for key 'C:\Users\neil/.ssh/id_rsa':
```

Enter the passphrase when prompted and complete the authentication process.

If an existing private key does not yet exist, generate a new private and public key pair within the PowerShell window using the *ssh-keygen* utility using the same steps as those outlined for Linux and macOS. Once the keys have been generated, the keys will once again be located in the *.ssh* directory of the current user's home folder, and the public key file *id_rsa.pub* will need to be installed on the remote CentOS 8 system. Unfortunately, Windows PowerShell does not include the *ssh-copy-id* utility, so this task will need to be performed manually.

Within the PowerShell window, change directory into the *.ssh* sub-directory and display the content of the public key *id_rsa.pub* file:

```
PS C:\Users\neil> cd .ssh
```

Configuring SSH Key-based Authentication on CentOS 8

```
PS C:\Users\neil\.ssh> type id_rsa.pub
ssh-rsa AAAAB3NzaC1yc2EAAAADAQABAAABAQDFgx1vzu591l16/uQw7FbmKVsQ3fzLz9MW1fgo4sdsx
Xp81wCHNAlqcjx1Pgr9BJPXWUMInQOi7BQ5I+vc2xQ2AS0kMq3ZH9ybWuQe/U2GjueXZd0FKrEXrT55wM
36Rm6Ii3roUCoGCzGR8mn95JvRB3VtCyDdzTWSi8JBpK5gV5oOxNTNPsewlLzouBlCT1qW3CKwEiIwu8S
9MTL7m3nrcaNeLewTTHevvHw4QDwzFQ+B0PDg96fzsYoTXVhzyHSWyo6H0gqrft7aK+gILBtEIhWTkSVE
MAzy1piKtCr1IYTmVK6engv0aoGtMUq6FnOeGp5FjvKkF4aQkh1QR28r neil@DESKTOP-S8P8D3N
```

Highlight the content of the file and copy it using the Ctrl-C keyboard shortcut.

Remaining within the PowerShell window, log into the remote system using password authentication:

```
PS C:\Users\neil\.ssh> ssh -l <username> <hostname>
```

Once signed in, check if the *.ssh* sub-directory exists. If it does not, create it as follows:

```
$ mkdir .ssh
```

Change directory into *.ssh* and check whether a file named *authorized_keys* already exists. If it does not, create it and paste the content of the public key file from the Windows 10 system into it.

If the *authorized_keys* file already exists it most likely already contains other keys. If this is the case, edit the file and paste the new public key at the end of the file. The following file, for example, contains two keys:

```
ssh-rsa AAAAB3NzaC1yc2EAAAADAQABAAABAQCzRWH27Xs8ZA5rIbZXKgxFY5XXauMv+6F5PljBLJ6j
+9nkmykVe3GjZTp3oD+KMRbT2kTEPbDpFD67DNL0eiX2ZuEEiYsxZfGCRCPBGYmQttFRHEAFnlS1Jx/
G4W5UNKvhAXWyMwDEKiWvqTVy6syB2Ritoak+D/Sc8nJflQ6dtw0jBs+S7Aim8TPfgpi4p5XJGruXNRS
camk68NgnPfTL3vT726EuABCk6C934KARd+/AXa8/5rNOh4ETPstjBRfFJ0tpmsWWhhNEnwJRqS2LD0
ug7E3yFI2qsNKGEzvAYUC8Up45MRP7liR3aMlCBilltsy9R+IB7oMEycZAe/qj neil@localhost.
localdomain
ssh-rsa AAAAB3NzaC1yc2EAAAADAQABAAABAQDFgx1vzu591l16/uQw7FbmKVsQ3fzLz9MW1fgo4sdsx
Xp81wCHNAlqcjx1Pgr9BJPXWUMInQOi7BQ5I+vc2xQ2AS0kMq3ZH9ybWuQe/U2GjueXZd0FKrEXrT55wM
36Rm6Ii3roUCoGCzGR8mn95JvRB3VtCyDdzTWSi8JBpK5gV5oOxNTNPsewlLzouBlCT1qW3CKwEiIwu8S
9MTL7m3nrcaNeLewTTHevvHw4QDwzFQ+B0PDg96fzsYoTXVhzyHSWyo6H0gqrft7aK+gILBtEIhWTkSVE
MAzy1piKtCr1IYTmVK6engv0aoGtMUq6FnOeGp5FjvKkF4aQkh1QR28r neil@DESKTOP-S8P8D3N
```

Once the public key is installed on the server, test the authentication by logging in to the server from within the Windows 10 PowerShell window, for example:

```
PS C:\Users\neil\.ssh> ssh -l neil 192.168.1.100
Enter passphrase for key 'C:\Users\neil/.ssh/id_rsa':
```

When key-based authentication has been set up for all the accounts and verified, disable password authentication on the CentOS 8 system as outlined at the end of the previous section.

14.7 SSH Key-based Authentication using PuTTY

For Windows systems that do not have OpenSSH available, or as a more flexible alternative to using PowerShell, the PuTTY tool is a widely used alternative. The first step in using PuTTY is to download and install it on any Windows systems that need an SSH client. PuTTY is a free utility and can be downloaded using the following link:

https://www.chiark.greenend.org.uk/~sgtatham/putty/latest.html

Download the Windows installer executable that matches your Windows system (32-bit and 64-bit versions are available) then execute the installer to complete installation.

If a private key already exists on another system, create the *.ssh* folder in the home folder of the current user and copy the private *id_rsa key* into it.

Next, the private key file needs to be converted to a PuTTY private key format file using the *PuTTYgen* tool. Locate this utility in the Windows Start menu and launch it:

Figure 14-2

Once launched, click on the *Load* button located in the *Actions* section and navigate to the private key file previously copied to the *.ssh* folder (note that it may be necessary to change the file type filter to *All Files (*.*)*) in order for the key file to be visible. Once located, select the file and load it into *PuttyGen*. When prompted, enter the passphrase originally used to encrypt the file. Once the private key has been imported, save it as a PuTTY key file by clicking on the *Save Private Key* button. For consistency, save the key file to the *.ssh* folder but give it a different name to differentiate it from the original key file.

Launch PuTTY from the Start menu and enter the IP address or host name of the remote server into the main screen before selecting the *Connection -> SSH -> Auth* category in the left-hand panel as highlighted in Figure 14-3:

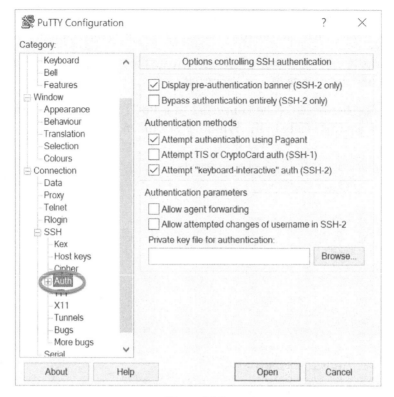

Figure 14-3

Click on the Browse button next to the *Private key for authentication* field and navigate to and select the previously saved PuTTY private key file. Optionally, scroll to the top of the left-hand panel, select the *Session* entry and enter a name for the session in the *Saved Sessions* field before clicking on the *Save* button. This will save the session configuration so that it can be used in future without having to re-enter the settings each time.

Finally, click on the *Open* button to establish the connection to the remote server, entering the user name and passphrase when prompted to do so to complete the authentication.

14.8 Generating a Private Key with PuTTYgen

The previous section explored the use of existing private and public keys when working with PuTTY. If keys do not already exist, they can be created using the *PuTTYgen* tool which is included with the main PuTTY installation.

To create new keys, launch *PuttyGen* and click on the *Generate* button highlighted in Figure 14-4:

Figure 14-4

Move the mouse pointer around to generate random data as instructed, then enter an optional passphrase with which to encrypt the private key. Once the keys have been generated, save the files to suitable locations using the *Save public key* and *Save private key* buttons. The private key can be used with PuTTY as outlined in the previous section. To install the public key on the remote server use the steps covered in the earlier section on using SSH within PowerShell on Windows 10.

14.9 Installing the Public Key for a Google Cloud Instance

If your CentOS 8 system is hosted by Google Cloud, for example as a Compute Engine instance, there are a number of different ways to gain SSH access to the server using key-based authentication. Perhaps the most straightforward is to add your public key to the metadata for your Google Cloud account. This will make the public key available for all Virtual Machine instances that you create within Google Cloud. To add the public key, log into the Google Cloud Platform console, select the *Metadata* option from the left-hand navigation panel as highlighted in Figure 14-5 and select the *SSH keys* tab:

Figure 14-5

On the SSH Keys screen, click on the *Edit* button (also highlighted in Figure 14-5) to edit the list of keys. Scroll down to the bottom of the current list and click on the *+ Add Item* button. A new field will appear into which you will need to paste the entire public key as it appears in your *id_rsa.pub* file. Once the key has been entered, click on the *Save* button to add the key.

The public key will now appear in the list of SSH Keys. Note that the key entry also includes the username which must be used when logging into any Google Cloud instances:

Figure 14-6

With the public key added to the metadata it should be possible to access any virtual machine instance from any client on which the corresponding private key has been installed and on which the user has an account. In fact, behind the scenes, all Google Cloud has done to enable this is add the public key to the *.ssh/authorized_keys* file in the user's home directory on any virtual machines on which the account exists.

14.10 Summary

It is important that any remote access to a CentOS 8 system be implemented in a way that provides a high level of security. By default, a CentOS 8 system allows SSH based access using password-based authentication. This leaves the system vulnerable to anyone who can either guess a password, or find out the password through other means. For this reason, the use of key-based authentication is recommended to protect system access. Key-based authentication uses the concept of public key encryption involving public and private keys. When implemented, users are only able to connect to a server if they are using a client which has a private key that matches a public key on the server. As an added layer of security, the private key may also be encrypted and password protected. Once key-based encryption has been implemented, the server system is then configured to disable support for the less secure password-based authentication.

This chapter has provided an overview of SSH key-based authentication and outlined the steps involved in generating keys and configuring clients on macOS, Linux and Windows, in addition to the installation and management of public keys on a CentOS 8 server.

15. CentOS 8 Remote Desktop Access with VNC

CentOS 8 can be configured to provide remote access to the graphical desktop environment over a network or internet connection. Although not enabled by default, it is relatively straightforward to display and access a CentOS 8 desktop from a system anywhere else on a network or the internet. This can be achieved regardless of whether that system is running Linux, Windows or macOS. In fact, there are even apps available for Android and iOS that will allow you to access your CentOS 8 desktop from just about anywhere that a data signal is available.

Remote desktop access can be useful in a number of scenarios. It enables you or another person, for example, to view and interact with your CentOS 8 desktop environment from another computer system either on the same network or over the internet. This is useful if you need to work on your computer when you are away from your desk such as while traveling. It is also useful in situations where a co-worker or IT support technician needs access to your desktop to resolve a problem.

In situations where the CentOS 8 system is running on a cloud-based server, it also allows access to the desktop environment as an alternative to performing administrative tasks using the command-line prompt or Cockpit web console.

The CentOS 8 remote desktop functionality is based on technology known as Virtual Network Computing (VNC) and in this chapter we will cover the key aspects of configuring and using remote desktops within CentOS 8.

15.1 Secure and Insecure Remote Desktop Access

In this chapter we will cover both secure and insecure remote desktop access methods. Assuming that you are accessing one system from another within the context of a secure internal network then it is generally safe to use the insecure access method. If, on the other hand, you plan to access your desktop remotely over any kind of public network you must use the secure method of access to avoid your system and data being compromised.

15.2 Installing the GNOME Desktop Environment

It is, of course, only possible to access the desktop environment if the desktop itself has been installed. If, for example, the system was initially configured as a server it is unlikely that the desktop packages were installed. The easiest way to install the packages necessary to run the GNOME desktop is to perform a *group install*. The key to installing groups of packages to enable a specific feature is knowing the name of the group. At the time of writing, the group for installing the desktop environment on CentOS 8 is named "Workstation". As the group names have a tendency to change from one CentOS release to another, it is useful to know that the list of groups that are either installed or available to be installed can be obtained using the *dnf* utility as follows:

```
# dnf grouplist

Available Environment Groups:
    Workstation
    Minimal Install
    Custom Operating System
Installed Environment Groups:
    Server with GUI
Installed Groups:
    Container Management
Available Groups:
    .NET Core Development
    RPM Development Tools
    Smart Card Support
    Scientific Support
    Security Tools
    Development Tools
    System Tools
    Headless Management
    Network Servers
    Legacy UNIX Compatibility
    Graphical Administration Tools
```

In the above example, the Workstation environment group is listed as being available (and therefore not already installed). To find out more information about the contents of a group prior to installation, use the following command:

```
# dnf groupinfo workstation

Environment Group: Workstation
 Description: Workstation is a user friendly desktop system for laptops and PCs.
 Mandatory Groups:
    Common NetworkManager submodules
    Core
    Fonts
    GNOME
    Guest Desktop Agents
    Internet Browser
    Multimedia
    Standard
    Workstation product core
    base-x
```

Having confirmed that this is the correct group, it can be installed as follows:

```
# dnf groupinstall workstation
```

Once installed, and assuming that the system has a display added, the desktop can be launched using the following command:

```
$ startx
```

If, on the other hand, the system is a server with no directly connected display, the only way to run and access the desktop will be to configure VNC support on the system.

15.3 Installing VNC on CentOS 8

Access to a remote desktop requires a VNC server installed on the remote system, a VNC viewer on the system from which access is being established and, optionally, a secure SSH connection. While a number of VNC server and viewer implementations are available, CentOS has standardized on TigerVNC which provides both server and viewer components for Linux-based operating systems. VNC viewer clients for non-Linux platforms include RealVNC and TightVNC.

To install the TigerVNC server package on CentOS 8, simply run the following command:

```
# dnf install tigervnc-server
```

If required, the TigerVNC viewer may also be installed as follows:

```
# dnf install tigervnc
```

Once the server has been installed the system will need to be configured to run one or more VNC services and to open the appropriate ports on the firewall.

15.4 Configuring the VNC Server

With the VNC server packages installed, the next step is to configure the server. The first step is to specify a password for the user that will be accessing the remote desktop environment. While logged in as root, execute the following command (where the user name is assumed to be demo):

```
# su - demo
[demo@demoserver ~]$ vncpasswd
Password:
Verify:
Would you like to enter a view-only password (y/n)? n
A view-only password is not used

[demo@demoserver ~]$ exit

#
```

Next, a VNC server configuration file named *vncserver@.service* needs to be created in the */etc/systemd/system* directory. The content of this file should read as follows, where all instances of <USER> are replaced with the username referenced when the VNC password was set:

```
[Unit]
escription=Remote desktop service (VNC)
After=syslog.target network.target

[Service]
Type=forking
```

```
WorkingDirectory=/home/<USER>
User=<USER>
Group=<USER>

ExecStartPre=/bin/sh -c '/usr/bin/vncserver -kill %i > /dev/null 2>&1 || :'
ExecStart=/usr/bin/vncserver -autokill %i
ExecStop=/usr/bin/vncserver -kill %i

Restart=on-success
RestartSec=15
[Install]
WantedBy=multi-user.target
```

Next, the firewall needs to be configured to provide external access to the VNC server for remote VNC viewer instances, for example:

```
# firewall-cmd --permanent --zone=public --add-port=5901/tcp
# firewall-cmd --reload
```

With the service configuration file created, the service needs to be enabled and started as follow:

```
# systemctl daemon-reload
# systemctl start  vncserver@:1.service
# systemctl enable  vncserver@:1.service
```

Note that *:1* is included in the service name to indicate that this is the service for VNC server display number 1. This matches port 5901 which was previously opened in the firewall.

Check that the service has started successfully as follows:

```
# systemctl status vncserver@:1.service
```

If the service fails to start, run the following command to check for error messages:

```
# journalctl -xe
```

Also try again after rebooting the system. If the service continues to fail, the VNC server can be started manually by logging in as the designated user and running the following command:

```
$ vncserver :1
```

15.5 Connecting to a VNC Server

VNC viewer implementations are available for a wide range of operating systems and a quick internet search will likely provide numerous links containing details on how to obtain and install this tool on your chosen platform.

From the desktop of a Linux system on which a VNC viewer such as TigerVNC is installed, a remote desktop connection can be established as follows from a Terminal window:

```
$ vncviewer <hostname>:<display number>
```

In the above example, <hostname> is either the hostname or IP address of the remote system and <display number> is the display number of the VNC server desktop, for example:

```
$ vncviewer 192.168.1.115:1
```

Alternatively, run the command without any options to be prompted for the details of the remote server:

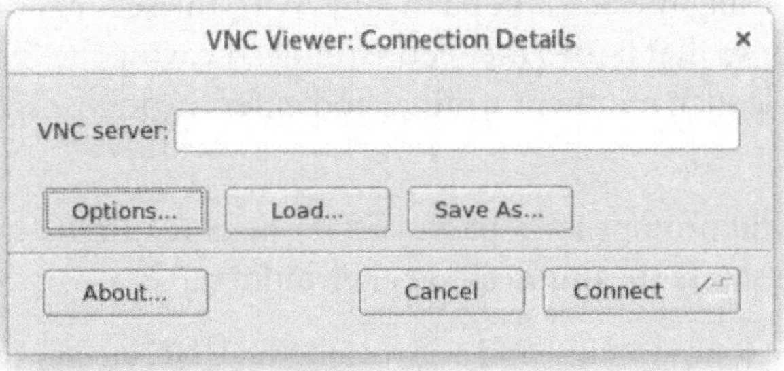

Figure 15-1

Enter the hostname or IP address followed by the display number (for example 192.168.1.115:1) into the VNC server field and click on the Connect button. The viewer will prompt for the user's VNC password to complete the connection, at which point a new window containing the remote desktop will appear.

This section assumed that the remote desktop was being accessed from a Linux or UNIX system, the same steps apply for most other operating systems.

Connecting to a remote VNC server using the steps in this section results in an insecure, unencrypted connection between the client and server. This means that the data transmitted during the remote session is vulnerable to interception. To establish a secure and encrypted connection a few extra steps are necessary.

15.6 Establishing a Secure Remote Desktop Session

The remote desktop configurations we have explored so far in this chapter are considered to be insecure because no encryption is used. This is acceptable when the remote connection does not extend outside of an internal network protected by a firewall. When a remote session is required over an internet connection, however, a more secure option is needed. This is achieved by tunneling the remote desktop through a secure shell (SSH) connection. This section will cover how to do this on Linux, UNIX and macOS client systems.

The SSH server is typically installed and activated by default on CentOS 8 systems. If this is not the case on your system, refer to the chapter entitled *"Configuring SSH Key-based Authentication on CentOS 8"*.

Assuming the SSH server is installed and active it is time to move to the other system. At the other system, log in to the remote system using the following command, which will establish the secure tunnel between the two systems:

```
$ ssh -l <username> -L 5901:localhost:5901 <remotehost>
```

In the above example, <username> references the user account on the remote system for which

CentOS 8 Remote Desktop Access with VNC

VNC access has been configured, and *<remotehost>* is either the host name or IP address of the remote system, for example:

```
$ ssh -l neilsmyth -L 5901:localhost:5901 192.168.1.115
```

When prompted, log in using the account password. With the secure connection established it is time to launch vncviewer so that it uses the secure tunnel. Leaving the SSH session running in the other terminal window, launch another terminal and enter the following command:

```
$ vncviewer localhost:5901
```

The vncviewer session will prompt for a password if one is required, and then launch the VNC viewer providing secure access to your desktop environment.

Although the connection is now secure and encrypted, the VNC viewer will most likely still report that the connection is insecure. Figure 15-2, for example, shows the warning dialog displayed by the RealVNC viewer running on a macOS system:

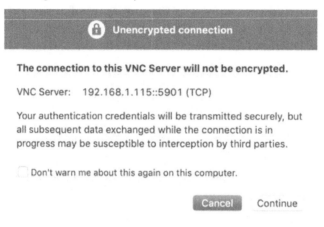

Figure 15-2

Unfortunately, although the connection is now secure, the VNC viewer software has no way of knowing this and consequently continues to issue warnings. Rest assured that as long as the SSH tunnel is being used, the connection is indeed secure.

In the above example we left the SSH tunnel session running in a terminal window. If you would prefer to run the session in the background, this can be achieved by using the –f and –N flags when initiating the connection:

```
$ ssh -l <username> -f -N -L 5901:localhost:5901 <remotehost>
```

The above command will prompt for a password for the remote server and then establish the connection in the background, leaving the terminal window available for other tasks.

If you are connecting to the remote desktop from outside the firewall keep in mind that the IP address for the SSH connection will be the external IP address provided by your ISP or cloud hosting provider, not the LAN IP address of the remote system (since this IP address is not visible to those outside the firewall). You will also need to configure your firewall to forward port 22 (for the SSH connection) to the IP address of the system running the desktop. It is not necessary to forward port 5900. Steps to perform port forwarding differ between firewalls, so refer to the documentation for your firewall, router or wireless base station for details specific to your configuration.

15.7 Establishing a Secure Tunnel on Windows using PuTTY

A similar approach is taken to establishing a secure desktop session from a Windows system to a CentOS 8 server. Assuming that you already have a VNC client such as TightVNC installed, the one remaining requirement is a Windows SSH client (in this case PuTTY).

Once PuTTY is downloaded and installed, the first step is to establish a secure connection between the Windows system and the remote CentOS 8 system with appropriate tunneling configured. When launched, PuTTY displays the following screen:

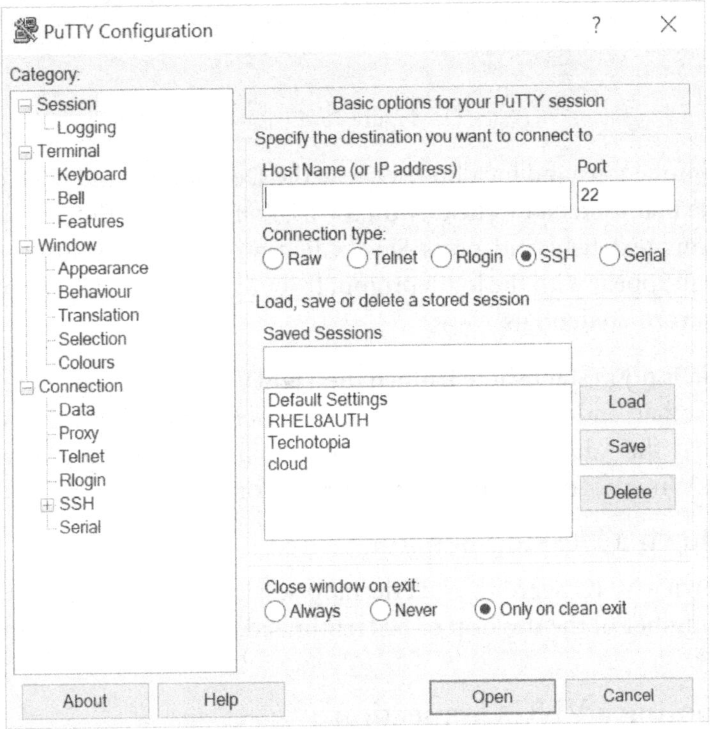

Figure 15-3

Enter the IP address or host name of the remote host (or the external IP address of the gateway if you are connecting from outside the firewall). The next step is to set up the tunnel. Click on the + next to SSH in the Category tree on the left-hand side of the dialog and click on Tunnels. The screen should subsequently appear as follows:

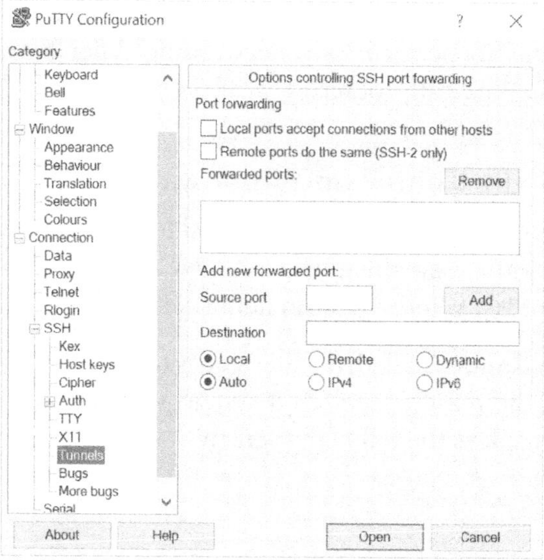

Figure 15-4

Enter 5901 as the Source port and localhost:5901 as the Destination and click on the *Add* button. Finally return to the main screen by clicking on the *Session* category. Enter a name for the session in the Saved Sessions text field and press *Save*. Click on *Open* to establish the connection. A terminal window will appear with the login prompt from the remote system. Enter the appropriate user login and password credentials.

The SSH connection is now established. Launch the TightVNC viewer and enter localhost:5901 in the VNC Server text field and click on *Connect*. The viewer will establish the connection, prompt for the password and then display the desktop. You are now accessing the remote desktop of a Linux system from Windows over a secure SSH tunnel connection.

15.8 Shutting Down a Desktop Session

In order to shut down a VNC Server hosted desktop session, use the –kill command-line option together with the number of the desktop to be terminated. For example, to kill desktop :1:

```
# vncserver -kill :1
```

15.9 Troubleshooting a VNC Connection

With so much happening in the background, VNC can sometimes seem opaque, particularly when problems arise and the server either fails to start, or attempts to connect remotely result in error messages. There are, however, a number of techniques for tracking down and resolving VNC problems:

If the VNC service fails to start, check the *systemctl* status of the service and check for error messages:

```
# systemctl status vncserver@:1.service
```

For more detailed information, check the systemd journal by running the following command:

```
# journalctl -xe
```

Additional information may be available in the log file located at:

```
/home/<username>/.vnc/<hostname>.<domain>:<display number>.log
```

For example:

```
/home/neilsmyth/.vnc/server01.localdomain:1.log
```

If the systemd VNC service is still unable to start the VNC server, try starting it manually using the following command:

```
# vncserver :<display number>
```

For example:

```
# vncserver :1
```

Check the output and log file for any errors that may help identify the problem. If the server starts successfully, try connecting again with a VNC viewer.

If the VNC server appears to be running but attempts to connect from a viewer fail, it may be worth checking that the correct firewall ports are open. Begin by identifying the default zone as follows:

```
# firewall-cmd --get-default-zone
public
```

Having obtained the default zone, check that the necessary ports are open:

```
# firewall-cmd --permanent --zone=public --list-ports
5901/tcp 5900/tcp
```

If a port used by VNC is not open, add the port as follows:

```
# firewall-cmd --permanent --zone=public --add-port=<port number>/tcp
```

15.10 Summary

Remote access to the GNOME desktop environment of a CentOS 8 system can be enabled by making use of Virtual Network Computing (VNC). Comprising the VNC server running on the remote server and a corresponding client on the local host, VNC allows remote access to multiple desktop instances running on the server.

When the VNC connection is being used over a public connection, the use of SSH tunneling is recommended to ensure that the communication between client and server is encrypted and secure.

16. Displaying CentOS 8 Applications Remotely (X11 Forwarding)

In the previous chapter we looked at how to display the entire CentOS 8 desktop on a remote computer. While this works well if you actually need to remotely display the entire desktop, it could be considered overkill if all you want to do is display a single application. In this chapter, therefore, we will look at displaying individual applications on a remote system.

16.1 Requirements for Remotely Displaying CentOS 8 Applications

In order to run an application on one CentOS 8 system and have it display on another system there are a couple of prerequisites. First, the system on which the application is to be displayed must be running an X server. If the system is a Linux or UNIX-based system with a desktop environment running then this is no problem. If the system is running Windows or macOS, however, then you must install an X server on it before you can display applications from a remote system. A number of commercial and free Windows based X servers are available for this purpose and a web search should provide you with a list of options.

Second, the system on which the application is being run (as opposed to the system on which the application is to be displayed) must be configured to allow SSH access. Details on configuring SSH on a CentOS 8 system can be found in the chapter entitled *"Configuring SSH Key-based Authentication on CentOS 8"*. This system must also be running the X Window system from X.org instead of Wayland. To find out which system is being used, open a terminal window and run the following command:

```
# echo $XDG_SESSION_TYPE
x11
```

If the above command outputs "wayland" instead of "x11", edit the */etc/gdm/custom.conf* file and uncomment the *WaylandEnable* line as follows and restart the system:

```
# Uncoment the line below to force the login screen to use Xorg
WaylandEnable=false
```

Finally, SSH must be configured to allow X11 forwarding. This is achieved by adding the following directive to the SSH configuration on the system from which forwarding is to occur. By default on CentOS 8, the */etc/ssh_config* file contains a directive to include all of the configuration files contained in the */etc/ssh/ssh_config.d* directory:

```
Include /etc/ssh/ssh_config.d/*.conf
```

On a newly installed system, the only file within */etc/ssh/ssh_config.d* is named *05-redhat.conf*. Edit this file and add a line to enable X11 forwarding as follows:

.

```
.

Host *

        GSSAPIAuthentication yes
        X11Forwarding yes

.

.
```

After making the change, save the file and restart the SSH service:

```
# systemctl restart sshd
```

Once the above requirements are met it should be possible to remotely display an X-based desktop application.

16.2 Remotely Displaying a CentOS 8 Application

The first step in remotely displaying an application is to move to the system where the application is to be displayed. At this system, establish an SSH connection to the remote system so that you have a command prompt. This can be achieved using the *ssh* command. When using the *ssh* command we need to use the -X flag to tell it that we plan to tunnel X11 traffic through the connection:

```
$ ssh -X user@hostname
```

In the above example *user* is the user name to use to log into the remote system and *hostname* is the hostname or IP address of the remote system. Enter your password at the login prompt and, once logged in, run the following command to see the DISPLAY setting:

```
$ echo $DISPLAY
```

The command should output something similar to the following:

```
localhost:10.0
```

To display an application simply run it from the command prompt. For example:

```
$ gedit
```

When executed, the above command should run the *gedit* tool on the remote system, but display the output on the local system.

16.3 Trusted X11 Forwarding

If the */etc/ssh/ssh_config.d/05-redhat.conf* file on the remote system contains the following line, then it is possible to use trusted X11 forwarding:

```
ForwardX11Trusted yes
```

Trusted X11 forwarding is slightly faster than untrusted forwarding but is less secure since it does not engage the X11 security controls. The -Y flag is needed when using trusted X11 forwarding:

```
$ ssh -Y user@hostname
```

16.4 Compressed X11 Forwarding

When using slower connections the X11 data can be compressed using the -C flag to improve performance:

```
$ ssh -X -C user@hostname
```

16.5 Displaying Remote CentOS 8 Apps on Windows

To display CentOS 8 based apps on Windows an SSH client and an X server will need to be installed on the Windows system. The subject of installing and using the PuTTY client on Windows was covered earlier in the book in the *"Configuring SSH Key-based Authentication on CentOS 8"* chapter. Refer to this chapter if you have not already installed PuTTY on your Windows system.

In terms of the X server, a number of options are available, though a popular choice appears to be VcXsrv which is available for free from the following URL:

https://sourceforge.net/projects/vcxsrv/

Once the VcXsrv X server has been installed, an application named *XLaunch* will appear on the desktop and in the start menu. Start XLaunch and select a display option (the most flexible being the *Multiple windows* option which allows each client app to appear in its own window):

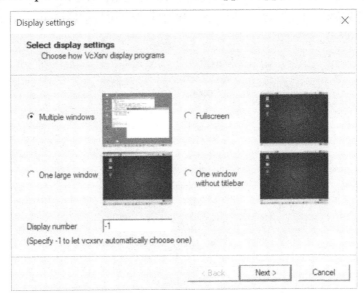

Figure 16-1

Click the *Next* button to proceed through the remaining screens, accepting the default configuration settings. On the final screen, click on the *Finish* button to start the X server. If the Windows Defender dialog appears click on the button to allow access to your chosen networks.

Once running, XLaunch will appear in the taskbar and can be exited by right-clicking on the icon and selecting the *Exit...* menu option:

Displaying CentOS 8 Applications Remotely (X11 Forwarding)

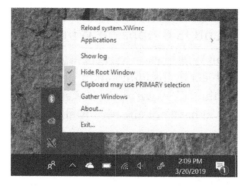

Figure 16-2

With the X server installed and running, launch PuTTY and either enter the connection information for the remote host or load a previously saved session profile. Before establishing the connection, however, X11 forwarding needs to be enabled. Within the PuTTY main window, scroll down the options in the left-hand panel, unfold the SSH section and select the X11 option as shown in Figure 16-3:

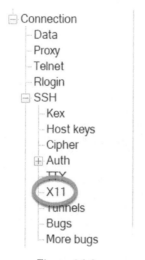

Figure 16-3

Turn on the *Enable X11 forwarding* checkbox highlighted in Figure 16-4, return to the sessions screen and open the connection (saving the session beforehand if you plan to use it again).

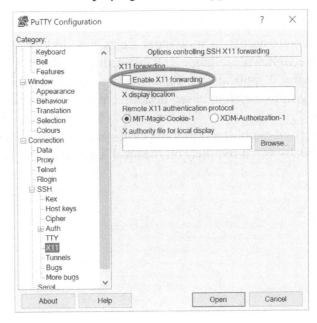

Figure 16-4

Log into the CentOS 8 system within the PuTTY session window and run a desktop app. After a short delay, the app will appear in the Windows desktop in its own window. Any dialogs that are opened by the app will also appear in separate windows, just as they would on the CentOS 8 GNOME desktop. Figure 16-5, for example, shows the CentOS 8 *nm-connection-editor* tool displayed on a Windows 10 system:

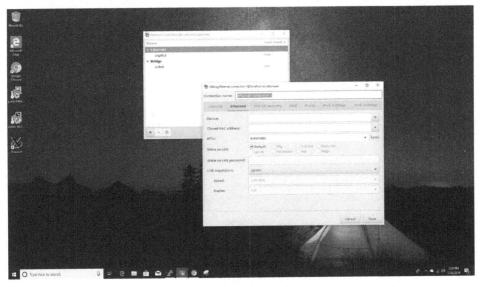

Figure 16-5

16.6 Summary

For situations where remote access to individual CentOS 8 desktop applications is required as opposed to the entire GNOME desktop, X11 forwarding provides a lightweight solution to remotely displaying graphical applications. The system on which the applications are to appear must be running an X Window System based desktop environment (such as GNOME) or have an X server installed and running. Once X11 forwarding has been enabled on the remote server and a secure SSH connection established from the local system using the X11 forwarding option, most applications can be displayed remotely on the local X server.

17. Using NFS to Share CentOS 8 Files with Remote Systems

CentOS 8 provides two mechanisms for sharing files and folders with other systems on a network. One approach is to use technology called Samba. Samba is based on Microsoft Windows Folder Sharing and allows Linux systems to make folders accessible to Windows systems, and also to access Windows based folder shares from Linux. This approach can also be used to share folders between other Linux and UNIX based systems as long as they too have Samba support installed and configured. This is by far the most popular approach to sharing folders in heterogeneous network environments. The topic of folder sharing using Samba is covered in *"Sharing Files between CentOS 8 and Windows Systems with Samba"*.

Another option, which is targeted specifically at sharing folders between Linux and UNIX based systems, uses technology called Network File System (NFS). NFS allows the file system on one Linux computer to be accessed over a network connection by another Linux or UNIX system. NFS was originally developed by Sun Microsystems (now part of Oracle Corporation) in the 1980s and remains the standard mechanism for sharing of remote Linux/UNIX file systems to this day.

NFS is very different to the Windows SMB resource sharing technology used by Samba. In this chapter we will be looking at network based sharing of folders between CentOS 8 and other UNIX/Linux based systems using NFS.

17.1 Ensuring NFS Services are running on CentOS 8

The first task is to verify that the NFS services are installed and running on your CentOS 8 system. This can be achieved either from the command-line, or using the Cockpit interface.

Behind the scenes, NFS makes use of Remote Procedure Calls (RPC) to share filesystems over a network between different computers in the form of the *rpcbind* service. Begin by installing both rpcbind and the NFS service by running the following command from a terminal window:

```
# dnf install rpcbind nfs-utils
```

Next, configure these services so that they automatically start at boot time:

```
# systemctl enable rpcbind
# systemctl enable nfs-server
```

Once the services have been enabled, start them as follows:

```
# systemctl start rpcbind
# systemctl start nfs-server
```

17.2 Configuring the CentOS 8 Firewall to Allow NFS Traffic

Next, the firewall needs to be configured to allow NFS traffic. To achieve this, run the following *firewall-cmd* commands where <zone> is replaced by the appropriate zone for your firewall and system configuration:

```
firewall-cmd --zone=<zone> --permanent --add-service=mountd
firewall-cmd --zone=<zone> --permanent --add-service=nfs
firewall-cmd --zone=<zone> --permanent --add-service=rpc-bind
firewall-cmd --reload
```

17.3 Specifying the Folders to be Shared

Now that NFS is running and the firewall has been configured, we need to specify which parts of the CentOS 8 file system may be accessed by remote Linux or UNIX systems. These settings can be declared in the */etc/exports* file, which will need to be modified to export the directories for remote access via NFS. The syntax for an export line in this file is as follows:

```
<export> <host1>(<options>) <host2>(<options>)...
```

In the above line, <export> is replaced by the directory to be exported, <host1> is the name or IP address of the system to which access is being granted and <options> represents the restrictions that are to be imposed on that access (read only, read write etc). Multiple host and options entries may be placed on the same line if required. For example, the following line grants read only permission to the */datafiles* directory to a host with the IP address of 192.168.2.38:

```
/datafiles 192.168.2.38(ro)
```

The use of wildcards is permitted in order to apply an export to multiple hosts. For example, the following line permits read write access to */home/demo* to all external hosts:

```
/home/demo *(rw)
```

A full list of options supported by the exports file may be found by reading the exports man page:

```
# man exports
```

For the purposes of this chapter, we will configure the */etc/exports* file as follows:

```
/tmp        *(rw,sync)
/vol1       192.168.2.21(ro,sync)
```

Once configured, the table of exported file systems maintained by the NFS server needs to be updated with the latest */etc/exports* settings using the *exportfs* command as follows:

```
# exportfs -a
```

It is also possible to view the current share settings from the command-line using the *exportfs* tool:

```
# exportfs
```

The above command will generate the following output:

```
/tmp            <world>
/vol1           192.168.2.21
```

17.4 Accessing Shared CentOS 8 Folders

The shared folders may be accessed from a client system by mounting them manually from the command-line. Before attempting to mount a remote NFS folder, the *nfs-utils* package should first be installed on the client system:

```
# dnf install nfs-utils
```

To mount a remote folder from the command-line, open a terminal window and create a folder where you would like the remote folder to be mounted:

```
# mkdir /home/demo/tmp
```

Next enter the command to mount the remote folder using either the IP address or hostname of the remote NFS server, for example:

```
# mount -t nfs 192.168.1.115:/tmp /home/demo/tmp
```

The remote */tmp* folder will then be mounted on the local system. Once mounted, the */home/demo/tmp* folder will contain the remote folder and all its contents.

Options may also be specified when mounting a remote NFS filesystem. The following command, for example, mounts the same folder, but configures it to be read-only:

```
# mount -t nfs -o ro 192.168.1.115:/tmp /home/demo/tmp
```

17.5 Mounting an NFS Filesystem on System Startup

It is also possible to configure a CentOS 8 system to automatically mount a remote file system each time the system starts up by editing the */etc/fstab* file. When loaded into an editor, it will likely resemble the following:

```
/dev/mapper/cl-root    /                      xfs    defaults    0 0
UUID=c2c3b49a-e1a1-4004 /boot                 xfs    defaults    0 0
/dev/mapper/cl-home    /home                  xfs    defaults    0 0
/dev/mapper/cl-swap    swap                   swap   defaults    0 0
```

To mount, for example, a folder with the path */tmp* which resides on a system with the IP address 192.168.1.115 in the local folder with the path */home/demo/tmp* (note that this folder must already exist) add the following line to the */etc/fstab* file:

```
192.168.1.115:/tmp      /home/demo/tmp        nfs    rw          0 0
```

Next time the system reboots the */tmp* folder located on the remote system will be mounted on the local */home/demo/tmp* mount point. All the files in the remote folder can then be accessed as if they reside on the local hard disk drive.

17.6 Unmounting an NFS Mount Point

Once a remote file system is mounted using NFS it can be unmounted using the *umount* command with the local mount point as the command-line argument. The following command, for example, will unmount our example filesystem mount point:

```
# umount /home/demo/tmp
```

17.7 Accessing NFS Filesystems in Cockpit

In addition to mounting a remote NFS file system on a client using the command-line, it is also possible to perform mount operations from within the Cockpit web interface. Assuming that Cockpit has been installed and configured on the client system, log into the Cockpit interface from within a web browser and select the *Storage* option from the left-hand navigation panel. If the Storage option is not listed, the *cockpit-storaged* package will need to be installed and the cockpit service restarted as follows:

```
# dnf install cockpit-storaged
# systemctl restart cockpit.socket
```

Once the Cockpit service has restarted, log back into the Cockpit interface at which point the Storage option should now be visible.

Once selected, the main storage page will include a section listing any currently mounted NFS file systems as illustrated in Figure 17-1:

Figure 17-1

To mount a remote filesystem, click on the '+' button highlighted above and enter information about the remote NFS server and file system share together with the local mount point and any necessary options into the resulting dialog before clicking on the *Add* button:

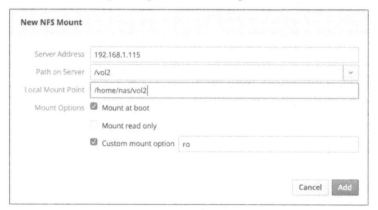

Figure 17-2

To modify, unmount or remove an NFS filesystem share, select the corresponding mount in the NFS Mounts list (Figure 17-1 above) to display the page shown in Figure 17-3 below:

Figure 17-3

Within this screen perform tasks such as changing the server or mount points or unmounting the file system. The Remove option unmounts the file system and deletes the entry from the */etc/fstab* file so that it does not re-mount next time the system reboots.

17.8 Summary

The Network File System (NFS) is a client/server-based system, originally developed by Sun Microsystems, which provides a way for Linux and Unix systems to share filesystems over a network. NFS allows a client system to access and (subject to permissions) modify files located on a remote server as though those files are stored on a local filesystem. This chapter has provided an overview of NFS and outlined the options available for configuring both client and server systems using the command-line or the Cockpit web interface.

18. Sharing Files between CentOS 8 and Windows Systems with Samba

Although Linux has made some inroads into the desktop market, its origins and future are very much server-based. It is not surprising therefore that CentOS 8 has the ability to act as a file server. It is also extremely common for CentOS and Windows systems to be used side by side in networked environments. It is a common requirement, therefore, that files on a CentOS 8 system be accessible to Linux, UNIX and Windows-based systems over network connections. Similarly, shared folders and printers residing on Windows systems may also need to be accessible from CentOS 8 based systems.

Windows systems share resources such as file systems and printers using a protocol known as Server Message Block (SMB). In order for a CentOS 8 system to serve such resources over a network to a Windows system and vice versa it must, therefore, support SMB. This is achieved using technology called Samba. In addition to providing integration between Linux and Windows systems, Samba may also be used to provide folder sharing between Linux systems (as an alternative to NFS which was covered in the previous chapter).

In this chapter we will look at the steps necessary to share file system resources and printers on a CentOS 8 system with remote Windows and Linux systems, and to access Windows resources from CentOS 8.

18.1 Samba and Samba Client

Samba allows both CentOS 8 resources to be shared with Windows systems and Windows resources to be shared with CentOS 8 systems. CentOS accesses Windows resources using the Samba client. CentOS resources, on the other hand, are shared with Windows systems by installing and configuring the Samba service.

18.2 Installing Samba on a CentOS 8 System

The default settings used during the CentOS 8 installation process do not typically install the necessary Samba packages. Unless you specifically requested that Samba be installed it is unlikely that you have Samba installed on your system. To check whether Samba is installed, open a terminal window and run the following *rpm* command:

```
# rpm -q samba samba-common samba-client
```

If any of the Samba packages are not installed, *rpm* will return with "package is not installed". That being the case, these can be installed using the *dnf* command-line tool:

```
# dnf install samba samba-common samba-client
```

18.3 Configuring the CentOS 8 Firewall to Enable Samba

Next, the firewall currently protecting the CentOS 8 system needs to be configured to allow Samba traffic. To achieve this, run the *firewall-cmd* command as follows:

```
# firewall-cmd --permanent --add-port={139/tcp,445/tcp}
# firewall-cmd --reload
```

Before starting the Samba service a number of configuration steps are necessary to define how the CentOS system will appear to Windows systems, and the resources which are to be shared with remote clients. The majority of these configuration tasks take place within the */etc/samba/smb.conf* file.

18.4 Configuring the *smb.conf* File

Prior to the introduction of CentOS 6, a user friendly graphical tool named *system-config-samba* was provided to assist in the configuration of Samba. In CentOS 7 and later, however, this tool has been removed. This means that the Samba environment must be configured manually within the */etc/samba/smb.conf* file and using the *smbpasswd* command-line tool. While the loss of *system-config-samba* may be mourned by those who relied on it, the tool's simplicity actually masked many of the more advanced features of Samba. In practice, much more can be achieved by taking the time to understand the intricacies of the *smb.conf* file.

Samba is a highly flexible and configurable system that provides many different options for controlling how resources are shared on Windows networks. This flexibility can lead to the sense that Samba is overly complex to work with. In reality, however, many of the configuration options are not needed by the typical installation, and the learning curve to set up a basic configuration is actually quite short.

For the purposes of this chapter we will look at joining a CentOS 8 system to a Windows workgroup and setting up a directory as a shared resource that can be accessed by a specific user. This is a configuration known as a *standalone* Samba server. More advanced configurations such as integrating Samba within an Active Directory environment are also available, though these are outside the scope of this book.

The first step in configuring Samba is to edit the */etc/samba/smb.conf* file.

18.4.1 Configuring the [global] Section

The *smb.conf* file is divided into sections. The first section is the [global] section where settings can be specified that apply to the entire Samba configuration. While these settings are global, each option may be overridden within other sections of the configuration file.

The first task is to define the name of the Windows workgroup on which the CentOS 8 resources are to be shared. This is controlled via the *workgroup* = directive of the [global] section which by default is configured as follows:

```
workgroup = SAMBA
```

Begin by changing this to the actual name of the workgroup. For example, if the workgroup is named WORKGROUP (the default for most Windows networks):

```
[global]
        workgroup = WORKGROUP
        security = user

        passdb backend = tdbsam
.
.
```

In addition to the workgroup setting, the other settings indicate that this is a standalone server on which the shared resources will be protected by user passwords. Before moving on to configuring the resources to be shared, a number of other parameters also need to be added to the [global] section as follows:

```
[global]
        workgroup = WORKGROUP
        security = user
        netbios name = LinuxServer
        passdb backend = tdbsam

        log file = /var/log/samba/%m.log
        log level = 1
.

.
```

The "netbios name" property specifies the name by which the server will be visible to other systems on the network, while the log settings simply specify a file location into which log output is to be recorded.

18.4.2 Configuring a Shared Resource

The next step is to configure the shared resources (in other words the resources that will be accessible from other systems on the Windows network). In order to achieve this, the section is given a name by which it will be referred to when shared. For example, if we plan to share the /*sampleshare* directory of our CentOS 8 system, we might entitle the section [sampleshare]. In this section a variety of configuration options are possible. For the purposes of this example, however, we will simply define the directory that is to be shared, indicate that the directory is both browsable and writable and declare the resource public so that guest users are able to gain access:

```
[sampleshare]
        comment = Example Samba share
        path = /sampleshare
        browseable = Yes
        public = yes
        writable = yes
```

To restrict access to specific users, the "valid users" property may be used, for example:

```
valid users = demo, bobyoung, marcewing
```

18.4.3 Removing Unnecessary Shares

The *smb.conf* file is pre-configured with sections for sharing printers and the home folders of the users on the system. If these resources do not need to be shared, the corresponding sections can be commented out so that they are ignored by Samba. In the following example, the [homes] section has been commented out:

```
.
.
#[homes]
#        comment = Home Directories
#        valid users = %S, %D%w%S
#        browseable = No
#        read only = No
#        inherit acls = Yes
.
.
```

18.5 Configuring SELinux for Samba

SELinux is a system integrated by default into the Linux kernel on all CentOS 8 systems and which provides an extra layer of security and protection to the operating system and user files.

Traditionally, Linux security has been based on the concept of allowing users to decide who has access to their files and other resources for which they have ownership. Consider, for example, a file located in the home directory of, and owned by, a particular user. That user is able to control the access permissions of that file in terms of whether other users on the system are able to read and write to or, in the case of a script or binary, execute the file. This type of security is referred to as *discretionary access control* since access to resources is left to the discretion of the user.

With SELinux, however, access is controlled by the system administrator and cannot be overridden by the user. This is referred to as *mandatory access control* and is defined by the administrator using SELinux *policy*. To continue the previous example, the owner of a file is only able to perform tasks on that file if SELinux policy defined either by default by the system, or by the administrator, permits it.

The current status of SELinux on a CentOS 8 system may be identified using the *sestatus* tool as follows:

```
# sestatus
SELinux status:                 enabled
SELinuxfs mount:                /sys/fs/selinux
SELinux root directory:         /etc/selinux
Loaded policy name:             targeted
Current mode:                   enforcing
Mode from config file:          enforcing
Policy MLS status:              enabled
Policy deny_unknown status:     allowed
```

```
Memory protection checking:     actual (secure)
Max kernel policy version:      31
```

SELinux can be run in either *enforcing* or *permissive* mode. When enabled, enforcing mode denies all actions that are not permitted by SELinux policy. Permissive mode, on the other hand, allows actions that would normally have been denied to proceed but records the violation in a log file.

SELinux security is based on the concept of *context labels*. All resources on a system (including processes and files) are assigned SELinux context labels consisting of user, role, type and optional security level. The SELinux context of files or folders, for example, may be viewed as follows:

```
$ ls -Z /home/demo
 unconfined_u:object_r:user_home_t:s0 Desktop
 unconfined_u:object_r:user_home_t:s0 Documents
```

Similarly, the *ps* command may be used to identify the context of a running process, in this case the *ls* command:

```
$ ps -eZ | grep ls
unconfined_u:unconfined_r:unconfined_t:s0-s0:c0.c1023 14311 tty1 00:00:18 ls
```

When a process (such as the above *ls* command) attempts to access a file or folder, the SELinux system will check the policy to identify whether or not access is permitted. Now consider the context of the Samba service:

```
$ ps -eZ | grep smb
system_u:system_r:smbd_t:s0     14129 ?        00:00:00 smbd
system_u:system_r:smbd_t:s0     14132 ?        00:00:00 smbd-notifyd
```

SELinux implements security in a number of ways, the most common of which is referred to as *type enforcement*. In basic terms, when a process attempts to perform a task on an object (for example writing to a file), SELinux checks the context types of both the process and the object and verifies that the security policy allows the action to be taken. If a process of type A, for example, attempts to write to a file of type B, it will only be permitted to do so if SELinux policy specifically states that a process of type A may perform a write operation to a file of type B. In SELinux enforcement, all actions are denied by default unless a rule exists specifically allowing the action to be performed.

The issue with SELinux and Samba is that SELinux policy is not configured to allow processes of type *smb_t* to perform actions on files of any type other than *samba_share_t*. The */home/demo* directory listed above, for example, will be inaccessible to the Samba service because it has a type of *user_home_t*. To make files or folders on the system accessible to the Samba service, the enforcement type of those specific resources must be changed to *samba_share_t*.

For the purposes of this example, we will create the */sampleshare* directory referenced previously in the *smb.conf* file and change the enforcement type so that it is accessible to the Samba service. Begin by creating the directory as follows:

```
# mkdir /sampleshare
```

Next, check the current SELinux context on the directory:

```
$ ls -aZ /sampleshare/
unconfined_u:object_r:default_t:s0 .
```

In this instance, the context label of the folder has been assigned a type of *default_t*. To make the folder sharable by Samba, the enforcement type needs to be set to *samba_share_t* using the *semanage* tool as follows:

```
# semanage fcontext -a -t samba_share_t "/sampleshare(/.*)?"
```

Note the use of a wildcard in the *semanage* command to ensure that the type is applied to any sub-directories and files contained within the */sampleshare* directory. Once added, the change needs to be applied using the *restorecon* command, making use of the -R flag to apply the change recursively through any sub-directories:

```
# restorecon -R -v /sampleshare
Relabeled /sampleshare from unconfined_u:object_r:default_t:s0 to
unconfined_u:object_r:samba_share_t:s0
```

Once these changes have been made, the folder is configured to comply with SELinux policy for the smb process and is ready to be shared by Samba.

18.6 Creating a Samba User

Any user that requires access to a Samba shared resource must be configured as a Samba User and assigned a password. This task is achieved using the *smbpasswd* command-line tool. Consider, for example, that a user named *demo* is required to be able to access the */sampleshare* directory of our CentOS 8 system from a Windows system. In order to fulfill this requirement we must add *demo* as a Samba user as follows:

```
# smbpasswd -a demo
New SMB password:
Retype new SMB password:
Added user demo.
```

Now that we have completed the configuration of a very basic Samba server, it is time to test our configuration file and then start the Samba services.

18.7 Testing the *smb.conf* File

The settings in the *smb.conf* file may be checked for errors using the *testparm* command-line tool as follows:

```
# testparm
Load smb config files from /etc/samba/smb.conf
rlimit_max: increasing rlimit_max (1024) to minimum Windows limit (16384)
Processing section "[sampleshare]"
Processing section "[homes]"
Processing section "[printers]"
Processing section "[print$]"
Loaded services file OK.
```

```
Server role: ROLE_STANDALONE

Press enter to see a dump of your service definitions

# Global parameters
[global]
        log file = /var/log/samba/%m.log
        netbios name = LINUXSERVER
        printcap name = cups
        security = USER
        wins support = Yes
        idmap config * : backend = tdb
        cups options = raw

[sampleshare]
        comment = Example Samba share
        guest ok = Yes
        path = /sampleshare
        read only = No

[homes]
        browseable = No
        comment = Home Directories
        inherit acls = Yes
        read only = No
        valid users = %S %D%w%S

[printers]
        browseable = No
        comment = All Printers
        create mask = 0600
        path = /var/tmp
        printable = Yes

[print$]
        comment = Printer Drivers
        create mask = 0664
        directory mask = 0775
        force group = @printadmin
        path = /var/lib/samba/drivers
        write list = @printadmin root
```

18.8 Starting the Samba and NetBIOS Name Services

In order for a CentOS 8 server to operate within a Windows network both the Samba (SMB) and NetBOIS nameservice (NMB) services must be started. Optionally, also enable the services so that they start each time the system boots:

```
# systemctl enable smb
# systemctl start smb
# systemctl enable nmb
# systemctl start nmb
```

Before attempting to connect from a Windows system, use the *smbclient* utility to verify that the share is configured:

```
# smbclient -U demo -L localhost
Enter WORKGROUP\demo's password:


        Sharename       Type        Comment
        ---------       ----        -------
        sampleshare     Disk        Example Samba share
        print$          Disk        Printer Drivers
        IPC$            IPC         IPC Service (Samba 4.9.1)
        demo            Disk        Home Directories
Reconnecting with SMB1 for workgroup listing.

        Server          Comment
        ---------       -------


        Workgroup       Master
        ---------       -------
        WORKGROUP       LINUXSERVER
```

18.9 Accessing Samba Shares

Now that the Samba resources are configured and the services are running, it is time to access the shared resource from a Windows system. On a suitable Windows system on the same workgroup as the CentOS 8 system, open Windows Explorer and navigate to the Network panel. At this point, explorer should search the network and list any systems using the SMB protocol that it finds. The following figure illustrates a CentOS 8 system named LINUXSERVER located using Windows Explorer on a Windows 10 system:

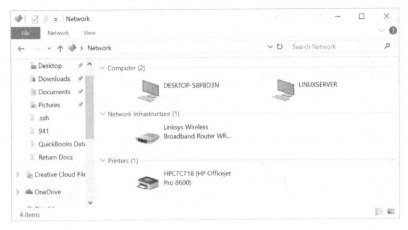

Figure 18-1

Double clicking on the LINUXSERVER host will prompt for the name and password of a user with access privileges. In this case it is the demo account that we configured using the *smbpasswd* tool:

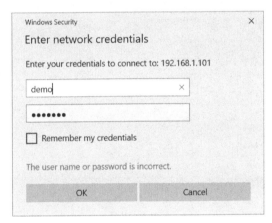

Figure 18-2

Entering the username and password will result in the shared resources configured for that user appearing in the explorer window, including the previously configured */sampleshare* resource:

sampleshare

Figure 18-3

Double clicking on the */sampleshare* shared resource will display a listing of the files and directories contained therein.

18.10 Accessing Windows Shares from CentOS 8

As previously mentioned, Samba is a two way street, allowing not only Windows systems to access files and printers hosted on a CentOS 8 system, but also allowing the CentOS 8 system to access shared resources on Windows systems. This is achieved using the samba-client package which was installed at the start of this chapter. If it is not currently installed, install it from a terminal window as follows:

```
# dnf install samba-client
```

Shared resources on a Windows system can be accessed either from the CentOS desktop using the Files application, or from the command-line prompt using the *smbclient* and *mount* tools. The steps in this section assume that appropriate network sharing settings have been enabled on the Windows system.

To access any shared resources on a Windows system using the desktop, begin by launching the Files application and selecting the *Other Locations* option. This will display the screen shown in Figure 18-4 below including an icon for the Windows Network (if one is detected):

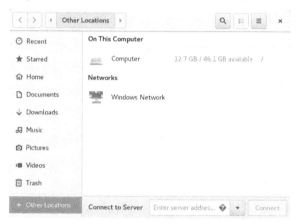

Figure 18-4

Selecting the Windows Network option will display the Windows systems detected on the network and allow access to any shared resources.

Figure 18-5

Alternatively, the *Connect to Server* option may be used to connect to a specific system. Note that the name or IP address of the remote system must be prefixed by *smb://* and may be followed by the path to a specific shared resource, for example:

```
smb://WinServer10/Documents
```

In the absence of a desktop environment, a remote Windows share may be mounted from the command-line using the *mount* command and specifying the *cifs* filesystem type. The following command, for example, mounts a share named Documents located on a Windows system named WinServer at a local mount point named */winfiles*:

```
# mount -t cifs //WinServer/Documents /winfiles -o user=demo
```

18.11 Summary

In this chapter we have looked at the steps necessary to configure a CentOS 8 system to act as both a Samba client and server allowing the sharing of resources with Windows based systems. Topics covered included the installation of Samba client and server packages and configuration of Samba as a standalone server. In addition, the basic concepts of SELinux were introduced together with the steps to provide Samba with access to a shared resource.

Chapter 19

19. An Overview of Virtualization Techniques

Virtualization is generically defined as the ability to run multiple operating systems simultaneously on a single computer system. While not necessarily a new concept, Virtualization has come to prominence in recent years because it provides a way to fully utilize the CPU and resource capacity of a server system while providing stability (in that if one virtualized guest system crashes, the host and any other guest systems continue to run).

Virtualization is also useful in terms of trying out different operating systems without having to configure dual boot environments. For example, you can run Windows in a virtual machine without having to re-partition the disk, shut down CentOS 8 and then boot from Windows. You simply start up a virtualized version of Windows as a guest operating system. Similarly, virtualization allows you to run other Linux distributions from within a CentOS 8 system, providing concurrent access to both operating systems.

When deciding on the best approach to implementing virtualization it is important to have a clear understanding of the different virtualization solutions that are currently available. The purpose of this chapter, therefore, is to describe in general terms the virtualization techniques in common use today.

19.1 Guest Operating System Virtualization

Guest OS virtualization, also referred to as application-based virtualization, is perhaps the easiest concept to understand. In this scenario the physical host computer system runs a standard unmodified operating system such as Windows, Linux, UNIX or macOS. Running on this operating system is a virtualization application which executes in much the same way as any other application such as a word processor or spreadsheet would run on the system. It is within this virtualization application that one or more virtual machines are created to run the guest operating systems on the host computer.

The virtualization application is responsible for starting, stopping and managing each virtual machine and essentially controlling access to physical hardware resources on behalf of the individual virtual machines. The virtualization application also engages in a process known as binary rewriting which involves scanning the instruction stream of the executing guest system and replacing any privileged instructions with safe emulations. This has the effect of making the guest system think it is running directly on the system hardware, rather than in a virtual machine within an application.

The following figure provides an illustration of guest OS based virtualization:

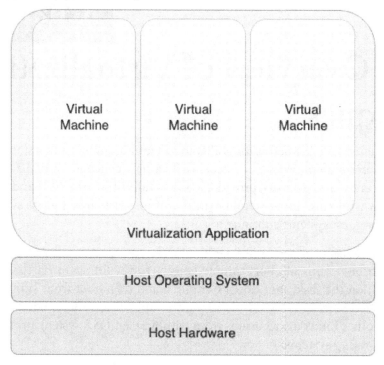

Figure 19-1

As outlined in the above diagram, the guest operating systems operate in virtual machines within the virtualization application which, in turn, runs on top of the host operating system in the same way as any other application. Clearly, the multiple layers of abstraction between the guest operating systems and the underlying host hardware are not conducive to high levels of virtual machine performance. This technique does, however, have the advantage that no changes are necessary to either host or guest operating systems and no special CPU hardware virtualization support is required.

19.2 Hypervisor Virtualization

In hypervisor virtualization, the task of a hypervisor is to handle resource and memory allocation for the virtual machines in addition to providing interfaces for higher level administration and monitoring tools. Hypervisor based solutions are categorized as being either Type-1 or Type-2.

Type-2 hypervisors (sometimes referred to as *hosted hypervisors*) are installed as software applications that run on top of the host operating system, providing virtualization capabilities by coordinating access to resources such as the CPU, memory and network for guest virtual machines. Figure 19-2 illustrates the typical architecture of a system using Type-2 hypervisor virtualization:

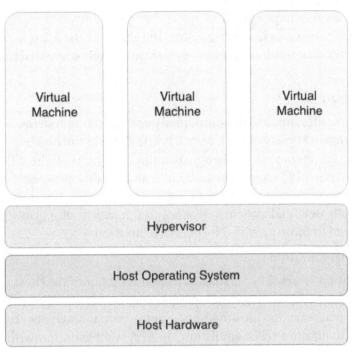

Figure 19-2

To understand how Type-1 hypervisors work, it helps to understand a little about Intel x86 processor architecture. The x86 family of CPUs provides a range of protection levels known as *rings* in which code can execute. Ring 0 has the highest level privilege and it is in this ring that the operating system kernel normally runs. Code executing in ring 0 is said to be running in system space, kernel mode or supervisor mode. All other code such as applications running on the operating system operate in less privileged rings, typically ring 3.

In contrast to Type-2 hypervisors, Type-1 hypervisors (also referred to as *metal* or *native hypervisors*) run directly on the hardware of the host system in ring 0. Clearly, with the hypervisor occupying ring 0 of the CPU, the kernels for any guest operating systems running on the system must run in less privileged CPU rings. Unfortunately, most operating system kernels are written explicitly to run in ring 0 for the simple reason that they need to perform tasks that are only available in that ring, such as the ability to execute privileged CPU instructions and directly manipulate memory. A number of different solutions to this problem have been devised in recent years, each of which is described below:

19.2.1 Paravirtualization

Under paravirtualization, the kernel of the guest operating system is modified specifically to run on the hypervisor. This typically involves replacing any privileged operations that will only run in ring 0 of the CPU with calls to the hypervisor (known as *hypercalls*). The hypervisor, in turn, performs the task on behalf of the guest kernel. This typically limits support to open source operating systems such as Linux which may be freely altered and proprietary operating

An Overview of Virtualization Techniques

systems where the owners have agreed to make the necessary code modifications to target a specific hypervisor. These issues notwithstanding, the ability of the guest kernel to communicate directly with the hypervisor results in greater performance levels compared to other virtualization approaches.

19.2.2 Full Virtualization

Full virtualization provides support for unmodified guest operating systems. The term unmodified refers to operating system kernels which have not been altered to run on a hypervisor and therefore still execute privileged operations as though running in ring 0 of the CPU. In this scenario, the hypervisor provides CPU emulation to handle and modify privileged and protected CPU operations made by unmodified guest operating system kernels. Unfortunately this emulation process requires both time and system resources to operate resulting in inferior performance levels when compared to those provided by paravirtualization.

19.2.3 Hardware Virtualization

Hardware virtualization leverages virtualization features built into the latest generations of CPUs from both Intel and AMD. These technologies, known as Intel VT and AMD-V respectively, provide extensions necessary to run unmodified guest virtual machines without the overheads inherent in full virtualization CPU emulation. In very simplistic terms these new processors provide an additional privilege mode (referred to as ring -1) above ring 0 in which the hypervisor can operate, thereby leaving ring 0 available for unmodified guest operating systems.

The following figure illustrates the Type-1 hypervisor approach to virtualization:

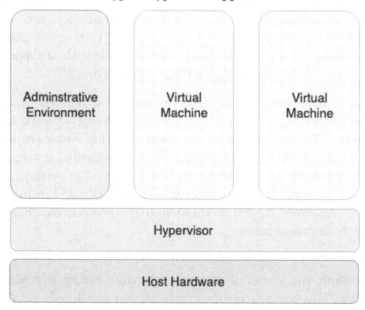

Figure 19-3

As outlined in the above illustration, in addition to the virtual machines, an administrative operating system and/or management console also runs on top of the hypervisor allowing the virtual machines to be managed by a system administrator.

19.3 Virtual Machine Networking

Virtual machines will invariably need to be connected to a network to be of any practical use. One option is for the guest to be connected to a virtual network running within the operating system of the host computer. In this configuration any virtual machines on the virtual network can see each other but access to the external network is provided by Network Address Translation (NAT). When using the virtual network and NAT, each virtual machine is represented on the external network (the network to which the host is connected) using the IP address of the host system. This is the default behavior for KVM virtualization on CentOS 8 and generally requires no additional configuration. Typically, a single virtual network is created by default, represented by the name *default* and the device *virbr0*.

In order for guests to appear as individual and independent systems on the external network (i.e. with their own IP addresses), they must be configured to share a physical network interface on the host. The quickest way to achieve this is to configure the virtual machine to use the "direct connection" network configuration option (also referred to as the MacVTap) which will provide the guest system with an IP address on the same network as the host. Unfortunately, while this gives the virtual machine access to other systems on the network, it is not possible to establish a connection between the guest and the host when using the MacVTap driver.

A better option is to configure a *network bridge* interface on the host system to which the guests can connect. This provides the guest with an IP address on the external network while also allowing the guest and host to communicate, a topic which is covered in the chapter entitled *"Creating a CentOS 8 KVM Networked Bridge Interface"*.

19.4 Summary

Virtualization is defined as the ability to run multiple guest operating systems within a single host operating system. A number of approaches to virtualization have been developed including guest operating system and hypervisor virtualization. Hypervisor virtualization falls into two categories known as Type-1 and Type-2. Type-2 virtualization solutions are categorized as para-virtualization, full virtualization and hardware virtualization, the latter making use of special virtualization features of some Intel and AMD processor models.

Virtual machine guest operating systems have a number of options in terms of networking including NAT, direct connection (MacVTap) and network bridge configurations.

20. Installing KVM Virtualization on CentOS 8

Prior to CentOS 6 two virtualization platforms were provided with CentOS in the form of Kernel-based Virtual Machine (KVM) and Xen. With the release of CentOS 6, support for Xen was removed leaving KVM as the only bundled virtualization option supplied with CentOS 8. In addition to KVM, third party solutions are available in the form of products such as VMware and Oracle VirtualBox. Since KVM is supplied with CentOS 8, however, this is the virtualization solution that will be covered in this and subsequent chapters.

Before plunging into installing and running KVM it is worth taking a little time to talk about how it fits into the various types of virtualization outlined in the previous chapter.

20.1 An Overview of KVM

KVM is categorized as a Type-1 hypervisor virtualization solution that implements full virtualization with support for unmodified guest operating systems using Intel VT and AMD-V hardware virtualization support.

KVM differs from many other Type-1 solutions in that it turns the host Linux operating system itself into the hypervisor, allowing bare metal virtualization to be implemented while still running a full, enterprise level host operating system.

20.2 KVM Hardware Requirements

Before proceeding with this chapter we need to take a moment to discuss the hardware requirements for running virtual machines within a KVM environment. First and foremost, KVM virtualization is only available on certain processor types. As previously discussed, these processors must include either Intel VT or AMD-V technology.

To check for virtualization support, run the following command in a terminal window:

```
# lscpu | grep Virtualization:
```

If the system contains a CPU with Intel VT support, the above command will provide the following output:

```
Virtualization:        VT-x
```

Alternatively, the following output will be displayed when a CPU with AMD-V support is detected:

```
Virtualization:        AMD-V
```

If the CPU does not support virtualization, no output will displayed by the *lscpu* command.

Note that while the above commands only report whether the processor supports the respective feature, it does not indicate whether the feature is currently enabled in the BIOS. In practice virtualization support is typically disabled by default in the BIOS of most systems. It is recommended, therefore, that you check your BIOS settings to ensure the appropriate virtualization technology is enabled before proceeding with this tutorial.

Unlike a dual booting environment, a virtualized environment involves the running of two or more complete operating systems concurrently on a single computer system. This means that the system must have enough physical memory, disk space and CPU processing power to comfortably accommodate all these systems in parallel. Before beginning the configuration and installation process check on the minimum system requirements for both CentOS 8 and your chosen guest operating systems and verify that your system has sufficient resources to handle the requirements of both systems.

20.3 Preparing CentOS 8 for KVM Virtualization

Unlike Xen, it is not necessary to run a special version of the kernel in order to support KVM. As a result KVM support is already available for use with the standard kernel via the installation of a KVM kernel module, thereby negating the need to install and boot from a special kernel.

To avoid conflicts, however, if a Xen enabled kernel is currently running on the system, reboot the system and select a non-Xen kernel from the boot menu before proceeding with the remainder of this chapter.

The tools required to setup and maintain a KVM-based virtualized system are not installed by default unless specifically selected during the CentOS 8 operating system installation process. To install KVM from the command prompt, execute the following command in a terminal window:

```
# dnf install qemu-kvm qemu-img libvirt virt-install libvirt-client
```

If you have access to a graphical desktop environment the *virt-manager* package is also recommended:

```
# dnf install virt-manager
```

20.4 Verifying the KVM Installation

It is worthwhile checking that the KVM installation worked correctly before moving forward. When KVM is installed and running, two modules will have been loaded into the kernel. The presence or otherwise of these modules can be verified in a terminal window by running the following command:

```
# lsmod | grep kvm
```

Assuming that the installation was successful the above command should generate output similar to the following:

```
# lsmod | grep kvm
kvm_intel              237568  0
kvm                    737280  1 kvm_intel
irqbypass               16384  1 kvm
```

Note that if the system contains an AMD processor the kvm module will likely read *kvm_amd* rather than *kvm_intel*.

The installation process should also have configured the libvirtd daemon to run in the background. Once again using a terminal window, run the following command to ensure libvirtd is running:

```
# systemctl status libvirtd
 libvirtd.service - Virtualization daemon
   Loaded: loaded (/usr/lib/systemd/system/libvirtd.service; enabled; vendor
preset: enabled)
   Active: active (running) since Wed 2019-03-06 14:41:22 EST; 3min 54s ago
```

If the process is not running, it may be started as follows:

```
# systemctl enable --now libvirtd
# systemctl start libvirtd
```

If the desktop environment is available, run the *virt-manager* tool by selecting Activities and entering "virt" into the search box. When the Virtual Machine Manager icon appears, click on it to launch it. When loaded, the manager should appear as illustrated in the following figure:

Figure 20-1

If the QEMU/KVM entry is not listed, select the *File -> Add Connection* menu option and, in the resulting dialog, select the QEMU/KVM Hypervisor before clicking on the Connect button:

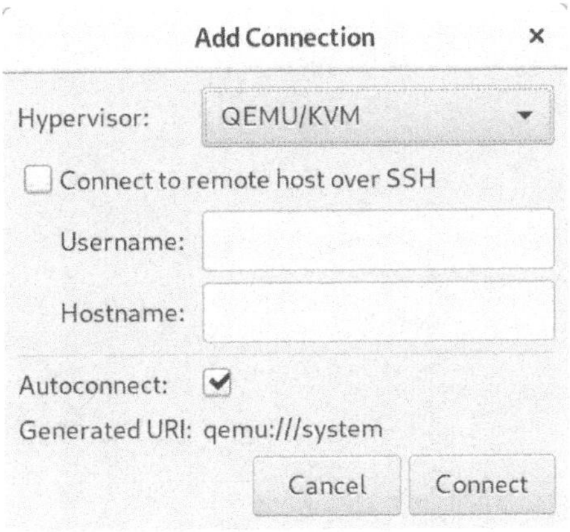

Figure 20-2

If the manager is not currently connected to the virtualization processes, right-click on the entry listed and select Connect from the popup menu.

20.5 Summary

KVM is a Type-1 hypervisor virtualization solution that implements full virtualization with support for unmodified guest operating systems using Intel VT and AMD-V hardware virtualization support. It is the default virtualization solution bundled with CentOS 8 and can be installed quickly and easily on any CentOS 8 system with appropriate processor support. With KVM support installed and enabled, the next few chapters will outline some of the options for installing and managing virtual machines on a CentOS 8 host.

21. Creating KVM Virtual Machines using Cockpit and virt-manager

KVM-based virtual machines can easily be configured on CentOS 8 using either the *virt-install* command-line tool, the *virt-manager* GUI tool or the Virtual Machines module of the Cockpit web console. For the purposes of this chapter we will use Cockpit and the *virt-manager* tool to install a Fedora distribution as a KVM guest on a CentOS 8 host. Before proceeding, however, it is important to note that *virt-manager* is now deprecated in CentOS 8 with the intention that it will be fully replaced by the Cockpit module in the future. As of CentOS 8, however, *virt-manager* is still available and includes features not yet integrated into the Cockpit virtual machine module.

The command-line approach to virtual machine creation will be covered in the next chapter entitled *"Creating KVM Virtual Machines with virt-install and virsh"*.

21.1 Installing the Cockpit Virtual Machines Module

By default, the virtual machines module is not included in a standard Cockpit installation. Assuming that Cockpit is installed and configured, the virtual machines module may be installed as follows:

```
# dnf install cockpit-machines
```

Once installed, the Virtual Machines option (marked A in *Figure 21-1*) will appear in the navigation panel next time you log into the Cockpit interface:

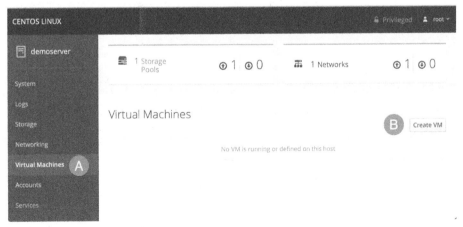

Figure 21-1

21.2 Creating a Virtual Machine in Cockpit

To create a virtual machine in Cockpit, simply click on the *Create VM* button marked B in *Figure 22-1* to display the creation dialog.

Creating KVM Virtual Machines using Cockpit and virt-manager

Within the dialog, enter a name for the machine and choose whether the installation media is in the form of an ISO accessible via a URL or a local filesystem path. Ideally, also select the vendor and operating system type information for the guest. While not essential, this will aid the system in optimizing the virtual machine for the guest.

Also specify the size of the virtual disk drive to be used for the operating system installation and the amount of memory to be allocated to the virtual machine:

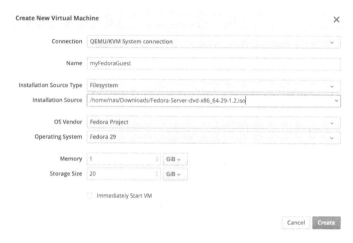

Figure 21-2

For this example, leave the *Immediately Start VM* option unselected and, once the new virtual machine has been configured, click on the *Create* button to build the virtual machine. After the creation process is complete, the new VM will appear in Cockpit as shown in *Figure 21-3*:

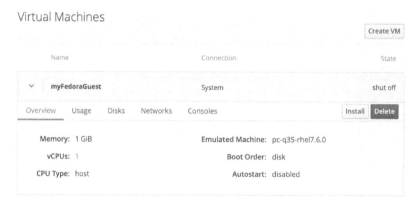

Figure 21-3

As described in *"An Overview of Virtualization Techniques"*, KVM provides virtual machines with a number of options in terms of network configuration. To view and change the network settings of a virtual machine, click on the Networks tab as shown in *Figure 21-4* followed by the Edit button located next to the network entry:

Figure 21-4

In the resulting dialog, the Network Type menu may be used to change the type of network connection, for example from virtual network (NAT) to direct connection (MacVTap).

21.3 Starting the Installation

To start the new virtual machine and begin installing the guest operating system from the designated installation media, click on the *Install* button highlighted in *Figure 21-3* above. Cockpit will start the virtual machine and switch to the Consoles view where the guest OS screen will appear:

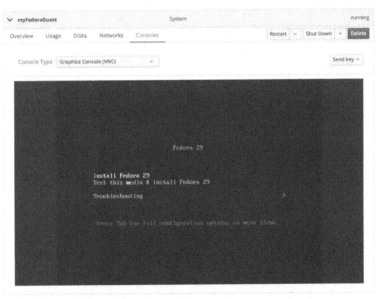

Figure 21-5

If the installation fails, check the message to see if it reads as follows:

```
Could not open '<path to iso image>': Permission denied
Domain installation does not appear to have been successful.
```

This usually occurs because the QEMU emulator runs as a user named qemu which does not have access to the directory in which the ISO installation image is located. To resolve this issue, change directory to the location of the ISO image file and add the qemu user to the access control list

Creating KVM Virtual Machines using Cockpit and virt-manager

(ACL) of the parent directory as follows:

```
# cd /path/to/iso/directory
# setfacl --modify u:qemu:x ..
```

After making this change, check the setting as follows:

```
# getfacl ..
# file: ..
# owner: demo
# group: demo
user::rwx
user:qemu:--x
group::---
mask::--x
other::---
```

Once these changes have been made, click on the Install button once again to complete the installation.

To complete the installation, interact with the screen in the Consoles view just as you would if you were installing the operating system on physical hardware.

It is also possible to connect with and display the graphical console for the VM from outside the Cockpit browser session using the *virt-viewer* tool. To install *virt-viewer* on a CentOS 8 system, run the following command:

```
# dnf install virt-viewer
```

The *virt-viewer* tool is also available for Windows systems and can be downloaded from the following URL:

https://virt-manager.org/download/

To connect with a virtual machine running on the local host, simply run *virt-viewer* and select the virtual machine to which you wish to connect from the resulting dialog:

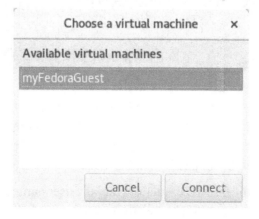

Figure 21-6

Alternatively, it is also possible to specify the virtual machine name and bypass the selection dialog, for example:

```
# virt-viewer myFedoraGuest
```

To connect a *virt-viewer* instance to a virtual machine running on a remote host using SSH, the following command can be used:

```
$ virt-viewer --connect qemu+ssh://<user>@<host>/system <guest name>
```

For example:

```
$ virt-viewer --connect qemu+ssh://root@192.168.1.122/system MyFedoraGuest
```

When using this technique it is important to note that you will be prompted twice for the user password before the connection will be fully established.

Once the virtual machine has been created, the Cockpit interface can be used to monitor the machine and perform tasks such as rebooting, shutting down or deleting the guest system. An option is also included on the *Disks* panel to add additional disks to the virtual machine configuration.

21.4 Creating a Virtual Machine using virt-manager

With the caveat that *virt-manager* is now deprecated and will be removed once the Virtual Machines Cockpit extension is fully implemented, the remainder of this chapter will explore the use of this tool to create new virtual machines.

21.5 Starting the Virtual Machine Manager

Begin by launching Virtual Machine Manager from the command-line in a terminal window by running *virt-manager*. Once loaded, the virtual machine manager will prompt for the password of the currently active user prior to displaying the following screen:

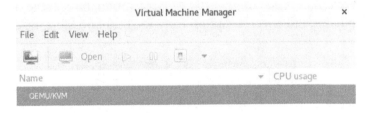

Figure 21-7

The main screen lists the current virtual machines running on the system. At this point there should only be one, the hypervisor running on the host system. By default the manager should be connected to the host. If it is not, connect to the host system by right-clicking on the entry in the list and selecting *Connect* from the popup menu.

To create a new virtual system, click on the new virtual machine button (the far left button on the toolbar) or right-click on the hypervisor entry and select *New* from the resulting menu to display the first screen of the New VM wizard. In the Name field enter a suitably descriptive

Creating KVM Virtual Machines using Cockpit and virt-manager

name for the virtual system. On this screen, also select the location of the media from which the guest operating system will be installed. This can either be a CD or DVD drive, an ISO image file accessible to the local host, a network install using HTTP, FTP, NFS or PXE or the disk image from an existing virtual machine:

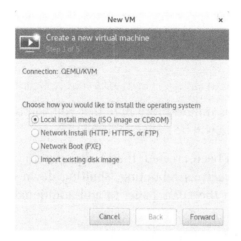

Figure 21-8

21.6 Configuring the KVM Virtual System

Clicking *Forward* will display a screen seeking additional information about the installation process. The screen displayed and information required will depend on selections made in the preceding screen. For example, if a CD, DVD or ISO was selected, this screen will ask for the specific location of the ISO file or physical media device. This screen also attempts to identify the type and version of the guest operating system to be installed (for example the Windows version or Linux distribution) based on the installation media specified. If it is unable to do so, uncheck the *Automatically detect from installation media / source* option, type in the first few character of the operating system name and select an option from the list of possible matches:

Figure 21-9

Once these settings are complete, click the *Forward* button to configure CPU and memory settings. The optimal settings will depend on the number of CPUs and amount of physical memory present in the host together with the requirements of other applications and virtual machines that will run in parallel with the new virtual machine:

Figure 21-10

The last item to configure before creating the virtual machine is the storage space for the guest operating system and corresponding user data. This takes the form of a virtual disk image or pre-existing storage. A virtual disk drive is essentially an image file located on the file system of the host computer which is seen by the virtual machine as a physical disk drive.

Options are available to create an image disk of a specified size, select a pre-existing volume or to create a storage volume of a specified format (raw, vmdk, ISO etc). Unless you have a specific need to use a particular format (for example you might need to use vmdk to migrate to a VMware based virtualization environment at a later date) or need to use a dedicated disk or partition, it is generally adequate to simply specify a size on this screen:

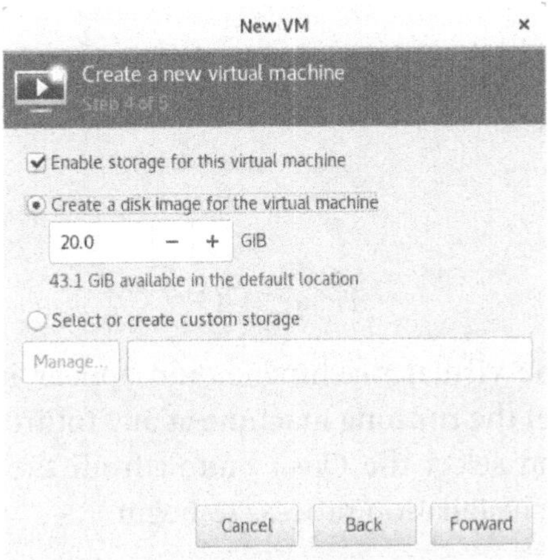

Figure 21-11

Creating KVM Virtual Machines using Cockpit and virt-manager

Once these settings are configured, click the *Forward* button once more. The final screen displays a summary of the configuration. Review the information displayed. Advanced options are also available to change the virtual network configuration for the guest as shown in *Figure 21-12*:

Figure 21-12

21.7 Starting the KVM Virtual Machine

Click on the *Finish* button to begin the creation process. The virtualization manager will create the disk and configure the virtual machine before starting the guest system. The new virtual machine will appear in the main *virt-manager* window with the status set to *Running* as illustrated in *Figure 21-13*:

Figure 21-13

By default, the console for the virtual machine should appear in the virtual machine viewer window. To view the console of the running machine at any future time, ensure that it is selected in the virtual machine list and select the *Open* button from the toolbar. The virtual machine viewer should be ready for the installation process to begin:

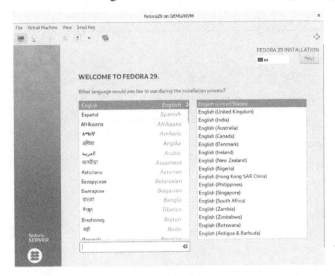

Figure 21-14

From this point on, simply follow the operating system installation instructions to install the guest OS in the KVM virtual machine.

21.8 Summary

This chapter has outlined two different ways to create new KVM-based virtual machines on a CentOS 8 host system. The first option covered involves the use of the Cockpit web-based interface to create and manage virtual machines. This has the advantage of not requiring access to a desktop environment running on the host system. An alternative option is to use the *virt-manager* graphical tool. Though deprecated in CentOS 8 and likely to be removed in later releases, *virt-manager* currently provides options not currently available in the Cockpit Virtual Machines extension. At the point that *virt-manager* is removed it is expected that Cockpit will provide equal or better functionality.

With these basics covered, the next chapter will cover the creation of virtual machines from the command-line.

22. Creating KVM Virtual Machines with virt-install and virsh

In the previous chapter we explored the creation of KVM guest operating systems on a CentOS 8 host using Cockpit and the *virt-manager* graphical tool. In this chapter we will turn our attention to the creation of KVM-based virtual machines using the *virt-install* and *virsh* command-line tools. These tools provide all the capabilities of the *virt-manager* and Cockpit options with the added advantage that they can be used within scripts to automate virtual machine creation. In addition, the *virsh* command allows virtual machines to be created based on a specification contained within a configuration file.

The *virt-install* tool is supplied to allow new virtual machines to be created by providing a list of command-line options. This chapter assumes that the necessary KVM tools are installed. For details on these requirements read the chapter entitled *"Installing KVM Virtualization on CentOS 8"*.

22.1 Running virt-install to build a KVM Guest System

The *virt-install* utility accepts a wide range of command-line arguments that are used to provide configuration information related to the virtual machine being created. Some of these command-line options are mandatory (specifically name, memory and disk storage must be provided) while others are optional.

At a minimum, a *virt-install* command will typically need the following arguments:

- **--name** - The name to be assigned to the virtual machine.

- **--memory** - The amount of memory to be allocated to the virtual machine.

- **--disk** - The name and location of an image file to be used as storage for the virtual machine. This file will be created by *virt-install* during the virtual machine creation unless the **--import** option is specified to indicate an existing image file is to be used.

- **--cdrom** or **--location** - Specifies the local path or the URL of a remote ISO image containing the installation media for the guest operating system.

A summary of all the arguments available for use when using *virt-install* can be found in the man page:

```
$ man virt-install
```

22.2 An Example CentOS 8 virt-install Command

With reference to the above command-line argument list, we can now look at an example command-line construct using the *virt-install* tool.

Note that in order to be able to display the virtual machine and complete the installation, a *virt-viewer* instance will need to be connected to the virtual machine after it is started by the *virt-install* utility. By default, *virt-install* will attempt to launch *virt-viewer* automatically once the virtual machine starts running. If *virt-viewer* is not available, *virt-install* will wait until a *virt-viewer* connection is established. The *virt-viewer* session may be running locally on the host system if it has a graphical desktop, or a connection may be established from a remote client as outlined in the chapter entitled *"Creating KVM Virtual Machines using Cockpit and virt-manager"*.

The following command creates a new KVM virtual machine configured to run Fedora 29 using KVM para-virtualization. It creates a new 10GB disk image, assigns 1024MB of RAM to the virtual machine and configures a virtual CD device for the installation media ISO image:

```
# virt-install --name MyFedora --memory 1024 --disk path=/tmp/myFedora.img,
size=10 --network network=default --os-variant fedora29 --cdrom /tmp/Fedora-
Server-dvd-x86_64-29-1.2.iso
```

As the creation process runs, the *virt-install* command will display status updates of the creation progress:

```
Starting install...
Allocating 'MyFedora.img'                              |  10 GB  00:00:01
Domain installation still in progress. Waiting for installation to complete.
```

Once the guest system has been created, the *virt-viewer* screen will appear containing the operating system installer loaded from the specified installation media:

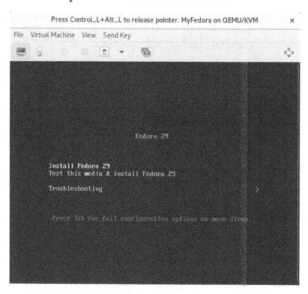

Figure 22-1

From this point, follow the standard installation procedure for the guest operating system.

22.3 Starting and Stopping a Virtual Machine from the Command-Line

Having created the virtual machine from the command-line it stands to reason that you may also need to start it from the command-line in the future. This can be achieved using the virsh command-line utility, referencing the name assigned to the virtual machine during the creation process. For example:

```
# virsh start MyFedora
```

Similarly, the virtual machine may be sent a shutdown signal as follows:

```
# virsh shutdown MyFedora
```

If the virtual machine fails to respond to the shutdown signal and does not begin a graceful shutdown the virtual machine may be destroyed (with the attendant risks of data loss) using the destroy directive:

```
# virsh destroy MyFedora
```

22.4 Creating a Virtual Machine from a Configuration File

The *virsh create* command can take as an argument the name of a configuration file on which to base the creation of a new virtual machine. The configuration file uses XML format. Arguably the easiest way to create a configuration file is to dump out the configuration of an existing virtual machine and modify it for the new one. This can be achieved using the *virsh dumpxml* command. The following command outputs the configuration data for a virtual machine domain named MyFedora to a file named *MyFedora.xml*:

```
# virsh dumpxml MyFedora > MyFedora.xml
```

Once the file has been generated, load it into an editor to review and change the settings for the new virtual machine.

At the very least, the <name>, <uuid> and image file path <source file> must be changed in order to avoid conflict with the virtual machine from which the configuration was taken. In the case of the UUID, this line can simply be deleted from the file.

The virtualization type, memory allocation and number of CPUs to name but a few options may also be changed if required. Once the file has been modified, the new virtual machine may be created as follows:

```
# virsh create MyFedora.xml
```

22.5 Summary

KVM provides the *virt-install* and *virsh* command-line tools as a quick and efficient alternative to using the Cockpit and *virt-manager* tools to create and manage virtual machine instances. These tools have the advantage that they can be used from within scripts to automate the creation and management of virtual machines. The *virsh* command also includes the option to create VM instances from XML-based configuration files.

23. Creating a CentOS 8 KVM Networked Bridge Interface

By default, the KVM virtualization environment on CentOS 8 creates a virtual network to which virtual machines may connect. It is also possible to configure a direct connection using a MacVTap driver, though as outlined in the chapter entitled *"An Overview of Virtualization Techniques"*, this approach does not allow the host and guest systems to communicate.

The goal of this chapter is to cover the steps involved in creating a network bridge on CentOS 8 enabling guest systems to share one or more of the host system's physical network connections while still allowing the guest and host systems to communicate.

In the remainder of this chapter we will cover the steps necessary to configure a CentOS 8 network bridge for use by KVM-based guest operating systems.

23.1 Getting the Current Network Settings

A network bridge can be created using the NetworkManager command-line interface tool (*nmcli*). The NetworkManager is installed and enabled by default on CentOS 8 systems and is responsible for detecting and connecting to network devices in addition to providing an interface for managing networking configurations.

A list of current network connections on the host system can be displayed as follows:

```
# nmcli con show
NAME        UUID                                   TYPE      DEVICE
eno1        99d40009-6bb1-4182-baad-a103941c90ff   ethernet  eno1
virbr0      7cb1265e-ffb9-4cb3-aaad-2a6fe5880d38   bridge    virbr0
```

In the above output we can see that the host has an Ethernet network connection established via a device named *eno1* and the default bridge interface named *virbr0* provides access to the NAT-based virtual network to which KVM guest systems are connected by default.

Similarly, the following command can be used to identify the devices (both virtual and physical) that are currently configured on the system:

```
# nmcli device show
GENERAL.DEVICE:                         eno1
GENERAL.TYPE:                           ethernet
GENERAL.HWADDR:                         AC:16:2D:11:16:73
GENERAL.MTU:                            1500
GENERAL.STATE:                          100 (connected)
GENERAL.CONNECTION:                     eno1
GENERAL.CON-PATH:                       /org/freedesktop/NetworkManager/
```

Creating a CentOS 8 KVM Networked Bridge Interface

```
ActiveConnection/1
WIRED-PROPERTIES.CARRIER:           on
IP4.ADDRESS[1]:                     192.168.86.59/24
IP4.GATEWAY:                        192.168.86.1
IP4.ROUTE[1]:                       dst = 0.0.0.0/0, nh = 192.168.86.1, mt =
100
IP4.ROUTE[2]:                       dst = 192.168.86.0/24, nh = 0.0.0.0, mt =
100
IP4.DNS[1]:                         192.168.86.1
IP4.DOMAIN[1]:                      lan
IP6.ADDRESS[1]:                     fe80::6deb:f739:7d67:2242/64
IP6.GATEWAY:                        --
IP6.ROUTE[1]:                       dst = fe80::/64, nh = ::, mt = 100
IP6.ROUTE[2]:                       dst = ff00::/8, nh = ::, mt = 256,
table=255

GENERAL.DEVICE:                     virbr0
GENERAL.TYPE:                       bridge
GENERAL.HWADDR:                     52:54:00:59:30:22
GENERAL.MTU:                        1500
GENERAL.STATE:                      100 (connected)
GENERAL.CONNECTION:                 virbr0
GENERAL.CON-PATH:                   /org/freedesktop/NetworkManager/
ActiveConnection/2
IP4.ADDRESS[1]:                     192.168.122.1/24
IP4.GATEWAY:                        --
IP4.ROUTE[1]:                       dst = 192.168.122.0/24, nh = 0.0.0.0, mt
= 0
IP6.GATEWAY:                        --
.

.
```

The above partial output indicates that the host system on which the command was executed contains a physical Ethernet device (eno1) and the virtual bridge (virbr0).

The *virsh* command may also be used to list the virtual networks currently configured on the system:

```
# virsh net-list --all
Name                  State     Autostart
----------------------------------------
default               active    yes
```

At this point, the only virtual network present is the default network provided by virbr0. Now that some basic information about the current network configuration has been obtained, the next step is to create a network bridge connected to the physical network device (in this case the device named eno1).

23.2 Creating a Network Bridge from the Command-Line

The first step in creating the network bridge is to add a new connection to the network configuration. This can be achieved using the *nmcli* tool, specifying that the connection is to be a bridge and providing names for both the connection and the interface:

```
# nmcli con add ifname br0 type bridge con-name br0
```

Once the connection has been added, a bridge slave interface needs to be established between physical device eno1 (the slave) and the bridge connection br0 (the master) as follows:

```
# nmcli con add type bridge-slave ifname eno1 master br0
```

At this point, the NetworkManager connection list should read as follows:

```
# nmcli con show
NAME                UUID                                  TYPE      DEVICE
eno1                66f0abed-db43-4d79-8f5e-2cbf8c7e3aff  ethernet  eno1
virbr0              0fa934d5-0508-47b7-a119-33a232b03f64  bridge    virbr0
br0                 59b6631c-a283-41b9-bbf9-56a60ec75653  bridge    br0
bridge-slave-eno1   395bb34b-5e02-427a-ab31-762c9f878908  ethernet  --
```

The next step is to start up the bridge interface. If the steps to configure the bridge are being performed over a network connection (i.e. via SSH) this step can be problematic because the current eno1 connection must be closed down before the bridge connection can be brought up. This means that the current connection will be lost before the bridge connection can be enabled to replace it, potentially leaving the remote host unreachable.

If you are accessing the host system remotely this problem can be avoided by creating a shell script to perform the network changes. This will ensure that the bridge interface is enabled after the eno1 interface is brought down, allowing you to reconnect to the host after the changes are complete. Begin by creating a shell script file named *bridge.sh* containing the following commands:

```
#!/bin/bash
nmcli con down eno1
nmcli con up br0
```

Once the script has been created, execute it as follows:

```
# sh ./bridge.sh
```

When the script executes, the connection will be lost when the eno1 connection is brought down. After waiting a few seconds, however, it should be possible to reconnect to the host once the br0 connection has been activated.

If you are working locally on the host, the two *nmcli* commands can be run within a terminal window without any risk of losing connectivity:

```
# nmcli con down eno1
# nmcli con up br0
```

Once the bridge is up and running, the connection list should now include both the bridge and the bridge-slave connections:

Creating a CentOS 8 KVM Networked Bridge Interface

```
# nmcli con show
NAME                UUID                                    TYPE       DEVICE
br0                 59b6631c-a283-41b9-bbf9-56a60ec75653    bridge     br0
bridge-slave-eno1   395bb34b-5e02-427a-ab31-762c9f878908    ethernet   eno1
virbr0              0fa934d5-0508-47b7-a119-33a232b03f64    bridge     virbr0
eno1                66f0abed-db43-4d79-8f5e-2cbf8c7e3aff    ethernet   --
```

Note that the eno1 connection is still listed but is actually no longer active. To exclude inactive connections from the list, simply use the --active flag when requesting the list:

```
# nmcli con show --active
NAME                UUID                                    TYPE       DEVICE
br0                 c2fa30cb-b1a1-4107-80dd-b1765878ab4f    bridge     br0
bridge-slave-eno1   21e8c945-cb94-4c09-99b0-17af9b5a7319    ethernet   eno1
virbr0              a877302e-ea02-42fe-a3c1-483440aae774    bridge     virbr0
```

23.3 Declaring the KVM Bridged Network

At this point, the bridge connection is present on the system but is not visible to the KVM environment. Running the *virsh* command should still list the default network as being the only available network option:

```
# virsh net-list --all
 Name                State      Autostart    Persistent
----------------------------------------------------------
 default             active     yes          yes
```

Before the bridge can be used by a virtual machine it must be declared and added to the KVM network configuration. This involves the creation of a definition file and, once again, the use of the *virsh* command-line tool.

Begin by creating a definition file for the bridge network named *bridge.xml* that reads as follows:

```
<network>
  <name>br0</name>
  <forward mode="bridge"/>
  <bridge name="br0" />
</network>
```

Next, use the file to define the new network:

```
# virsh net-define ./bridge.xml
```

Once the network has been defined, start it and, if required, configure it to autostart each time the system reboots:

```
# virsh net-start br0
# virsh net-autostart br0
```

Once again list the networks to verify that the bridge network is now accessible within the KVM environment:

```
# virsh net-list --all
```

Name	State	Autostart	Persistent
br0	active	yes	yes
default	active	yes	yes

23.4 Using a Bridge Network in a Virtual Machine

To create a virtual machine that makes use of the bridge network, use the *virt-install* --network option and specify the br0 bridge name. For example:

```
# virt-install --name MyFedora --memory 1024 --disk path=/tmp/myFedora.
img,size=10 --network network=br0 --os-variant fedora29 --cdrom /home/demo/
Downloads/Fedora-Server-dvd-x86_64-29-1.2.iso
```

When the guest operating system is running it will appear on the same physical network as the host system and will no longer be on the NAT-based virtual network.

To modify an existing virtual machine so that it uses the bridge, use the *virsh edit* command. This command loads the XML definition file into an editor where changes can be made and saved:

```
# virsh edit GuestName
```

By default, the file will be loaded into the vi editor. To use a different editor, simply change the $EDITOR environment variable, for example:

```
# export EDITOR=gedit
```

To change from the default virtual network, locate the <interface> section of the file which will read as follows for a NAT based configuration:

```
<interface type='network'>
    <mac address='<your mac address here>'/>
    <source network='default'/>
    <model type='virtio'/>
    <address type='pci' domain='0x0000' bus='0x01' slot='0x00' function='0x0'/>
</interface>
```

Alternatively, if the virtual machine was using a direct connection, the entry may read as follows:

```
<interface type='direct'>
    <mac address='<your mac address here>'/>
    <source dev='eno1' mode='vepa'/>
    <model type='virtio'/>
    <address type='pci' domain='0x0000' bus='0x01' slot='0x00' function='0x0'/>
```

To use the bridge, change the source network property to read as follows before saving the file:

```
<interface type='network'>
    <mac address='<your mac address here>'/>
    <source network='br0'/>
    <model type='virtio'/>
    <address type='pci' domain='0x0000' bus='0x01' slot='0x00' function='0x0'/>
</interface>
```

If the virtual machine is already running, the change will not take effect until it is restarted.

23.5 Creating a Bridge Network using nm-connection-editor

If either local or remote desktop access is available on the host system, much of the bridge configuration process can be performed using the *nm-connection-editor* graphical tool. To use this tool, open a Terminal window within the desktop and enter the following command:

```
# nm-connection-editor
```

When the tool has loaded, the window shown in Figure 23-1 will appear listing the currently configured network connections (essentially the same output as that generated by the *nmcli con show* command):

Figure 23-1

To create a new connection, click on the '+' button located in the bottom left-hand corner of the window. From the resulting dialog (Figure 23-2) select the Bridge option from the menu:

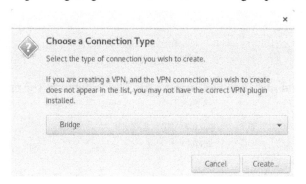

Figure 23-2

With the bridge option selected, click on the *Create...* button to proceed to the bridge configuration screen. Begin by changing both the connection and interface name fields to br0 before clicking on the *Add* button located to the right of the Bridge connections list as highlighted in Figure 23-3:

Figure 23-3

From the connection type dialog (Figure 23-4) change the menu setting to *Ethernet* before clicking on the *Create...* button:

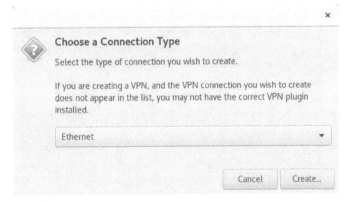

Figure 23-4

Another dialog will now appear in which the bridge slave connection needs to be configured. Within this dialog, select the physical network to which the bridge is to connect (for example *eno1*) from the Device menu:

Creating a CentOS 8 KVM Networked Bridge Interface

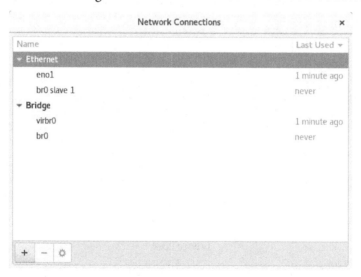

Figure 23-5

Click on the *Save* button to apply the changes and return to the *Editing br0* dialog (as illustrated in Figure 23-3 above). Within this dialog, click on the *Save* button to create the bridge. On returning to the main window, the new bridge and slave connections should now be listed:

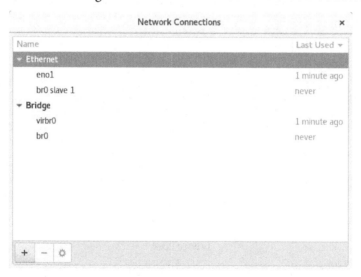

Figure 23-6

All that remains is to bring down the original eno1 connection and bring up the br0 connection using the steps outlined in the previous chapter (remembering to perform these steps in a shell script if the host is being accessed remotely):

```
# nmcli con down eno1
```

```
# nmcli con up br0
```

It will also be necessary, as it was when creating the bridge using the command-line tool, to add this bridge to the KVM network configuration. To do so, simply repeat the steps outlined in the section above entitled *"Declaring the KVM Bridged Network"*. Once this step has been taken, the bridge is ready to be used by guest virtual machines.

23.6 Summary

By default, KVM virtual machines are connected to a virtual network that uses NAT to provide access to the network to which the host system is connected. If the guests are required to appear on the network with their own IP addresses, the guests need to be configured to share the physical network interface of the host system. As outlined in this chapter, this can be achieved using either the *nmcli* or *nm-connection-editor* tools to create a networked bridge interface.

24. Managing KVM using the virsh Command-Line Tool

In previous chapters we have covered the steps necessary to install and configure KVM-based guest operating systems on CentOS 8. This chapter is dedicated to exploring some additional areas of the *virsh* tool that have not been covered in previous chapters, and how it may be used to manage KVM-based guest operating systems from the command-line.

24.1 The virsh Shell and Command-Line

The *virsh* tool is both a command-line tool and an interactive shell environment. When used in the command-line mode, the command is simply issued at the command prompt with sets of arguments appropriate to the task to be performed.

To use the options as command-line arguments, use them at a terminal command prompt as shown in the following example:

```
# virsh <option>
```

The *virsh* tool, when used in shell mode, provides an interactive environment from which to issue sequences of commands.

To run commands in the *virsh* shell, run the following command:

```
# virsh
Welcome to virsh, the virtualization interactive terminal.

Type:  'help' for help with commands
       'quit' to quit


virsh #
```

At the *virsh* # prompt enter the options you wish to run. The following *virsh* session, for example, lists the current virtual machines, starts a virtual machine named FedoraVM and then obtains another listing to verify the VM is running:

```
# virsh
Welcome to virsh, the virtualization interactive terminal.

Type:  'help' for help with commands
       'quit' to quit


virsh # list
 Id    Name                           State
```

185

```
------------------------------------------------------
 8      RHEL8VM                          running
 9      CentOS7VM                        running

virsh # start FedoraVM
Domain FedoraVM started

virsh # list
 Id     Name                            State
------------------------------------------------------
 8      RHEL8VM                          running
 9      CentOS7VM                        running
10      FedoraVM                         running

virsh#
```

The *virsh* tool supports a wide range of commands, a full listing of which may be obtained using the help option:

```
# virsh help
```

Additional details on the syntax for each command may be obtained by specifying the command after the help directive:

```
# virsh help restore
  NAME
    restore - restore a domain from a saved state in a file

  SYNOPSIS
    restore <file> [--bypass-cache] [--xml <string>] [--running] [--paused]

  DESCRIPTION
    Restore a domain.

  OPTIONS
    [--file] <string>  the state to restore
    --bypass-cache     avoid file system cache when restoring
    --xml <string>     filename containing updated XML for the target
    --running          restore domain into running state
    --paused           restore domain into paused state
```

In the remainder of this chapter we will look at some of these commands in more detail.

24.2 Listing Guest System Status

The status of the guest systems on a CentOS 8 virtualization host may be viewed at any time using the *list* option of the *virsh* tool. For example:

```
# virsh list
```

The above command will display output containing a line for each guest similar to the following:

```
virsh # list
 Id    Name                        State
----------------------------------------------------
 8     RHEL8VM                     running
 9     CentOS7VM                   running
 10    FedoraVM                    running
```

24.3 Starting a Guest System

A guest operating system can be started using the *virsh* tool combined with the start option followed by the name of the guest operating system to be launched. For example:

```
# virsh start myGuestOS
```

24.4 Shutting Down a Guest System

The *shutdown* option of the *virsh* tool, as the name suggests, is used to shutdown a guest operating system:

```
# virsh shutdown guestName
```

Note that the shutdown option allows the guest operating system to perform an orderly shutdown when it receives the shutdown instruction. To instantly stop a guest operating system the *destroy* option may be used (with all the attendant risks of file system damage and data loss):

```
# virsh destroy guestName
```

24.5 Suspending and Resuming a Guest System

A guest system can be suspended and resumed using the *virsh* tool's suspend and resume options. For example, to suspend a specific system:

```
# virsh suspend guestName
```

Similarly, to resume the paused system:

```
# virsh resume guestName
```

Note that a suspended session will be lost if the host system is rebooted. Also, be aware that a suspended system continues to reside in memory. To save a session such that it no longer takes up memory and can be restored to its exact state (even after a reboot), it is necessary to save and restore the guest.

24.6 Saving and Restoring Guest Systems

A running guest operating system can be saved and restored using the *virsh* utility. When saved, the current status of the guest operating system is written to disk and removed from system memory. A saved system may subsequently be restored at any time (including after a host system reboot):

To save a guest:

```
# virsh save guestName path_to_save_file
```

To restore a saved guest operating system session:

```
# virsh restore path_to_save_file
```

24.7 Rebooting a Guest System

To reboot a guest operating system:

```
# virsh reboot guestName
```

24.8 Configuring the Memory Assigned to a Guest OS

To configure the memory assigned to a guest OS, use the *setmem* option of the *virsh* command. For example, the following command reduces the memory allocated to a guest system to 256Mb:

```
# virsh setmem guestName 256
```

Note that acceptable memory settings must fall within the memory available to the current Domain. This may be increased using the *setmaxmem* option.

24.9 Summary

The *virsh* tool provides a wide range of options for creating, monitoring and managing guest virtual machines. As outlined in this chapter, the tool can be used in either command-line or interactive modes.

25. An Introduction to Linux Containers

The preceding chapters covered the concept of virtualization with a particular emphasis on creating and managing virtual machines using KVM. This chapter will introduce a related technology in the form of Linux Containers. While there are some similarities between virtual machines and containers, there are also some key differences that will be outlined in this chapter along with an introduction to the concepts and advantages of Linux Containers. The chapter will also provide an overview of some of the CentOS 8 container management tools. Once the basics of containers have been covered in this chapter, the next chapter will work through some practical examples of creating and running containers on CentOS 8.

25.1 Linux Containers and Kernel Sharing

In simple terms, Linux containers can be thought of as a lightweight alternative to virtualization. In a virtualized environment, a virtual machine is created that contains and runs the entire guest operating system. The virtual machine, in turn, runs on top of an environment such as a hypervisor that manages access to the physical resources of the host system.

Containers work by using a concept referred to as *kernel sharing* which takes advantage of the architectural design of Linux and UNIX-based operating systems.

In order to understand how kernel sharing and containers work it helps to first understand the two main components of Linux or UNIX operating systems. At the core of the operating system is the kernel. The kernel, in simple terms, handles all the interactions between the operating system and the physical hardware. The second key component is the root file system which contains all the libraries, files and utilities necessary for the operating system to function. Taking advantage of this structure, containers each have their own root file system but share the kernel of the host operating system. This structure is illustrated in the architectural diagram in Figure 25-1 below.

This type of resource sharing is made possible by the ability of the kernel to dynamically change the current root file system (a concept known as *change root* or *chroot*) to a different root file system without having to reboot the entire system. Linux containers are essentially an extension of this capability combined with a *container runtime*, the responsibility of which is to provide an interface for executing and managing the containers on the host system. A number of container runtimes are available including Docker, lxd, containerd and CRI-O. Earlier versions of CentOS used Docker by default but this has been supplanted by Podman as the default in CentOS 8.

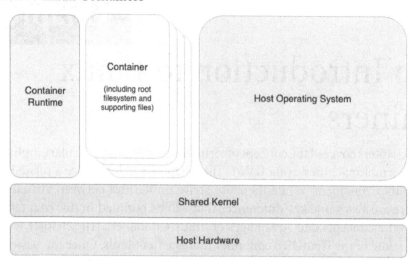

Figure 25-1

25.2 Container Uses and Advantages

The main advantage of containers is that they require considerably less resource overhead than virtualization allowing many container instances to be run simultaneously on a single server, and can be started and stopped rapidly and efficiently in response to demand levels. Containers run natively on the host system providing a level of performance that cannot be matched by a virtual machine.

Containers are also extremely portable and can be migrated between systems quickly and easily. When combined with a container management system such as Docker, OpenShift and Kubernetes, it is possible to deploy and manage containers on a vast scale spanning multiple servers and cloud platforms, potentially running thousands of containers.

Containers are frequently used to create lightweight execution environments for applications. In this scenario, each container provides an isolated environment containing the application together with all of the runtime and supporting files required by that application to run. The container can then be deployed to any other compatible host system that supports container execution and run without any concerns that the target system may not have the necessary runtime configuration for the application - all of the application's dependencies are already in the container.

Containers are also useful when bridging the gap between development and production environments. By performing development and QA work in containers, those containers can then be passed to production and launched safe in the knowledge that the applications are running in the same container environments in which they were developed and tested.

Containers also promote a modular approach to deploying large and complex solutions. Instead of developing applications as single monolithic entities, containers can be used to design applications as groups of interacting modules, each running in a separate container.

One possible drawback of containers is the fact that the guest operating systems must be

190

compatible with the version of the kernel which is being shared. It is not, for example, possible to run Microsoft Windows in a container on a Linux system. Nor is it possible for a Linux guest system designed for the 2.6 version of the kernel to share a 2.4 version kernel. These requirements are not, however, what containers were designed for. Rather than being seen as limitations, therefore, these restrictions should be viewed as some of the key advantages of containers in terms of providing a simple, scalable and reliable deployment platform.

25.3 CentOS 8 Container Tools

CentOS 8 provides a number of tools for creating, inspecting and managing containers. The main tools are as follows:

- **buildah** – A command-line tool for building container images.

- **podman** – A command-line based container runtime and management tool. Performs tasks such as downloading container images from remote registries and inspecting, starting and stopping images.

- **skopeo** – A command-line utility used to convert container images, copy images between registries and inspect images stored in registries without the need to download them.

- **runc** – A lightweight container runtime for launching and running containers from the command-line.

- **OpenShift** – An enterprise level container application management platform consisting of command-line and web-based tools.

All of the above tools are compliant with the Open Container Initiative (OCI), a set of specifications designed to ensure that containers conform to the same standards between competing tools and platforms.

25.4 The Docker Registry

Although CentOS is provided with a set of tools designed to be used in place of those provided by Docker, those tools still need access to CentOS images for use when building containers. For this purpose, the CentOS project maintains a set of CentOS container images within the Docker Hub. The Docker Hub is an online container *registry* made of multiple *repositories*, each containing a wide range of container images available for download when building containers. The images within a repository are each assigned a *repository tag* (for example, centos8, centos7.7, latest etc) which can be referenced when performing an image download. The following, for example, is the URL of the centos8 image contained within the Docker Hub:

```
docker://docker.io/library/centos:centos8
```

In addition to downloading (referred to as "pulling" in container terminology) container images from Docker and other third party hosts registries, you can also use registries to store your own images. This can be achieved either by hosting your own registry, or by making use of existing services such as those provided by Docker, Amazon AWS, Google Cloud, Microsoft Azure and IBM Cloud to name a few of the many options.

25.5 Container Networking

By default, containers are connected to a network using a Container Networking Interface (CNI) bridged network stack. In the bridged configuration, all the containers running on a server belong to the same subnet (10.88.0.0/16 by default) and, as such, are able to communicate with each other. The containers are also connected to the external network by bridging the host system's network connection. Similarly, the host is able to access the containers via a virtual network interface (usually named cni0) which will have been created as part of the container tool installation.

25.6 Summary

Linux Containers offer a lightweight alternative to virtualization and take advantage of the structure of the Linux and Unix operating systems. Linux Containers essentially share the kernel of the host operating system, with each container having its own root file system containing the files, libraries and applications. Containers are highly efficient and scalable and provide an ideal platform for building and deploying modular enterprise level solutions. A number of tools and platforms are available for building, deploying and managing containers including third-party solutions and those provided with CentOS.

26. Working with Containers on CentOS 8

Now that the basics of Linux Containers have been covered in the previous chapter, the goal of this chapter is to demonstrate how to create and manage containers using the Podman, Skopeo and Buildah tools included with CentOS 8. It is intended that by the end of this chapter you will have a clearer understanding of how to create and manage containers on CentOS 8 and will have gained a knowledge foundation on which to continue exploring the power of Linux Containers.

26.1 Pulling a Container Image

For this example, the CentOS 8 Base image will be pulled from the registry. Before pulling an image, however, information about the image repository can be obtained using the *skopeo* tool, for example:

```
# skopeo inspect docker://docker.io/library/centos
{
    "Name": "docker.io/library/centos",
    "Digest": "sha256:f94c1d992c193b3dc09e297ffd54d8a4f1dc946c37cbeceb26d35ce1647
f88d9",
    "RepoTags": [
        "5.11",
        "5",
        "6.10",
        "6.6",
        "6.7",
        "6.8",
        "6.9",
        "6",
        "7.0.1406",
        "7.1.1503",
        "7.2.1511",
        "7.3.1611",
        "7.4.1708",
        "7.5.1804",
        "7.6.1810",
        "7.7.1908",
        "7",
        "8",
        "centos5.11",
        "centos5",
```

```
        "centos6.10",
        "centos6.6",
        "centos6.7",
        "centos6.8",
        "centos6.9",
        "centos6",
        "centos7.0.1406",
        "centos7.1.1503",
        "centos7.2.1511",
        "centos7.3.1611",
        "centos7.4.1708",
        "centos7.5.1804",
        "centos7.6.1810",
        "centos7.7.1908",
        "centos7",
        "centos8",
        "latest"
    ],
    "Created": "2019-10-01T23:19:57.105928163Z",
    "DockerVersion": "18.06.1-ce",
    "Labels": {
        "org.label-schema.build-date": "20190927",
        "org.label-schema.license": "GPLv2",
        "org.label-schema.name": "CentOS Base Image",
        "org.label-schema.schema-version": "1.0",
        "org.label-schema.vendor": "CentOS"
    },
    "Architecture": "amd64",
    "Os": "linux",
    "Layers": [
        "sha256:729ec3a6ada3a6d26faca9b4779a037231f1762f759ef34c08bdd61bf52cd704"
    ]
}
```

Having verified that the repository has the images we need, the podman command can be used to download an image for the required CentOS version using the following syntax where <RepoTag> is replaced by the tag for the CentOS version as shown in the skopeo output:

```
# podman pull docker://docker.io/library/centos:<RepoTag>
```

For example, to pull the CentOS 7 image:

```
# podman pull docker://docker.io/library/centos:centos7
```

Alternatively, to default to the latest release of CentOS:

```
# podman pull docker://docker.io/library/centos:latest
Trying to pull docker://docker.io/library/centos:latest...Getting image source
```

```
signatures
Skipping blob 729ec3a6ada3 (already present): 68.21 MiB / 68.21 MiB [=======] 0s
Copying config 0f3e07c0138f: 2.13 KiB / 2.13 KiB [==========================] 0s
Writing manifest to image destination
Storing signatures
0f3e07c0138fbe05abcb7a9cc7d63d9bd4c980c3f61fea5efa32e7c4217ef4da
```

Verify that the image has been stored by asking *podman* to list all local images:

```
# podman images
REPOSITORY                  TAG      IMAGE ID       CREATED       SIZE
docker.io/library/centos    latest   0f3e07c0138f   8 weeks ago   227 MB
```

Details about a local image may be obtained by running the *podman inspect* command:

```
# podman inspect centos:latest
```

26.2 Running the Image in a Container

The image pulled from the registry is a fully operational image that is ready to run in a container without modification. To run the image, use the *podman run* command. In this case the *–rm* option will be specified to indicate that we want to run the image in a container, execute one command and then have the container exit. In this case, the *cat* tool will be used to output the content of the */etc/passwd* file located on the container root filesystem:

```
# podman run --rm centos:latest cat /etc/passwd
root:x:0:0:root:/root:/bin/bash
bin:x:1:1:bin:/bin:/sbin/nologin
daemon:x:2:2:daemon:/sbin:/sbin/nologin
adm:x:3:4:adm:/var/adm:/sbin/nologin
lp:x:4:7:lp:/var/spool/lpd:/sbin/nologin
sync:x:5:0:sync:/sbin:/bin/sync
shutdown:x:6:0:shutdown:/sbin:/sbin/shutdown
halt:x:7:0:halt:/sbin:/sbin/halt
mail:x:8:12:mail:/var/spool/mail:/sbin/nologin
operator:x:11:0:operator:/root:/sbin/nologin
games:x:12:100:games:/usr/games:/sbin/nologin
ftp:x:14:50:FTP User:/var/ftp:/sbin/nologin
nobody:x:65534:65534:Kernel Overflow User:/:/sbin/nologin
dbus:x:81:81:System message bus:/:/sbin/nologin
systemd-coredump:x:999:997:systemd Core Dumper:/:/sbin/nologin
systemd-resolve:x:193:193:systemd Resolver:/:/sbin/nologin
```

Compare the content of the */etc/passwd* file within the container with the */etc/passwd* file on the host system and note that it lacks all of the additional users that are present on the host confirming that the *cat* command was executed within the container environment. Also note that the container started, ran the command and exited all within a matter of seconds. Compare this to the amount of time it takes to start a full operating, perform a task and shutdown a virtual machine and you begin to appreciate the speed and efficiency of containers.

Working with Containers on CentOS 8

To launch a container, keep it running and access the shell, the following command can be used:

```
$ podman run --name=mycontainer -it centos:latest /bin/bash
[root@965acf617e6e /]#
```

Note that an additional command-line option is used to assign the name "mycontainer" to the container. Though optional, this makes the container easier to recognize and reference as an alternative to using the automatically generated container ID.

While the container is running, run *podman* in a different terminal window to see the status of all containers on the system

```
# podman ps -a
CONTAINER ID  IMAGE                             COMMAND     CREATED
STATUS                   PORTS   NAMES
965acf617e6e  docker.io/library/centos:latest  /bin/bash  About a minute ago  Up
About a minute ago           mycontainer
```

To execute a command in a running container from the host, simply use the *podman exec* command, referencing the name of the running container and the command to be executed. The following command, for example, starts up a second bash session in the container named *mycontainer*:

```
# podman exec -it mycontainer /bin/bash
bash-4.4#
```

Note that though the above example referenced the container name the same result can be achieved using the container ID as listed by the *podman ps -a* command:

```
# podman exec -it 965acf617e6e /bin/bash
bash-4.4#
```

Alternatively, the *podman attach* command will also attach to a running container and access the shell prompt:

```
# podman attach mycontainer
bash-4.4#
```

Once the container is up and running, any additional configuration changes can be made and packages installed just like any other CentOS 8 system.

26.3 Managing a Container

Once launched, a container will continue to run until it is stopped via *podman*, or the command that was launched when the container was run exits. Running the following command on the host, for example, will cause the container to exit:

```
# podman stop mycontainer
```

Alternatively, pressing the Ctrl-D keyboard sequence within the last remaining bash shell of the container would cause both the shell and container to exit. Once it has exited, the status of the container will change accordingly:

```
# podman ps -a
```

```
CONTAINER ID   IMAGE                            COMMAND      CREATED       STATUS
PORTS   NAMES
965acf617e6e   docker.io/library/centos:latest  /bin/bash   10 minutes ago  Exited
(0) 21 seconds ago         mycontainer
```

Although the container is no longer running, it still exists and contains all of the changes that were made to the configuration and file system. If you installed packages, made configuration changes or added files, these changes will persist within "mycontainer". To verify this, simply restart the container as follows:

```
# podman start mycontainer
```

After starting the container, use the *podman exec* command once again to execute commands within the container as outlined previously. For example, to once again gain access to a shell prompt:

```
# podman exec -it mycontainer /bin/bash
```

A running container may also be paused and resumed using the *podman pause* and *unpause* commands as follows:

```
# podman pause my container
# podman unpause my container
```

26.4 Saving a Container to an Image

Once the container guest system is configured to your requirements there is a good chance that you will want to create and run more than one container of this particular type. To do this, the container needs to be saved as an image to local storage so that it can be used as the basis for additional container instances. This is achieved using the *podman commit* command combined with the name or ID of the container and the name by which the image will be stored, for example:

```
$ podman commit mycontainer  mycentos_image
```

Once the image has been saved, check that it now appears in the list of images in the local repository:

```
$ podman images
REPOSITORY                    TAG      IMAGE ID       CREATED        SIZE
localhost/mycentos_image      latest   c32c45218143   5 seconds ago  227 MB
docker.io/library/centos      latest   0f3e07c0138f   8 weeks ago    227 MB
```

The saved image can now be used to create additional containers identical to the original:

```
$ podman run --name=mycontainer2 -it localhost/mycentos_image /bin/bash
```

26.5 Removing an Image from Local Storage

To remove an image from local storage once it is no longer needed, simply run the *podman rmi* command, referencing either the image name or ID as output by the *podman images* command. For example, to remove the image named *mycentos_image* created in the previous section, run *podman* as follows:

```
$ podman rmi localhost/mycentos_image
```

Note before an image can be removed, any containers based on that image must first be removed.

26.6 Removing Containers

Even when a container has exited or been stopped, it still exists and can be restarted at any time. If a container is no longer needed, it can be deleted using the *podman rm* command as follows after the container has been stopped:

```
# podman rm mycontainer2
```

26.7 Building a Container with Buildah

Buildah allows new containers to be built either from existing containers, an image or entirely from scratch. Buildah also includes the ability to mount the file system of a container so that it can be accessed and modified from the host.

The following *buildah* command, for example, will build a container from the CentOS 8 Base image (if the image has not already been pulled from the registry, *buildah* will download it before creating the container):

```
$ buildah from docker://docker.io/library/centos:centos8
```

The result of running this command will be a container named *centos-working-container* that is ready to run:

```
$ buildah run centos-working-container cat /etc/passwd
```

26.8 Building a Container from Scratch

Building a container from scratch essentially creates an empty container. Once created, packages may be installed to meet the requirements of the container. This approach is useful when creating a container that will only need the minimum of packages installed.

The first step in building from scratch is to run the following command to build the empty container:

```
# buildah from scratch
working-container
```

After the build is complete, a new container will have been created named *working-container*:

```
$ buildah containers
CONTAINER ID  BUILDER  IMAGE ID     IMAGE NAME                         CONTAINER
NAME
00f81b68f03f     *       0f3e07c0138f docker.io/library/centos:centos8 centos-
working-container
d7dd4b652379     *                    scratch                          working-
container
```

The empty container is now ready to have some packages installed. Unfortunately this cannot be performed from within the container because not even the *bash* or *dnf* tools exist at this point. Instead the container filesystem needs to be mounted on the host system and the installation of the packages performed using *dnf* with the system root set to the mounted container filesystem. Begin this process by mounting the container's filesystem as follows:

```
# buildah mount working-container
/var/lib/containers/storage/overlay/20b46cf0e2994d1ecdc4487b89f93f6ccf41f72788da6
3866b6bf80984081d9a/merge
```

If the file system was successfully mounted, *buildah* will output the mount point for the container file system. Now that we have access to the container filesystem, the *dnf* command can be used to install packages into the container using the *–installroot* option to point to the mounted container file system. The following command, for example, installs the bash, CoreUtils and dnf packages on the container filesystem (where *<container_fs_mount>* is the mount path output previously by the *buildah mount* command) :

```
# dnf install --releasever=8 --installroot <container_fs_mount> bash coreutils
dnf
```

Note that the --releasever option is used to indicate to dnf that the packages for CentOS version 8 are to be installed within the container.

After the installation completes, unmount the scratch filesystem as follows:

```
# buildah umount working-container
```

Once *dnf* has performed the package installation, the container can be run and the bash command prompt accessed as follows:

```
# buildah run working-container bash
bash-4.4#
```

26.9 Container Bridge Networking

As outlined in the previous chapter, container networking is implemented using the Container Networking Interface (CNI) bridged network stack. The following command shows the typical network configuration on a host system on which containers are running:

```
# ip a
1: lo: <LOOPBACK,UP,LOWER_UP> mtu 65536 qdisc noqueue state UNKNOWN group default
qlen 1000
    link/loopback 00:00:00:00:00:00 brd 00:00:00:00:00:00
    inet 127.0.0.1/8 scope host lo
      valid_lft forever preferred_lft forever
    inet6 ::1/128 scope host
      valid_lft forever preferred_lft forever
2: enp0s3: <BROADCAST,MULTICAST,UP,LOWER_UP> mtu 1500 qdisc fq_codel state UP
group default qlen 1000
    link/ether 08:00:27:20:dc:2f brd ff:ff:ff:ff:ff:ff
    inet 192.168.0.33/24 brd 192.168.0.255 scope global dynamic noprefixroute
enp0s3
      valid_lft 3453sec preferred_lft 3453sec
    inet6 2606:a000:4307:f000:aa6:6da1:f8a9:5f95/64 scope global dynamic
noprefixroute
      valid_lft 3599sec preferred_lft 3599sec
    inet6 fe80::4275:e186:85e2:d81f/64 scope link noprefixroute
```

```
        valid_lft forever preferred_lft forever
3: cni0: <BROADCAST,MULTICAST,UP,LOWER_UP> mtu 1500 qdisc noqueue state UP group
default qlen 1000
    link/ether 7e:b6:04:22:4f:22 brd ff:ff:ff:ff:ff:ff
    inet 10.88.0.1/16 scope global cni0
        valid_lft forever preferred_lft forever
    inet6 fe80::7cb6:4ff:fe22:4f22/64 scope link
        valid_lft forever preferred_lft forever
12: veth2a07dc55@if3: <BROADCAST,MULTICAST,UP,LOWER_UP> mtu 1500 qdisc noqueue
master cni0 state UP group default
    link/ether 42:0d:69:13:89:af brd ff:ff:ff:ff:ff:ff link-netns cni-61ba825e-
e596-b2ef-a59f-b0743025e448
    inet6 fe80::400d:69ff:fe13:89af/64 scope link
        valid_lft forever preferred_lft forever
```

In the above example, the host has an interface named enp0s3 which is connected to the external network with an IP address of 192.168.0.33. In addition, a virtual interface has been created named cni0 and assigned the IP address of 10.88.0.1. Running the same *ip* command on a container running on the host might result in the following output:

```
# ip a
1: lo: <LOOPBACK,UP,LOWER_UP> mtu 65536 qdisc noqueue state UNKNOWN group default
qlen 1000
    link/loopback 00:00:00:00:00:00 brd 00:00:00:00:00:00
    inet 127.0.0.1/8 scope host lo
        valid_lft forever preferred_lft forever
    inet6 ::1/128 scope host
        valid_lft forever preferred_lft forever
3: eth0@if12: <BROADCAST,MULTICAST,UP,LOWER_UP> mtu 1500 qdisc noqueue state UP
group default
    link/ether 3e:52:22:4b:e0:d8 brd ff:ff:ff:ff:ff:ff link-netnsid 0
    inet 10.88.0.28/16 scope global eth0
        valid_lft forever preferred_lft forever
    inet6 fe80::3c52:22ff:fe4b:e0d8/64 scope link
        valid_lft forever preferred_lft forever
```

In this case, the container has an IP address of 10.88.0.28. Running the *ping* command on the host will verify that the host and containers are indeed on the same subnet:

```
# ping 10.88.0.28
PING 10.88.0.28 (10.88.0.28) 56(84) bytes of data.
64 bytes from 10.88.0.28: icmp_seq=1 ttl=64 time=0.056 ms
64 bytes from 10.88.0.28: icmp_seq=2 ttl=64 time=0.039 ms
.
.
```

The CNI configuration settings can be found in the */etc/cni/net.d/87-podman-bridge.conflist* file on the host system which, by default, will read as follows:

```
{
    "cniVersion": "0.3.0",
    "name": "podman",
    "plugins": [
      {
        "type": "bridge",
        "bridge": "cni0",
        "isGateway": true,
        "ipMasq": true,
        "ipam": {
            "type": "host-local",
            "subnet": "10.88.0.0/16",
            "routes": [
                { "dst": "0.0.0.0/0" }
            ]
        }
      },
      {
        "type": "portmap",
        "capabilities": {
          "portMappings": true
        }
      }
    ]
}
```

Changes can be made to this file to change the subnet address range, and also to change the plugin type (set to bridge for this example) for implementing different network configurations.

26.10 Summary

This chapter has worked through the creation and management of Linux Containers on CentOS 8 using the *skopeo* and *buildah* tools, including the use of container images obtained from a repository and the creation of a new image built entirely from scratch.

27. Setting Up a CentOS 8 Web Server

Among the many packages that make up the CentOS 8 operating system is the Apache web server. In fact the scalability and resilience of CentOS 8 makes it an ideal platform for hosting even the most heavily trafficked web sites.

In this chapter we will explain how to configure a CentOS 8 system using Apache to act as a web server, including both secure (HTTPS) and insecure (HTTP) configurations.

27.1 Requirements for Configuring a CentOS 8 Web Server

To set up your own web site you need a computer (or cloud server instance), an operating system, a web server, a domain name, a name server and an IP address.

In terms of an operating system, we will, of course, assume you are using CentOS 8. As previously mentioned, CentOS 8 supports the Apache web server which can easily be installed once the operating system is up and running. A domain name can be registered with any domain name registration service.

If you are running CentOS 8 on a cloud instance, the IP address assigned by the provider will be listed in the server overview information. If you are hosting your own server and your internet service provider (ISP) has assigned a static IP address then you will need to associate your domain with that address. This is achieved using a name server and all domain registration services will provide this service for you.

If you do not have a static IP address (i.e. your ISP provides you with a dynamic address which changes frequently) then you can use one of a number of free Dynamic DNS (DDNS or DynDNS for short) services which map your dynamic IP address to your domain name.

Once you have your domain name and your name server configured the next step is to install and configure your web server.

27.2 Installing the Apache Web Server Packages

The current release of CentOS typically does not install the Apache web server by default. To check whether the server is already installed, run the following command:

```
# rpm -q httpd
```

If *rpm* generates output similar to the following, the apache server is already installed:

```
httpd-2.4.35-6.el8+2089+57a79027.x86_64
```

Alternatively, if *rpm* generates a "package httpd is not installed" message then the next step, obviously, is to install it. To install Apache, run the following command at the command prompt:

```
# dnf install httpd
```

27.3 Configuring the Firewall

Before starting and testing the Apache web server, the firewall will need to be modified to allow the web server to communicate with the outside world. By default, the HTTP and HTTPS protocols use ports 80 and 443 respectively so, depending on which protocols are being used, either one or both of these ports will need to be opened. When opening the ports, be sure to specify the firewall zone that applies to the internet facing network connection:

```
# firewall-cmd --permanent --zone=<zone> --add-port=80/tcp
# firewall-cmd --permanent --zone=<zone> --add-port=443/tcp
```

After opening the necessary ports, be sure to reload the firewall settings:

```
# firewall-cmd --reload
```

On cloud hosted servers, it may also be necessary to enable the appropriate port for the server instance within the cloud console. Check the documentation for the cloud provider for steps on how to do this.

27.4 Port Forwarding

If the CentOS 8 system hosting the web server sits on a network protected by a firewall (either another computer running a firewall, or a router or wireless base station containing built-in firewall protection) you will need to configure the firewall to forward port 80 and/or port 443 to your web server system. The mechanism for performing this differs between firewalls and devices so check your documentation to find out how to configure port forwarding.

27.5 Starting the Apache Web Server

Once the Apache server is installed and the firewall configured, the next step is to verify that the server is running and start it if necessary.

To check the status of the Apache httpd service from the command-line, enter the following at the command-prompt:

```
# systemctl status httpd
```

If the above command indicates that the httpd service is not running, it can be launched from the command-line as follows:

```
# systemctl start httpd
```

If you would like the Apache httpd service to start automatically when the system boots, run the following command:

```
# systemctl enable  httpd
```

27.6 Testing the Web Server

Once the installation is complete the next step is to verify the web server is up and running.

The first step is to add a file to the default web site folder. In a terminal window, change directory to /var/www/html and create a new file named *index.html* with the following HTML content:

```
<html>
<title>CentOS Apache Test Page</title>
<body>
<h1>Welcome to CentOS</h1>
<p>Apache is working.</p>
</body>
</html>
```

If you have access (either locally or remotely) to the desktop environment of the server, simply start up a web browser and enter *http://127.0.0.1* in the address bar (127.0.0.1 is the loop-back network address which tells the system to connect to the local machine). If everything is set up correctly, the browser should load the page shown in Figure 27-1:

Figure 27-1

If the desktop environment is not available, connect either from another system on the same local network as the server, or using the external IP address assigned to the system if it is hosted remotely.

27.7 Configuring the Apache Web Server for Your Domain

The next step in setting up your web server is to configure it for your domain name. To configure the web server, begin by changing directory to */etc/httpd* which, in turn, contains a number of sub-directories. Change directory into the *conf* sub-directory where you will find a file named *httpd.conf* containing the configuration settings for the Apache server.

Edit the *httpd.conf* file using your preferred editor with super-user privileges to ensure you have write permission to the file. Once loaded, there are a number of settings that need to be changed to match your environment.

The most common way to configure Apache for a specific domain is to add *virtual host* entries to the *httpd.conf* file. This has the advantage of allowing a single Apache server to support multiple web sites simply by adding a virtual host entry for each site domain. Within the *httpd.conf* file, add a virtual host entry for your domain as follows:

```
<VirtualHost *:80>
    ServerAdmin feedback@myexample.com
    ServerName www.myexample.com
    DocumentRoot /var/www/myexample
    ErrorLog logs/myexample_error_log
    CustomLog logs/myexample_access_log combined
</VirtualHost>
```

The ServerAdmin directive in the above virtual host entry defines an administrative email address for people wishing to contact the web master for your site. Change this to an appropriate email address where you can be contacted.

Next, the ServerName is declared so that the web server knows the domain name associated with this virtual host.

Since each web site supported by the server will have its own set of files, the DocumentRoot setting is used to specify the location of the files for this web site domain. The tradition is to use */var/www/domain-name*, for example:

```
DocumentRoot /var/www/myexample
```

Finally, entries are added for the access history and error log files.

Create the */var/www/<domain name>* directory as declared in the *httpd.conf* file and place an *index.html* file in it containing some basic HTML. For example:

```
<html>
<title>Sample Web Page</title>
<body>
Welcome to MyExample.com
</body>
</html>
```

The last step is to restart the httpd service to make sure it picks up our new settings:

```
# systemctl restart httpd
```

Finally, check that the server configuration is working by opening a browser window and navigating to the site using the domain name instead of the IP address. The web page that loads should be the one defined in the *index.html* file created above.

27.8 The Basics of a Secure Web Site

The web server and web site created so far in this chapter use the HTTP protocol on port 80 and, as such, is considered to be insecure. The problem is that the traffic between the web server and the client (typically a user's web browser) is transmitted in *clear text*. In other words the data is unencrypted and susceptible to interception. While not a problem for general web browsing, this is a serious weakness when performing tasks such as logging into web sites or transferring sensitive information such as identity or credit card details.

These days, web sites are expected to use HTTPS which uses either Secure Socket Layer (SSL) or Transport Layer Security (TLS) to establish secure, encrypted communication between web server and client. This security is established through the use of public, private and session encryption together with certificates.

To support HTTPS, a web site must have a certificate issued by a trusted authority known as a Certificate Authority (CA). When a browser connects to a secure web site, the web server sends back a copy of the web site's SSL certificate which also contains a copy of the site's public key. The browser then validates the authenticity of the certificate with trusted certificate authorities.

If the certificate is found to be valid, the browser uses the public key sent by the server to encrypt a session key and passes it to the server. The server decrypts the session key using the private key and uses it to send an encrypted acknowledgment to the browser. Once this process is complete, the browser and server use the session key to encrypt all subsequent data transmissions until the session ends.

27.9 Configuring Apache for HTTPS

By default, the Apache server does not include the necessary module to implement a secure HTTPS web site. The first step, therefore, is to install the Apache *mod_ssl* module on the server system as follows:

```
# dnf install mod_ssl
```

Restart httpd after the installation completes to load the new module into the Apache server:

```
# systemctl restart httpd
```

Check that the module has loaded into the server using the following command:

```
# apachectl -M | grep ssl_module
 ssl_module (shared)
```

Assuming that the module is installed, the next step is to generate an SSL certificate for the web site.

27.10 Obtaining an SSL Certificate

The certificate for a web site must be obtained from a Certificate Authority. A number of options are available at a range of prices. By far the best option, however, is to obtain a free certificate from Let's Encrypt at the following URL:

https://letsencrypt.org/

The process of obtaining a certificate from Let's Encrypt simply involves installing and running the *Certbot* tool. This tool will scan the *httpd.conf* file on the server and provides the option to generate certificates for any virtual hosts configured on the system. It will then generate the certificate and add virtual host entries to the Apache configuration specifically for the corresponding web sites.

Setting Up a CentOS 8 Web Server

Follow the steps on the Let's Encrypt web site to download and install Certbot on your CentOS 8 system, then run the *certbot* tool as follows to generate and install the certificate:

```
# certbot --apache
```

After requesting an email address and seeking terms of service acceptance, Certbot will list the domains found in the *httpd.conf* file and provide the option to select one or more of those sites for which a certificate is to be installed. Certbot will then perform some checks before obtaining and installing the certificate on the system:

```
Which names would you like to activate HTTPS for?
- - - - - - - - - - - - - - - - - - - - - - - - - - - - - - - - - - - - -
1: www.myexample.com
- - - - - - - - - - - - - - - - - - - - - - - - - - - - - - - - - - - - -
Select the appropriate numbers separated by commas and/or spaces, or leave input
blank to select all options shown (Enter 'c' to cancel): 1
Obtaining a new certificate
Performing the following challenges:
http-01 challenge for www.myexample.com
Waiting for verification...
Cleaning up challenges
Created an SSL vhost at /etc/httpd/conf/httpd-le-ssl.conf
Deploying Certificate to VirtualHost /etc/httpd/conf/httpd-le-ssl.conf
Enabling site /etc/httpd/conf/httpd-le-ssl.conf by adding Include to root
configuration
```

Certbot will also have created a new file named *httpd-le-ssl.conf* in the */etc/httpd/conf* directory containing a secure virtual host entry for each domain name for which a certificate has been generated. These entries will be similar to the following:

```
<IfModule mod_ssl.c>
<VirtualHost *:443>
    ServerAdmin feedback@myexample.com
    ServerName www.myexample.com
    DocumentRoot /var/www/myexample
    ErrorLog logs/myexample_error_log
    CustomLog logs/myexample_access_log combined


SSLCertificateFile /etc/letsencrypt/live/www.myexample.com/fullchain.pem
SSLCertificateKeyFile /etc/letsencrypt/live/www.myexample.com/privkey.pem
Include /etc/letsencrypt/options-ssl-apache.conf
</VirtualHost>
</IfModule>
```

Finally, Certbot will ask whether future HTTP web requests should be redirected by the server to HTTPS. In other words, if a user attempts to access *http://www.myexample.com* the web server will redirect the user to *https://www.myexample.com*:

```
Please choose whether or not to redirect HTTP traffic to HTTPS, removing HTTP
```

```
access.
- - - - - - - - - - - - - - - - - - - - - - - - - - - - - - - - - - - - - - - -
1: No redirect - Make no further changes to the webserver configuration.
2: Redirect - Make all requests redirect to secure HTTPS access. Choose this for
new sites, or if you're confident your site works on HTTPS. You can undo this
change by editing your web server's configuration.
- - - - - - - - - - - - - - - - - - - - - - - - - - - - - - - - - - - - - - - -
Select the appropriate number [1-2] then [enter] (press 'c' to cancel): 2
```

If you are currently testing the HTTPS configuration and would like to keep the HTTP version live until later, select the *No redirect* option. Otherwise, redirecting to HTTPS is generally recommended.

Once the certificate has been installed, test it in a browser at the following URL (replacing myexample.com with your own domain name):

```
https://www.ssllabs.com/ssltest/analyze.html?d=www.myexample.com
```

If the certificate configuration was successful, the SSL Labs report will provide a high rating as shown in Figure 27-2:

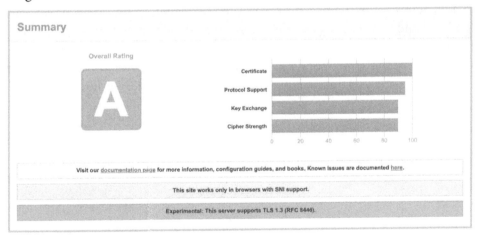

Figure 27-2

As a final test, open a browser window and navigate to your domain using the https:// prefix. The page should load as before and the browser should indicate that the connection between the browser and server is secure (usually indicated by a padlock icon in the address bar which can be clicked for additional information):

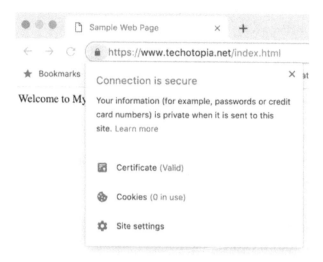

Figure 27-3

27.11 Summary

A CentOS 8 system can be used to host web sites by installing the Apache web server. Both insecure (HTTP) and secure (HTTPS) web sites can be deployed on CentOS 8. Secure web sites use either Secure Socket Layer (SSL) or Transport Layer Security (TLS) to establish encrypted communication between the web server and client through the use of public, private and session encryption together with a certificate issued by a trusted Certificate Authority.

28. Configuring a CentOS 8 Postfix Email Server

Along with acting as a web server, email is one of the primary uses of a CentOS 8 system, particularly in business environments. Given both the importance and popularity of email it is surprising to some people to find out how complex the email structure is on a Linux system and this complexity can often be a little overwhelming to the CentOS 8 newcomer.

The good news is that much of the complexity is there to allow experienced email administrators to implement complicated configurations for large scale enterprise installations. The fact is, for most Linux administrators it is relatively straight forward to set up a basic email system so that users can send and receive electronic mail.

In this chapter of CentOS 8 Essentials, we will explain the basics of Linux-based email configuration and step through configuring a basic email environment. In the interests of providing the essentials, we will leave the complexities of the email system for more advanced books on the subject.

28.1 The structure of the Email System

There are a number of components that make up a complete email system. Below is a brief description of each one:

28.1.1 Mail User Agent

This is the part of the system that the typical user is likely to be most familiar with. The Mail User Agent (MUA), or mail client, is the application that is used to write, send and read email messages. Anyone who has written and sent a message on any computer has used a Mail User Agent of one type or another.

Typical Graphical MUA's on Linux are Evolution, Thunderbird and KMail. For those who prefer a text based mail client, there are also the more traditional *pine* and *mail* tools.

28.1.2 Mail Transfer Agent

The Mail Transfer Agent (MTA) is the part of the email system that does much of the work of transferring the email messages from one computer to another (either on the same local network or over the internet to a remote system). Once configured correctly, most users will not have any direct interaction with their chosen MTA unless they wish to re-configure it for any reason. There are many choices of MTA available for Linux including sendmail, Postfix, Fetchmail, Qmail and Exim.

28.1.3 Mail Delivery Agent

Another part of the infrastructure that is typically hidden from the user, the Mail Delivery Agent (MDA) sits in the background and performs filtering of the email messages between the Mail Transfer Agent and the mail client (MUA). The most popular form of MDA is a spam filter to remove all the unwanted email messages from the system before they reach the inbox of the user's mail client (MUA). Popular MDAs are Spamassassin and Procmail. It is important to note that some Mail User Agent applications (such as Evolution, Thunderbird and KMail) include their own MDA filtering. Others, such as Pine and Basla, do not. This can be a source of confusion to the Linux beginner.

28.1.4 SMTP

SMTP is an acronym for Simple Mail Transport Protocol. This is the protocol used by the email systems to transfer mail messages from one server to another. This protocol is essentially the communications language that the MTAs use to talk to each other and transfer messages back and forth.

28.1.5 SMTP Relay

SMTP Relay is a protocol that allows an external SMTP server to be used to send emails instead of hosting a local SMTP server. This will typically involve using a service such as MailJet, SendGrid or MailGun. These services avoid the necessity to configure and maintain your own SMTP server and often provide additional benefits such as analytics.

28.2 Configuring a CentOS 8 Email Server

Many systems use the Sendmail MTA to transfer email messages and on many Linux distributions this is the default Mail Transfer Agent. Sendmail is, however, a complex system that can be difficult for beginner and experienced user alike to understand and configure. It is also falling from favor because it is considered to be slower at processing email messages than many of the more recent MTAs available.

Many system administrators are now using Postfix or Qmail to handle email. Both are faster and easier to configure than Sendmail.

For the purposes of this chapter, therefore, we will look at Postfix as an MTA because of its simplicity and popularity. If you would prefer to use Sendmail there are many books that specialize in the subject and that will do the subject much more justice than we can in this chapter.

As a first step, this chapter will cover the configuration of a CentOS 8 system to act as a full email server. Later in the chapter, the steps to make use of an SMTP Relay service will also be covered.

28.3 Postfix Pre-Installation Steps

The first step before installing Postfix is to make sure that Sendmail is not already running on your system. You can check for this using the following command:

```
# systemctl status sendmail
```

If sendmail is not installed, the tool will display a message similar to the following:

```
Unit sendmail.service could not be found.
```

If sendmail is running on your system it is necessary to stop it before installing and configuring Postfix. To stop sendmail, run the following command:

```
# systemctl stop sendmail
```

The next step is to ensure that sendmail does not get restarted automatically when the system is rebooted:

```
# systemctl disable  sendmail
```

Sendmail is now switched off and configured so that it does not auto start when the system is booted. Optionally, to completely remove sendmail from the system, run the following command:

```
# dnf remove sendmail
```

28.4 Firewall/Router Configuration

Since the sending and receiving of email messages involves network connections, the *firewall-cmd* tool will need to be used to add the *smtp* service to the firewall as follows:

```
# firewall-cmd --permanent --add-service=smtp
```

It will also be important to configure any other firewall or router between the server and the internet to allow connections on port 25, 143 and 587 and, if necessary, to configure port forwarding for those ports to the corresponding ports on the email server.

With these initial steps completed, we can now move on to installing Postfix.

28.5 Installing Postfix on CentOS 8

By default, the CentOS 8 installation process installs postfix for most configurations. To verify if postfix is already installed, use the following *rpm* command:

```
# rpm -q postfix
```

If *rpm* reports that postfix is not installed, it may be installed as follows:

```
# dnf install postfix
```

The *dnf* tool will download and install postfix, and configure a special postfix user in the */etc/passwd* file.

28.6 Configuring Postfix

The main configuration settings for postfix are located in the */etc/postfix/main.cf* file. There are many resources on the internet that provide detailed information on postfix so this section will focus on the basic options required to get email up and running.

The key options in the *main.cf* file are:

```
myhostname = mta1.domain.com
mydomain = domain.com
myorigin = $mydomain
mydestination = mydestination = $myhostname, localhost.$mydomain, localhost,
$mydomain
```

Configuring a CentOS 8 Postfix Email Server

```
inet_interfaces = $myhostname
mynetworks = subnet
```

Other settings will have either been set up for you by the installation process or are not needed unless you are feeling adventurous and want to configure a more sophisticated email system.

The format of *myhostname* is *host.domain.extension*. If, for example, your Linux system is named MyLinuxHost and your internet domain is MyDomain.com you would set the myhostname option as follows:

```
myhostname = mylinuxhost.mydomain.com
```

The *mydomain* setting is just the domain part of the above setting. For example:

```
mydomain = mydomain.com
```

The *myorigin* setting defines the name of the domain from which output email appears to come from when it arrives in the recipient's inbox and should be set to your domain name:

```
myorigin = $mydomain
```

Perhaps one of the most crucial parameters, *mydestination* relates to incoming messages and declares the domains for which this server is the final delivery destination. Any incoming email messages addressed to a domain name not on this list will be considered a relay request which, subject to the *mynetworks* setting (outlined below), will typically result in a delivery failure.

The *inet_interfaces* setting defines the network interfaces on the system via which postfix is permitted to receive email and is generally set to *all*:

```
inet_interfaces = all
```

The *mynetworks* setting defines which external systems are trusted to use the server as an SMTP relay. Possible values for this setting are as follows:

- **host** - Only the local system is trusted. Attempts by all external clients to use the server as a relay will be rejected.

- **subnet** - Only systems on the same network subnet are permitted to use the server as a relay. If, for example, the server has an IP address of 192.168.1.29, a client system with an IP address of 192.168.1.30 would be able to use the server as a relay.

- **class** - Any systems within the same IP address class (A, B and C) may use the server as a relay.

Trusted IP addresses may also be defined manually by specifying subnets, address ranges or referencing pattern files. The following example declares the local host and the subnet 192.168.0.0 as trusted IP addresses.

```
mynetworks = 192.168.0.0/24, 127.0.0.0/8
```

For this example, set the property to *subnet* so that any other systems on the same local network as the server are able to send email via SMTP relay while external systems are prevented from doing so.

```
mynetworks = subnet
```

28.7 Configuring DNS MX Records

When you registered and configured your domain name with a registrar, a number of default values will have been configured in the DNS settings. One of these is the so-called *Mail Exchanger (MX)* record. This record essentially defines where email addressed to your domain should be sent and is usually set by default to a mail server provided by your registrar. If you are hosting your own mail server, the MX record should be set to your domain or the address of your mail server. The steps on how to make this change will depend on your domain registrar but generally involves editing the DNS information for the domain and either adding or editing an existing MX record so that it points to your email server.

28.8 Starting Postfix on a CentOS 8 System

Once the */etc/postfix/main.cf* file is configured with the correct settings it is now time to start up postfix. This can be achieved from the command-line as follows:

```
# systemctl start postfix
```

To configure postfix to start automatically at system startup, run the following command:

```
# systemctl enable postfix
```

The postfix process should now start up. The best way to verify that everything is working is to check your mail log. This is typically in the */var/log/maillog* file and should now contain an entry resembling the following output:

```
Mar 25 11:21:48 demo-server postfix/postfix-script[5377]: starting the Postfix mail
system
Mar 25 11:21:48 demo-server postfix/master[5379]: daemon started -- version 3.3.1,
configuration /etc/postfix
```

As long as no error messages have been logged, you have successfully installed and started postfix and are ready to test the postfix configuration.

28.9 Testing Postfix

An easy way to test the postfix configuration is to send an email message between local users on the system. To perform a quick test, use the *mail* tool as follows (where *name* and *mydomain* are replaced by the name of a user on the system and your domain name respectively):

```
# mail name@mydomain.com
```

When prompted, enter a subject for the email message and then enter message body text. To send the email message, simply press Ctrl-D. For example:

```
# mail neil@mydomain.com
Subject: Test email message
This is a test message.
EOT
```

Run the *mail* command again, this time as the other user and verify that the message was sent and received:

```
$ mail
```

Configuring a CentOS 8 Postfix Email Server

```
Heirloom Mail version 12.5 7/5/10.   Type ? for help.
"/var/spool/mail/neilsmyth": 1 message 1 new
>N  1 root                    Mon Mar 25 13:36   18/625    "Test email message"
&                 .
```

If the message does not appear, check the log file (*/var/log/maillog*) for errors. A successful mail delivery will appear in the log file as follows:

```
Mar 25 13:41:37 demo-server postfix/pickup[7153]: 94FAF61E8F4A: uid=0 from=<root>
Mar 25 13:41:37 demo-server postfix/cleanup[7498]: 94FAF61E8F4A: message-
id=<20190325174137.94FAF61E8F4A@demo-server.mydomain.com>
Mar 25 13:41:37 demo-server postfix/qmgr[7154]: 94FAF61E8F4A: from=<root@mydomain.
com>, size=450, nrcpt=1 (queue active)
Mar 25 13:41:37 demo-server postfix/local[7500]: 94FAF61E8F4A: to=<neil@mydomain.
com>, relay=local, delay=0.12, delays=0.09/0.01/0/0.02, dsn=2.0.0, status=sent
(delivered to mailbox)
Mar 25 13:41:37 demo-server postfix/qmgr[7154]: 94FAF61E8F4A: removed
```

Once local email is working, try sending an email to an external address (such as a GMail account), Also, test that incoming mail works by sending an email from an external account to a user on your domain. In each case, check the */var/log/maillog* file for explanations of any errors.

28.10 Sending Mail via an SMTP Relay Server

An alternative to configuring a mail server to handle outgoing email messages is to use an SMTP Relay service. As previously discussed, a number of services are available, most of which can be found by performing a web search for "SMTP Relay Service". Most of these services will require you to verify your domain in some way and will provide MX records with which to update your DNS settings. You will also be provided with a username and password which need to be added to the postfix configuration. The remainder of this section makes the assumption that postfix is already installed on your system and that all of the initial steps required by your chosen SMTP Relay provider have been completed.

Begin by editing the */etc/postfix/main.cf* file and configuring the *myhostname* parameter with your domain name:

```
myhostname = mydomain.com
```

Next, create a new file in */etc/postfix* named *sasl_passwd* and add a line containing the mail server host provided by the relay service and the user name and password. For example:

```
[smtp.myprovider.com]:587 neil@mydomain.com:mypassword
```

Note that port 587 has also been specified in the above entry. Without this setting, postfix will default to using port 25 which is blocked by default by most SMTP relay service providers.

With the password file created, use the *postmap* utility to generate the hash database containing the mail credentials:

```
# postmap /etc/postfix/sasl_passwd
```

Before proceeding, take some additional steps to secure your postfix credentials:

```
# chown root:root /etc/postfix/sasl_passwd /etc/postfix/sasl_passwd.db
# chmod 0600 /etc/postfix/sasl_passwd /etc/postfix/sasl_passwd.db
```

Edit the *main.cf* file once again and add an entry to specify the relay server:

```
relayhost = [smtp.myprovider.com]:587
```

Remaining within the *main.cf* file, add the following lines to configure the authentication settings for the SMTP server:

```
smtp_use_tls = yes
smtp_sasl_auth_enable = yes
smtp_sasl_password_maps = hash:/etc/postfix/sasl_passwd
smtp_tls_CAfile = /etc/ssl/certs/ca-bundle.crt
smtp_sasl_security_options = noanonymous
smtp_sasl_tls_security_options = noanonymous
```

Finally, restart the postfix service:

```
# systemctl restart postfix
```

Once the service has restarted, try sending and receiving mail using either the *mail* tool or your preferred mail client.

28.11 Summary

A complete, end-to-end email system consists of a Mail User Agent (MUA), Mail Transfer Agent (MTA), Mail Delivery Agent (MDA) and the SMTP protocol. CentOS 8 provides a number of options in terms of MTA solutions, one of the more popular being Postfix. This chapter has outlined how to install, configure and test postfix on a CentOS 8 system both to act as a mail server and to send and receive email using a third party SMTP relay server.

29. Adding a New Disk Drive to a CentOS 8 System

One of the first problems encountered by users and system administrators these days is that systems tend to run out of disk space to store data. Fortunately disk space is now one of the cheapest IT commodities. In the next two chapters we will look at the steps necessary to configure CentOS 8 to use the space provided via the installation of a new physical or virtual disk drive.

29.1 Mounted File Systems or Logical Volumes

There are two ways to configure a new disk drive on a CentOS 8 system. One very simple method is to create one or more Linux partitions on the new drive, create Linux file systems on those partitions and then mount them at specific mount points so that they can be accessed. This approach will be covered in this chapter.

Another approach is to add the new space to an existing volume group or create a new volume group. When CentOS 8 is installed a volume group is created and named *cl*. Within this volume group are three logical volumes named *root*, *home* and *swap* that are used to store the / and /home file systems and swap partition respectively. By configuring the new disk as part of a volume group we are able to increase the disk space available to the existing logical volumes. Using this approach we are able, therefore, to increase the size of the /home file system by allocating some or all of the space on the new disk to the *home* volume. This topic will be discussed in detail in *"Adding a New Disk to a CentOS 8 Volume Group and Logical Volume"*.

29.2 Finding the New Hard Drive

This tutorial assumes that a new physical or virtual hard drive has been installed on the system and is visible to the operating system. Once added, the new drive should automatically be detected by the operating system. Typically, the disk drives in a system are assigned device names beginning hd or sd followed by a letter to indicate the device number. For example, the first device might be */dev/sda*, the second */dev/sdb* and so on.

The following is output from a system with only one disk drive connected to a SATA controller:

```
# ls /dev/sd*
/dev/sda   /dev/sda1   /dev/sda2
```

This shows that the disk drive represented by */dev/sda* is itself divided into 2 partitions, represented by */dev/sda1* and */dev/sda2*.

The following output is from the same system after a second hard disk drive has been installed:

```
# ls /dev/sd*
/dev/sda /dev/sda1 /dev/sda2 /dev/sdb
```

Adding a New Disk Drive to a CentOS 8 System

As shown above, the new hard drive has been assigned to the device file */dev/sdb*. Currently the drive has no partitions shown (because we have yet to create any).

At this point we have a choice of creating partitions and file systems on the new drive and mounting them for access or adding the disk as a physical volume as part of a volume group. To perform the former continue with this chapter, otherwise read *"Adding a New Disk to a CentOS 8 Volume Group and Logical Volume"* for details on configuring Logical Volumes.

29.3 Creating Linux Partitions

The next step is to create one or more Linux partitions on the new disk drive. This is achieved using the *fdisk* utility which takes as a command-line argument the device to be partitioned:

```
# fdisk /dev/sdb
Welcome to fdisk (util-linux 2.32.1).
Changes will remain in memory only, until you decide to write them.
Be careful before using the write command.


Device does not contain a recognized partition table.
Created a new DOS disklabel with disk identifier 0xbd09c991.


Command (m for help):
```

In order to view the current partitions on the disk enter the p command:

```
Command (m for help): p
Disk /dev/sdb: 8 GiB, 8589934592 bytes, 16777216 sectors
Units: sectors of 1 * 512 = 512 bytes
Sector size (logical/physical): 512 bytes / 512 bytes
I/O size (minimum/optimal): 512 bytes / 512 bytes
Disklabel type: dos
Disk identifier: 0xbd09c991
```

As we can see from the above *fdisk* output, the disk currently has no partitions because it is a previously unused disk. The next step is to create a new partition on the disk, a task which is performed by entering n (for new partition) and p (for primary partition):

```
Command (m for help): n
Partition type
   p   primary (0 primary, 0 extended, 4 free)
   e   extended (container for logical partitions)
Select (default p): p
Partition number (1-4, default 1):
```

In this example we only plan to create one partition which will be partition 1. Next we need to specify where the partition will begin and end. Since this is the first partition we need it to start at the first available sector and since we want to use the entire disk we specify the last sector as the end. Note that if you wish to create multiple partitions you can specify the size of each partition by sectors, bytes, kilobytes or megabytes.

```
Partition number (1-4, default 1): 1
First sector (2048-16777215, default 2048):
Last sector, +sectors or +size{K,M,G,T,P} (2048-16777215, default 16777215):

Created a new partition 1 of type 'Linux' and of size 8 GiB.

Command (m for help):
```

Now that we have specified the partition, we need to write it to the disk using the w command:

```
Command (m for help): w
The partition table has been altered.
Calling ioctl() to re-read partition table.
Syncing disks.
```

If we now look at the devices again we will see that the new partition is visible as */dev/sdb1*:

```
# ls /dev/sd*
/dev/sda /dev/sda1 /dev/sda2 /dev/sdb /dev/sdb1
```

The next step is to create a file system on our new partition.

29.4 Creating a File System on a CentOS 8 Disk Partition

We now have a new disk installed, it is visible to CentOS 8 and we have configured a Linux partition on the disk. The next step is to create a Linux file system on the partition so that the operating system can use it to store files and data. The easiest way to create a file system on a partition is to use the *mkfs.xfs* utility:

```
# mkfs.xfs /dev/sdb1
meta-data=/dev/sdb1              isize=512    agcount=4, agsize=524224 blks
         =                       sectsz=512   attr=2, projid32bit=1
         =                       crc=1        finobt=1, sparse=1, rmapbt=0
         =                       reflink=1
data     =                       bsize=4096   blocks=2096896, imaxpct=25
         =                       sunit=0      swidth=0 blks
naming   =version 2              bsize=4096   ascii-ci=0, ftype=1
log      =internal log           bsize=4096   blocks=2560, version=2
         =                       sectsz=512   sunit=0 blks, lazy-count=1
realtime =none                   extsz=4096   blocks=0, rtextents=0
```

In this case we have created an XFS file system. XFS is a high performance file system which is the default filesystem type on CentOS 8 and includes a number of advantages in terms of parallel I/O performance and the use of journaling.

29.5 An Overview of Journaled File Systems

A journaling filesystem keeps a journal or log of the changes that are being made to the filesystem during disk writing that can be used to rapidly reconstruct corruptions that may occur due to events such as a system crash or power outage.

There are a number of advantages to using a journaling file system. Both the size and volume of data stored on disk drives has grown exponentially over the years. The problem with a non-journaled file system is that following a crash the *fsck* (filesystem consistency check) utility has to be run. The *fsck* utility will scan the entire filesystem validating all entries and making sure that blocks are allocated and referenced correctly. If it finds a corrupt entry it will attempt to fix the problem. The issues here are two-fold. First, the *fsck* utility will not always be able to repair damage and you will end up with data in the *lost+found* directory. This is data that was being used by an application but the system no longer knows where it was referenced from. The other problem is the issue of time. It can take a very long time to complete the *fsck* process on a large file system, potentially leading to unacceptable down time.

A journaled file system, on the other hand, records information in a log area on a disk (the journal and log do not need to be on the same device) during each write. This is a essentially an "intent to commit" data to the filesystem. The amount of information logged is configurable and ranges from not logging anything, to logging what is known as the "metadata" (i.e. ownership, date stamp information etc), to logging the "metadata" and the data blocks that are to be written to the file. Once the log is updated the system then writes the actual data to the appropriate areas of the filesystem and marks an entry in the log to say the data is committed.

After a crash the filesystem can very quickly be brought back on-line using the journal log, thereby reducing what could take minutes using *fsck* to seconds with the added advantage that there is considerably less chance of data loss or corruption.

29.6 Mounting a File System

Now that we have created a new file system on the Linux partition of our new disk drive we need to mount it so that it is accessible and usable. In order to do this we need to create a mount point. A mount point is simply a directory or folder into which the file system will be mounted. For the purposes of this example we will create a */backup* directory to match our file system label (although it is not necessary that these values match):

```
# mkdir /backup
```

The file system may then be manually mounted using the *mount* command:

```
# mount /dev/sdb1 /backup
```

Running the *mount* command with no arguments shows us all currently mounted file systems (including our new file system):

```
# mount
sysfs on /sys type sysfs (rw,nosuid,nodev,noexec,relatime,seclabel)
proc on /proc type proc (rw,nosuid,nodev,noexec,relatime)
.

.

/dev/sdb1 on /backup type xfs (rw,relatime,seclabel,attr2,inode64,noquota)
```

29.7 Configuring CentOS 8 to Automatically Mount a File System

In order to set up the system so that the new file system is automatically mounted at boot time an entry needs to be added to the */etc/fstab* file. The format for an fstab entry is as follows:

```
<device>        <dir>  <type> <options>     <dump> <fsck>
```

These entries can be summarized as follows:

- **<device>** - The device on which the filesystem is to be mounted.

- **<dir>** - The directory that is to act as the mount point for the filesystem.

- **<type>** - The filesystem type (xfs, ext4 etc.)

- **<options>** - Additional filesystem mount options, for example making the filesystem read-only or controlling whether the filesystem can be mounted by any user. Run *man mount* to review a full list of options. Setting this value to *defaults* will use the default settings for the filesystem (rw, suid, dev, exec, auto, nouser, async).

- **<dump>** - Dictates whether the content of the filesystem is to be included in any backups performed by the dump utility. This setting is rarely used and can be disabled with a 0 value.

- **<fsck>** - Whether the filesystem is checked by fsck after a system crash and the order in which filesystems are to be checked. For journaled filesystems such as XFS this should be set to 0 to indicate that the check is not required.

The following example shows an *fstab* file configured to automount our */backup* partition on the /dev/sdb1 partition:

```
/dev/mapper/cl-root    /                       xfs     defaults        0 0
UUID=b4fc85a1-0b25-4d64-8100-d50ea23340f7 /boot                 xfs
defaults           0 0
/dev/mapper/cl-home    /home                   xfs     defaults        0 0
/dev/mapper/cl-swap    swap                    swap    defaults        0 0
/dev/sdb1              /backup                 xfs     defaults        0 0
```

The */backup* filesystem will now automount each time the system restarts.

29.8 Adding a Disk Using Cockpit

In addition to working with storage using the command-line utilities outlined in this chapter, it is also possible to configure a new storage device using the Cockpit web console. To view the current storage configuration, log into the Cockpit console and select the Storage option as shown in Figure 29-1:

Adding a New Disk Drive to a CentOS 8 System

Figure 29-1

To locate the newly added storage, scroll to the bottom of the Storage page until the Drives section comes into view:

Figure 29-2

In the case of the above figure, the new drive is the 8 GiB drive. Select the new drive to display the Drive screen as shown in Figure 29-3:

Figure 29-3

Click on the *Create Partition Table* button and, in the resulting dialog accept the default settings clicking on the *Format* button:

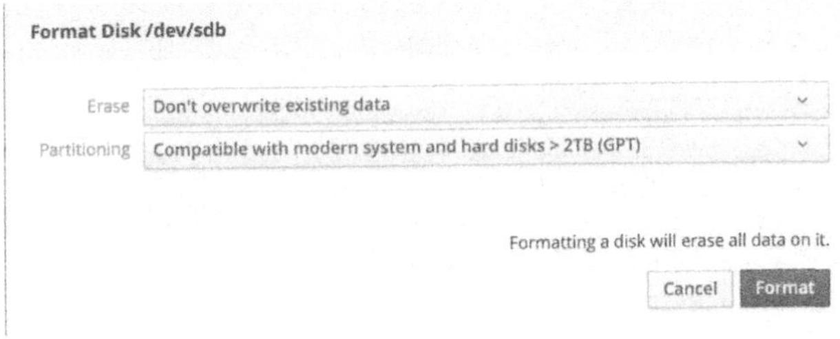

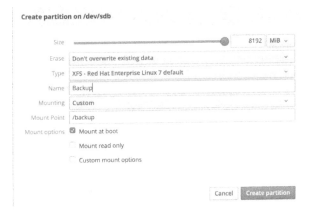

Figure 29-4

Click on the *Create Partition* button and use the dialog to specify how much space is to be allocated to this partition, the filesystem type (XFS is recommended) and an optional label, filesystem mount point and mount options. Note that if this new partition does not use all of the available space, additional partitions may subsequently be added to the drive. To change settings such as whether the filesystem is read-only or mounted at boot time, change the Mounting menu option to *Custom* and adjust the toggle button settings:

Figure 29-5

Once the settings have been selected, click on the *Create partition* button to commit the change. On completion of the creation process the new partition will be added to the disk, the corresponding filesystem created and mounted at the designated mount point and appropriate changes made to the */etc/fstab* file.

29.9 Summary

This chapter has covered the topic of adding an additional physical or virtual disk drive to an existing CentOS 8 system. This is a relatively simple process of making sure the new drive has been detected by the operating system, creating one or more partitions on the drive and then making filesystems on those partitions. Although a number of different filesystem types are available on CentOS 8, XFS is generally the recommended option. Once the filesystems are ready, they can be mounted using the *mount* command. So that the newly created filesystems mount automatically on system startup, additions can be made to the */etc/fstab* configuration file.

30. Adding a New Disk to a CentOS 8 Volume Group and Logical Volume

In the previous chapter we looked at adding a new disk drive to a CentOS 8 system, creating a partition and file system and then mounting that file system so that the disk can be accessed. An alternative to creating fixed partitions and file systems is to use Logical Volume Management (LVM) to create logical disks made up of space from one or more physical or virtual disks or partitions. The advantage of using LVM is that space can be added to or removed from logical volumes as needed without the need to spread data over multiple file systems.

Let us take, for example, the root (*/home*) file system of a CentOS 8-based server. Without LVM this file system would be created with a certain size when the operating system is installed. If a new disk drive is installed there is no way to allocate any of that space to the */home* file system. The only option would be to create new file systems on the new disk and mount them at particular mount points. In this scenario you would have plenty of space on the new file system but the */home* file system would still be nearly full. The only option would be to move files onto the new file system. With LVM, the new disk (or part thereof) can be assigned to the logical volume containing the root file system thereby dynamically extending the space available.

In this chapter we will look at the steps necessary to add new disk space to both a volume group and a logical volume for the purpose of adding additional space to the root file system of a CentOS 8 system.

30.1 An Overview of Logical Volume Management (LVM)

LVM provides a flexible and high level approach to managing disk space. Instead of each disk drive being split into partitions of fixed sizes onto which fixed size file systems are created, LVM provides a way to group together disk space into logical volumes which can be easily resized and moved. In addition, LVM allows administrators to carefully control disk space assigned to different groups of users by allocating distinct volume groups or logical volumes to those users. When the space initially allocated to the volume is exhausted the administrator can simply add more space without having to move the user files to a different file system.

LVM consists of the following components:

30.1.1 Volume Group (VG)

The Volume Group is the high level container which holds one or more logical volumes and physical volumes.

30.1.2 Physical Volume (PV)

A physical volume represents a storage device such as a disk drive or other storage media.

30.1.3 Logical Volume (LV)

A logical volume is the equivalent to a disk partition and, as with a disk partition, can contain a file system.

30.1.4 Physical Extent (PE)

Each physical volume (PV) is divided into equal size blocks known as physical extents.

30.1.5 Logical Extent (LE)

Each logical volume (LV) is divided into equal size blocks called logical extents.

Suppose we are creating a new volume group called VolGroup001. This volume group needs physical disk space in order to function so we allocate three disk partitions */dev/sda1*, */dev/sdb1* and */dev/sdb2*. These become physical volumes in VolGroup001. We would then create a logical volume called LogVol001 within the volume group made up of the three physical volumes.

If we run out of space in LogVol001 we simply add more disk partitions as physical volumes and assign them to the volume group and logical volume.

30.2 Getting Information about Logical Volumes

As an example of using LVM with CentOS 8 we will work through an example of adding space to the / file system of a standard CentOS 8 installation. Anticipating the need for flexibility in the sizing of the root partition, CentOS 8 sets up the / file system as a logical volume (called *root*) within a volume group called *cl*. Before making any changes to the LVM setup, however, it is important to first gather information.

Running the *mount* command will output information about a range of mount points, including the following entry for the root filesystem:

```
/dev/mapper/cl-root on / type xfs (rw,relatime,seclabel,attr2,inode64,noquota)
```

Information about the volume group can be obtained using the *vgdisplay* command:

```
# vgdisplay
  --- Volume group ---
  VG Name               cl
  System ID
  Format                lvm2
  Metadata Areas        1
  Metadata Sequence No  3
  VG Access             read/write
  VG Status             resizable
  MAX LV                0
  Cur LV                2
  Open LV               2
  Max PV                0
  Cur PV                1
  Act PV                1
```

```
VG Size                <44.70 GiB
PE Size                4.00 MiB
Total PE               11442
Alloc PE / Size        11442 / <44.70 GiB
Free  PE / Size        0 / 0
VG UUID                fANXsd-810S-0zO1-BJVN-rnBa-gNf4-eIgjG8
```

As we can see in the above example, the *cl* volume group has a physical extent size of 4.00MB and has a total of 44.7GB available for allocation to logical volumes. Currently 11442 physical extents are allocated equaling the total 44.7GB capacity. If we want to increase the space allocated to any logical volumes in the *cl* volume group, therefore, we will need to add one or more physical volumes. The *vgs* tool is also useful for displaying a quick overview of the space available in the volume groups on a system:

```
# vgs
 VG #PV #LV #SN Attr   VSize    VFree
 cl   1   2   0 wz--n- <44.70g     0
```

Information about logical volumes in a volume group may similarly be obtained using the *lvdisplay* command:

```
# lvdisplay
  --- Logical volume ---
  LV Path                /dev/cl/swap
  LV Name                swap
  VG Name                cl
  LV UUID                FDSEXC-XawV-QhsZ-0CIq-IwV5-rxH6-Q6ATg2
  LV Write Access        read/write
  LV Creation host, time localhost, 2019-11-15 15:59:58 -0500
  LV Status              available
  # open                 2
  LV Size                4.57 GiB
  Current LE             1170
  Segments               1
  Allocation             inherit
  Read ahead sectors     auto
  - currently set to     8192
  Block device           253:1

  --- Logical volume ---
  LV Path                /dev/cl/root
  LV Name                root
  VG Name                cl
  LV UUID                Nysd1Y-483C-IKLf-P4ez-c3Kq-s2hZ-eumSB5
  LV Write Access        read/write
  LV Creation host, time localhost, 2019-11-15 15:59:58 -0500
  LV Status              available
```

Adding a New Disk to a CentOS 8 Volume Group and Logical Volume

```
# open                   1
LV Size                  40.12 GiB
Current LE               10272
Segments                 1
Allocation               inherit
Read ahead sectors       auto
- currently set to       8192
Block device             253:0
```

As shown in the above example 40.12 GiB of the space in volume group *cl* is allocated to logical volume *root* (for the / file system) and 4.57 GiB to *swap* (for swap space).

Now that we know what space is being used it is often helpful to understand which devices are providing the space (in other words which devices are being used as physical volumes). To obtain this information we need to run the *pvdisplay* command:

```
# pvdisplay
  --- Physical volume ---
  PV Name               /dev/sda2
  VG Name               cl
  PV Size               <44.70 GiB / not usable 3.00 MiB
  Allocatable           yes (but full)
  PE Size               4.00 MiB
  Total PE              11442
  Free PE               0
  Allocated PE          11442
  PV UUID               Gq547r-HUyj-hPeZ-7be0-CvFx-206v-Hy2xmj
```

Clearly the space controlled by logical volume *cl* is provided via a physical volume located on /*dev/sda2*.

Now that we know a little more about our LVM configuration we can embark on the process of adding space to the volume group and the logical volume contained within.

30.3 Adding Additional Space to a Volume Group from the Command-Line

Just as with the previous steps to gather information about the current Logical Volume Management configuration of a CentOS 8 system, changes to this configuration can be made from the command-line.

In the remainder of this chapter we will assume that a new disk has been added to the system and that it is being seen by the operating system as /*dev/sdb*. We shall also assume that this is a new disk that does not contain any existing partitions. If existing partitions are present they should be backed up and then the partitions deleted from the disk using the *fdisk* utility. For example, assuming a device represented by /*dev/sdb* containing two partitions as follows:

```
# fdisk -l /dev/sdb
Disk /dev/sdb: 8 GiB, 8589934592 bytes, 16777216 sectors
Units: sectors of 1 * 512 = 512 bytes
```

```
Sector size (logical/physical): 512 bytes / 512 bytes
I/O size (minimum/optimal): 512 bytes / 512 bytes
Disklabel type: dos
Disk identifier: 0xbd09c991

Device     Boot   Start      End  Sectors   Size Id Type
/dev/sdb1          2048  5678545  5676498   2.7G 83 Linux
/dev/sdb2       5679104 16777215 11098112   5.3G 83 Linux
```

Once the filesystems on these partitions have been unmounted, they can be deleted as follows:

```
# fdisk /dev/sdb

Welcome to fdisk (util-linux 2.32.1).
Changes will remain in memory only, until you decide to write them.
Be careful before using the write command.

Command (m for help): d
Partition number (1,2, default 2): 1

Partition 1 has been deleted.

Command (m for help): d
Selected partition 2
Partition 2 has been deleted.

Command (m for help): w
The partition table has been altered.
Calling ioctl() to re-read partition table.
Syncing disks.
```

Before moving to the next step, be sure to remove any entries in the */etc/fstab* file for these filesystems so that the system does not attempt to mount them on the next reboot.

Once the disk is ready, the next step is to convert this disk into a physical volume using the *pvcreate* command (also wiping the dos signature if one exists):

```
# pvcreate /dev/sdb
  Physical volume "/dev/sdb" successfully created.
```

If the creation fails with a message that reads "Device /dev/<device> excluded by a filter", it may be necessary to wipe the disk using the *wipefs* command before creating the physical volume:

```
# wipefs -a /dev/sdb
/dev/sdb: 8 bytes were erased at offset 0x00000200 (gpt): 45 46 49 20 50 41 52 54
/dev/sdb: 8 bytes were erased at offset 0x1ffffffe00 (gpt): 45 46 49 20 50 41 52
54
/dev/sdb: 2 bytes were erased at offset 0x000001fe (PMBR): 55 aa
/dev/sdb: calling ioctl to re-read partition table: Success
```

Adding a New Disk to a CentOS 8 Volume Group and Logical Volume

With the physical volume created we now need to add it to the volume group (in this case *cl*) using the *vgextend* command:

```
# vgextend cl /dev/sdb
  Volume group "cl" successfully extended
```

The new physical volume has now been added to the volume group and is ready to be allocated to a logical volume. To do this we run the *lvextend* tool providing the size by which we wish to extend the volume. In this case we want to extend the size of logical volume *root* by 7 GB. Note that we need to provide the path to the logical volume which can be obtained from the *lvdisplay* command (in this case */dev/cl/root*):

```
# lvextend -L+7G /dev/cl/root
  Size of logical volume cl/root changed from 40.12 GiB (10272 extents) to 47.12
GiB (12064 extents).
  Logical volume cl/root successfully resized.
```

The last step in the process is to resize the file system residing on the logical volume so that it uses the additional space. Since we are assuming a default CentOS 8 installation using the XFS filesystem, this can be achieved using the *xfs_growfs* utility:

```
# xfs_growfs /
meta-data=/dev/mapper/cl-root    isize=512     agcount=4, agsize=2629632 blks
         =                       sectsz=512    attr=2, projid32bit=1
         =                       crc=1         finobt=1, sparse=1, rmapbt=0
         =                       reflink=1
data     =                       bsize=4096    blocks=10518528, imaxpct=25
         =                       sunit=0       swidth=0 blks
naming   =version 2              bsize=4096    ascii-ci=0, ftype=1
log      =internal log           bsize=4096    blocks=5136, version=2
         =                       sectsz=512    sunit=0 blks, lazy-count=1
realtime =none                   extsz=4096    blocks=0, rtextents=0
data blocks changed from 10518528 to 12353536
```

If, on the other hand, the filesystem is of type ext2, ext3, or ext4, the *resize2fs* utility should be used instead when performing the filesystem resize:

```
# resize2fs /dev/cl/root
```

Once the resize completes, the file system will have been extended to use the additional space provided by the new disk drive. All this has been achieved without moving a single file or even having to restart the server. As far as any users on the system are concerned nothing has changed (except, of course, that there is now more disk space).

30.4 Adding Additional Space to a Volume Group using Cockpit

In addition to the command-line utilities outlined so far in this chapter, it is also possible to access information about logical volumes and make volume group and logical volume changes from within the Cockpit web interface using the Storage page as shown in Figure 30-1:

Figure 30-1

If the Storage option is not listed, the *cockpit-storaged* package will need to be installed and the cockpit service restarted as follows:

```
# dnf install cockpit-storaged
# systemctl restart cockpit.socket
```

Once the Cockpit service has restarted, log back into the Cockpit interface at which point the Storage option should now be visible.

To add a new disk drive to an existing volume group from within the Cockpit console, start at the above Storage page and click on a filesystem associated with the volume group to be extended from the list marked A above.

On the resulting screen, click on the + button highlighted in Figure 30-2 below to add a physical volume:

Figure 30-2

Select the new drive to be added to the volume group and click on the *Add* button:

Adding a New Disk to a CentOS 8 Volume Group and Logical Volume

Figure 30-3

On returning to the volume group screen, scroll down to the logical volume that is to be extended and click on it to unfold additional information. Figure 30-4, for example, shows details of the *root* logical volume:

Figure 30-4

To extend the logical volume using the new space, click on the *Grow* button and use the slider in the resulting dialog to select how much space should be added to the volume. Click the *Grow* button to commit the change (the available space can be shared among different volume groups if required):

Figure 30-5

Once these steps are complete, the volume group will have been configured to use the newly added space.

30.5 Summary

Volume groups and logical volumes provide an abstract layer on top of the physical storage devices on a CentOS 8 system to provide a flexible way to allocate the space provided by multiple disk drives. This allows disk space allocations to be made and changed dynamically without the need to repartition disk drives and move data between filesystems. This chapter has outlined the basic concepts of volume groups, logical volumes and physical volumes while demonstrating how to manage these using both command-line tools and the Cockpit web interface.

31. Adding and Managing CentOS 8 Swap Space

An important part of maintaining the performance of a CentOS 8 system involves ensuring that adequate swap space is available comparable to the memory demands placed on the system. The goal of this chapter, therefore, is to provide an overview of swap management on CentOS 8.

31.1 What is Swap Space?

Computer systems have a finite amount of physical memory that is made available to the operating system. When the operating system begins to approach the limit of the available memory it frees up space by writing memory pages to disk. When any of those pages are required by the operating system they are subsequently read back into memory. The area of the disk allocated for this task is referred to as *swap space*.

31.2 Recommended Swap Space for CentOS 8

The amount of swap recommended for CentOS 8 depends on a number of factors including the amount of memory in the system, the workload imposed on that memory and whether the system is required to support hibernation. The current guidelines for CentOS 8 swap space are as follows:

Amount of installed RAM	Recommended swap space	Recommended swap space if hibernation enabled
2GB or less	Installed RAM x 2	Installed RAM x 3
2GB - 8GB	Installed RAM x 1	Installed RAM x 2
8GB - 64GB	At least 4GB	Installed RAM x 1.5
64GB or more	At least 4GB	Hibernation not recommended

Table 31-1

When a system enters hibernation, the current system state is written to the hard disk and the host machine is powered off. When the machine is subsequently powered on, the state of the system is restored from the hard disk drive. This differs from suspension where the system state is stored in RAM. The machine then enters a sleep state whereby power is maintained to the system RAM while other devices are shut down.

31.3 Identifying Current Swap Space Usage

The current amount of swap used by a CentOS 8 system may be identified in a number of ways. One option is to output the */proc/swaps* file:

```
# cat /proc/swaps
```

```
Filename                    Type        Size      Used      Priority
/dev/dm-1                   partition   4169724   41484     -2
```

Alternatively, the *swapon* command may be used:

```
# swapon
NAME        TYPE        SIZE   USED PRIO
/dev/dm-1   partition   4G   40.5M   -2
```

To view the amount of swap space relative to the overall available RAM, the *free* command may be used:

```
# free
              total        used        free      shared  buff/cache   available
Mem:        4035436     1428276     2224596       21968      382564     2360172
Swap:       4169724       41484     4128240
```

31.4 Adding a Swap File to a CentOS 8 System

Additional swap may be added to the system by creating a file and assigning it as swap. Begin by creating the swap file using the *dd* command. The size of the file can be changed by adjusting the *count=* variable. The following command-line, for example, creates a 2.0 GB file:

```
# dd if=/dev/zero of=/newswap bs=1024 count=2000000
2000000+0 records in
2000000+0 records out
2048000000 bytes (2.0 GB, 1.9 GiB) copied, 3.62697 s, 565 MB/s
```

Before converting the file to a swap file, it is important to make sure the file has secure permissions set:

```
# chmod 0600 /newswap
```

Once a suitable file has been created, it needs to be converted into a swap file using the *mkswap* command:

```
# mkswap /newswap
Setting up swapspace version 1, size = 1.9 GiB (2047995904 bytes)
no label, UUID=4ffc238d-7fde-4367-bd98-c5c46407e535
```

With the swap file created and configured it can be added to the system in real-time using the *swapon* utility:

```
# swapon /newswap
```

Rerunning swapon should now report that the new file is now being used as swap:

```
# swapon
NAME        TYPE        SIZE USED PRIO
/dev/dm-1   partition   4G    0B   -2
/newswap    file       1.9G   0B   -3
```

The swap space may be removed dynamically by using the *swapoff* utility as follows:

```
# swapoff /newswap
```

Finally, modify the */etc/fstab* file to automatically add the new swap at system boot time by adding the following line:

```
/newswap     swap     swap    defaults 0 0
```

31.5 Adding Swap as a Partition

As an alternative to designating a file as swap space, entire disk partitions may also be designated as swap. The steps to achieve this are largely the same as those for adding a swap file. Before allocating a partition to swap, however, make sure that any existing data on the corresponding filesystem is either backed up or no longer needed and that the filesystem has been unmounted.

Assuming that a partition exists on a disk drive represented by */dev/sdb1*, for example, the first step would be to convert this into a swap partition, once again using the *mkswap* utility:

```
# mkswap /dev/sdb1
mkswap: /dev/sdb1: warning: wiping old xfs signature.
Setting up swapspace version 1, size = 8 GiB (8587833344 bytes)
no label, UUID=a899c8ec-c410-4569-ba18-ddea03370c7f
```

Next, add the new partition to the system swap and verify that it has indeed been added:

```
# swapon /dev/sdb1
# swapon
NAME        TYPE        SIZE USED PRIO
/dev/dm-1 partition     4G   0B   -2
/dev/sdb1 partition     8G   0B   -3
```

Once again, the */etc/fstab* file may be modified to automatically add the swap partition at boot time as follows:

```
/dev/sdb1     swap     swap    defaults 0 0
```

31.6 Adding Space to a CentOS 8 LVM Swap Volume

By default, CentOS 8 configures swap space using Logical Volume Management (LVM). An alternative to adding swap via file or disk partition, therefore, is to extend the logical volume used for the swap space.

The first step is to identify the current amount of swap available and the volume group and logical volume used for the swap space using the *lvdisplay* utility (for more information on LVM, refer to the chapter entitled *"Adding a New Disk to a CentOS 8 Volume Group and Logical Volume"*):

```
# lvdisplay
   --- Logical volume ---
   LV Path                /dev/cl/swap
   LV Name                swap
   VG Name                cl
   LV UUID                fwOZsF-ROwu-6eLe-2KDR-JZ0d-Pn4o-K5B0Vb
   LV Write Access        read/write
   LV Creation host, time demoserver, 2019-02-14 11:12:07 -0500
   LV Status              available
```

```
  # open                    2
  LV Size                   <3.98 GiB
  Current LE                1018
  Segments                  1
  Allocation                inherit
  Read ahead sectors        auto
  - currently set to        256
  Block device              253:1
  .
  .
  .
```

Clearly the swap resides on a logical volume named *swap* which is part of the volume group named *cl*. The next step is to verify if there is any space available on the volume group that can be allocated to swap volume:

```
# vgs
  VG    #PV #LV #SN Attr    VSize    VFree
  cl     2   3   0 wz--n- 197.66g <22.00g
```

If the amount of space available is sufficient to meet additional swap requirements, turn off the swap and extend the swap logical volume to use as much of the available space as needed to meet the system's swap requirements:

```
# swapoff /dev/cl/swap
# lvextend -L+8GB /dev/cl/swap
    Logical volume cl/swap successfully resized.
```

Next, reformat the swap volume and turn the swap back on:

```
# mkswap /dev/cl/swap
mkswap: /dev/cl/swap: warning: wiping old swap signature.
Setting up swapspace version 1, size = 12 GiB (12754874368 bytes)
no label, UUID=241a4818-e51c-4b8c-9bc9-1697fc2ce26e

# swapon /dev/cl/swap
```

Having made the changes, check that the swap space has increased:

```
# swapon
NAME        TYPE        SIZE USED PRIO
/dev/dm-1 partition    12G    0B   -2
```

31.7 Adding Swap Space to the Volume Group

In the above section we extended the swap logical volume to use space that was already available in the volume group. If no space is available in the volume group then it will need to be added before the swap can be extended.

Begin by checking the status of the volume group:

```
# vgs
  VG    #PV #LV #SN Attr    VSize    VFree
```

```
cl     1    3    0 wz--n- <189.67g     0
```

The above output indicates that no space is available within the volume group. Suppose, however, that we have a requirement to add 8 GB to the swap on the system. Clearly, this will require the addition of more space to the volume group. For the purposes of this example it will be assumed that a disk that is 8 GB in size and represented by */dev/sdb* is available for addition to the volume group. The first step is to turn this partition into a physical volume:

```
# pvcreate /dev/sdb
  Physical volume "/dev/sdb" successfully created.
```

If the creation fails with a message similar to "Device /dev/sdb excluded by a filter", it may be necessary to wipe the disk before creating the physical volume:

```
# wipefs -a /dev/sdb
/dev/sdb: 8 bytes were erased at offset 0x00000200 (gpt): 45 46 49 20 50 41 52 54
/dev/sdb: 8 bytes were erased at offset 0x1ffffffe00 (gpt): 45 46 49 20 50 41 52
54
/dev/sdb: 2 bytes were erased at offset 0x000001fe (PMBR): 55 aa
/dev/sdb: calling ioctl to re-read partition table: Success
```

Next, the volume group needs to be extended to use this additional physical volume:

```
# vgextend cl /dev/sdb
  Volume group "cl" successfully extended
```

At this point the *vgs* command should report the addition of the 8 GB of space to the volume group:

```
# vgs
  VG   #PV #LV #SN Attr   VSize   VFree
  cl    2   3   0 wz--n- 197.66g <8.00g
```

Now that the additional space is available in the volume group, the swap logical volume may be extended to utilize the space. First, turn off the swap using the *swapoff* utility:

```
# swapoff /dev/cl/swap
```

Next, extend the logical volume to use the new space:

```
## lvextend -L+7.9GB /dev/cl/swap
  Rounding size to boundary between physical extents: 7.90 GiB.
  Size of logical volume cl/swap changed from <3.98 GiB (1018 extents) to <11.88
GiB (3041 extents).
  Logical volume cl/swap successfully resized.
```

Re-create the swap on the logical volume:

```
# mkswap /dev/cl/swap
mkswap: /dev/cl/swap: warning: wiping old swap signature.
Setting up swapspace version 1, size = 11.9 GiB (12754874368 bytes)
no label, UUID=241a4818-e51c-4b8c-9bc9-1697fc2ce26e
```

Next, turn swap back on:

Adding and Managing CentOS 8 Swap Space

```
# swapon /dev/cl/swap
```

Finally, use the *swapon* command to verify the addition of the swap space to the system:

```
# swapon
NAME        TYPE        SIZE USED PRIO
/dev/dm-1 partition 11.9G    0B   -2
```

31.8 Summary

Swap space is a vital component of just about any operating system in terms of handling situations where memory resources become constrained. By swapping out areas of memory to disk, the system is able to continue to function and meet the needs of the processes and applications running on it.

CentOS 8 has a set of guidelines recommending the amount of disk-based swap space that should be allocated depending on the amount of RAM installed in the system. In situations where these recommendations prove to be insufficient, additional swap space can be added to the system, typically without the need to reboot. As outlined in this chapter, swap space can be added in the form of a file, disk or disk partition or by extending existing logical volumes that have been configured as swap space.

Index

Symbols

05-redhat.conf file 127
.bashrc file 63
/etc/exports file 134
/etc/fstab 29, 31
/etc/fstab file 223
/etc/yum.repos.d/ directory 72
/home directory 65
/proc/swaps file 235
.requires folder 82
.ssh 107
.wants folder 82

A

ACC Corporation 4
AMD-V 154
    checking availability 157
Apache web server 203
    configure firewall 204
    domain configuration 205
    httpd.conf file 206
    HTTPS 206, 207
    installation 203
    Secure web site 206
    SSL certificate 207
    starting 204
    testing 204
Application Stream 71
AppStream 71, 73
    modules 73
    packages 73
    profiles 73
AppStream repository 71

B

BaseOS repository 71, 72
Bash shell 57
    Aliases 61
    .bashrc file 63
    command-line editing 58
    Environment Variables 62
    filename shorthand 60
    history 59
    I/O redirection 60
    path completion 60
    pattern matching 60
    pipes 61
    shell scripts 63
basic.target 78
Boot Menu
    editing 25, 35
Bourne shell 57
buildah 191, 198
    from scratch 198
    mount 199
    run 199

C

CA 207
cat 60
CentOS 5
Certificate Authority (CA) 207
change root 189
chmod 64
chroot 189
CNI 192, 199
Cockpit
    accessing 46
    account management 49
    add disk 223
    applications 50
    cockpit-storaged 233
    create VM 161
    dashboard 52

Index

diagnostic reports 50

enabling 46

extensions 45, 50

firewall management 102

installing 46

kernel dump 51

logs 47

Multiple Servers 52

networking 48

NFS management 136

overview 45

persistent metrics 54

port 46

SELinux 51

services 50

software updates 51

storage 48

system 47

systemd units 82

terminal access 52

user management 67

virtual machines 49

virtual machines module 161

volume group management 233

cockpit-pcp 55

cockpit-storaged 233

Connection profiles 90

containerd 189

Container Networking Interface 192, 199

container runtime 189

Containers 189

  buildah 191

  build from scratch 198

  change root 189

  chroot 189

  CNI 192

  cni0 192

  containerd 189

  container runtime 189

  CRI-O 189

  Docker 189

  kernel sharing 189

  lxd 189

  networking 192

  OpenShift 191

  overview 189

  podman 191

  Podman 189

  pull image 193

  runc 191

  running image 195

  save to image 197

  skopeo 191

context labels 143

CRI-O 189

C shell 57

D

daemon 77

dd 9, 236

default.target file 80

discretionary access control 142

disk drive

  adding 219

  detecting 219

Disk partition

  formatting 34

diskutil 9

dmesg 8

dnf 20

dnf.conf file 72

DNS MX Records 215

Docker 189

dual boot 23, 31

E

Email server 211

  configuration 212

  MX Records 215

Email system

  overview 211

encryption

disk 18

env 62

Environment variables 62

EPEL 28

Errata 2

export 62

Extra Packages for Enterprise Linux 28

F

FAT16 23

FAT32 23

fdisk 31, 220, 230

Fedora Linux 5

Fedora Media Writer 10

Fedora Project 5

file system
   create 221
   mounting 222

findmnt 8

Firewall
   email settings 213
   overview 95
   web server settings 204

firewall-cmd 97
   NFS settings 134
   Samba settings 140

firewall-config 102

firewalld
   default zone 98
   display zone information 98
   firewall-cmd 97
   firewall-config 102
   ICMP rules 100
   interfaces 95, 96
   list services 99
   overview 95
   permanent settings 97
   port forwarding 101
   port rules 99
   ports 95, 97
   reload 98

   runtime settings 97
   services 95, 97
   status 97
   zone creation 100
   zone/interface assignments 100
   zones 95
   zone services 99

free 236

Free Software Foundation 4

fsck 222

Full Virtualization 154

Fuse NTFS driver 28

G

GDM 20

GNOME 3 37

GNOME Desktop 37
   installation 37
   installing the 117
   starting 37

GNOME Display Manager 20

GNU/Linux 4

Google Cloud 113

graphical.target 78

groupadd 66

groupdel 66

groups 66
   adding 66
   listing members 66
   removing 66
   wheel 66

grub 26

grub2-mkconfig 26

Guest OS virtualization 151

H

Hardware Virtualization 154

hibernation 235

history 58, 59

HOME 62

hosted hypervisors 152

Index

httpd 203

httpd.conf file 206

httpd-le-ssl.conf file 208

httpd.service 81

HTTPS 206

hypercalls 153

Hypervisor Virtualization 152

   Type-1 152

   Type-2 152

I

id_rsa 106, 107, 109

id_rsa.pub 109

installation

   disk partitioning 15

Installation

   clean disk 7

install packages

   listing 72

Intel VT 154

   checking availability 157

ip 88

   address 88

iptables 95

ISO image

   write to USB drive 8

J

journaled file system 221

K

Kdump 15

KDump 51

kernel sharing 189

KVM 157

   create VM in Cockpit 161

   hardware requirements 157

   installing 158

   kvm_amd 159

   kvm_intel 159

   libvirtd 159

   network bridge interface 175

   overview 157

   verification 158

   virsh 185

   virt-manager 158, 159

   virt-viewer 164

kvm_amd 159

kvm_intel 159

L

libvirtd 159

Linus Torvalds 4

Linux Containers. *See* Containers

Logical Extents 228

Logical Volume Management 17

   swap space 237

Logical Volumes 227, 228

   extending 232

   getting information 228

   management 227

ls 58

lvdisplay 229, 237

lvextend 232

LVM 17, 227

lxd 189

M

macOS

   writing ISO to USB drive 9

Mail Delivery Agent 212

Mail Transfer Agent 211

Mail User Agent 211

main.cf file 213

man 58

mandatory access control 142

Marc Ewing 4

Martin Hellman 105

MDA 212

metal hypervisors 153

mkfs.xfs 34

mkswap 236, 237

mount 228

MTA 211

MUA 211

multi-user.target 78

MX Records 215

N

NAT 155

native hypervisors 153

NetBIOS Name Services 146

Network Address Translation 155

network bridge interface 175

Network File System 133

NetworkManager 85

  check status 86

  Connection profiles 90

  connections 87

  devices 87

  device status 86

  enabling 86

  installing 86

  manage connections 89

  modify connections 89

  network-scripts folder 90

  nmcli 85

  nm-connection-editor 85

  nmtui 85

  permissions 94

network-scripts

  folder 90

network-scripts folder 90

NFS 133

  Cockpit management 136

  exporting filesystems 134

  firewall settings 134

  mounting filesystems 135

  starting services 133

  unmounting filesystems 135

nfs-client.target 78

NMB 146

nmcli 85, 175

basic commands 86

connection permissions 94

Connection profiles 90

interactive editing 92

manage connections 89

network bridge creation 177

permissions 94

show connections 89

Wi-Fi scan 89

nm-connection-editor 85, 180

  networked bridge interface 180

nmtui 85

NTFS 23, 28, 32

O

OpenShift 191

P

Paravirtualization 153

Partition

  mounting 34

passwd 65

PATH 62

pcp-libs 55

pcp-selinux 55

Physical Extents 228

Physical Volumes 227

  creating 231

podman 191

  attach 196

  exec 196

  list images 195

  pause 197

  ps -a 196

  rm 198

  start 197

  stop 196

  unpause 197

Podman 189

Port Forwarding 101

postfix

Index

configuration 212, 213

  installation 213

  log file 215

  main.cf file 213

  SMTP Relay Server 216

  staring 215

  testing 215

Postfix 211

poweroff.target 77

ps 61

public key encryption 105

PuTTY 110

  secure tunnel 123

PuTTYgen 111, 112

pvcreate 231

pvdisplay 230

pwd 58

Q

QEMU/KVM 159

R

RealVNC 119

reboot.target 78

Red Hat, Inc. 3

Red Hat Package Manager 72

Red Hat Support 4

Remote Desktop Access 117

  secure vs. insecure 117

remote-fs.target 78

remote installation 14

Remote Procedure Calls 133

repositories

  listing 71

Repositories 71

rescue.target 78

resize2fs 232

restorecon 144

Richard Stallman 4

root password

  specifying during installation 19

root user 1

RPC 133

rpcbind service 133

rpm 72

RPM 72

runc 191

runlevel 77

S

samba 139

Samba 139

  client 139

  configure shared resource 141

  create user 144

  discretionary access control 142

  firewall settings 140

  installing 139

  mandatory access control 142

  NetBIOS Name Services 146

  NMB 146

  samba-client 148

  SELinux 142

  smb:// 149

  smbclient 146

  smb.conf file 140

  smbpasswd 140

  testing smb.conf file 144

  workgroup 140

samba-client 139, 148

Samba Client 139

samba-common 139

SATA controller 219

Secure Socket Layer (SSL) 207

Secure web site

  configuring 206

SELinux 142

  context labels 143

  enforcing 143

  permissive 143

  restorecon 144

  Samba 142

semanage 144

    sestatus 142

    smbpasswd 144

    type enforcement 143

semanage 144

Server Message Block 139

services 77

    disable 82

    enable 81

    mask 82

    start 81

    stop 81

sestatus 142

sh 64

shadow file 67

Shell

    history 59

    overview 57

shell scripts 63

skopeo 191, 193

    get image info 193

smb:// 149

SMB 139

smbclient 146

smb.conf 144

smb.conf file 140

    [global] section 140

    testing 144

smbpasswd 140, 144

SMTP 212

SMTP Relay 212

SMTP Relay Server 216

    configuration 216

sockets.target 78

Software Updates 51

SSH 105

SSH authentication 106

    from Linux 106

    from macOS 106

    from Windows 109

    Google Cloud 113

    multiple keys 108

    PuTTY 110

    PuTTYgen 111, 112

    ssh_config file 108

    ssh-copy-id 107

    ssh-keygen 106

ssh_config.d file 127

ssh_config file 108

ssh-copy-id 107

sshd.service 108

ssh-keygen 106

SSL 207

SSL Certificate 207

startx 37, 119

stderr 61

stdin 60

stdout 60

storage devices

    identify 8

su - command 1

sudo 1, 66

sudoers file 67

Superuser 1

swapoff 236

swapoff u 239

swapon 236, 240

swap space

    add partition 237

    add swap file 236

    add to volume group 238

    current usage 235

    extend logical swap volume 237

    recommended 235

systemctl 78, 79

systemd

    default target 77

    targets 77

    units 77

systemd targets

    basic.target 78

    changing dynamically 80

Index

get default 79

graphical.target 78

list dependencies 78

multi-user.target 78

nfs-client.target 78

poweroff.target 77

reboot.target 78

remote-fs.target 78

rescue.target 78

set default 79

sockets.target 78

systemd unit

configuration files 80

disable 81

enable 81

mask 81

status 79

types 80

systemd units 77

T

targets 77

TigerVNC 119

TightVNC 123, 124

TLS 207

Transport Layer Security (TLS) 207

Type-1 virtualization 152

Type-2 virtualization 152

U

umount 8

update packages 73

updates

installing 20

USB drive

device name 8

useradd 65

userdel 65

usermod 66

users

adding and deleting 65

adding to groups 66

Users and Groups 65

V

VcXsrv 129

vgdisplay 228

vgextend 232

virsh

interactive mode 185

reboot guest 188

restore guest 187

resume guest 187

save guest 187

setmem 188

shell 185

suspend guest 187

virt-install 161

virt-manager 158, 159, 161, 165

create VM 165

start VM 168

Virtualization 151

AMD-V 154

Full Virtualization 154

Guest OS virtualization 151

Hardware Virtualization 154

hosted hypervisors 152

hypercalls 153

Hypervisor Virtualization 152

Intel VT 154

KVM 157

metal hypervisors 153

native hypervisors 153

Paravirtualization 153

virt-viewer 164

installing 164

remote SSH connection 165

VNC

connecting to server 120

firewall settings 120

secure access 121

server installation 119

server shutdown 124

    troubleshooting 124

Volume Groups 227

W

wc 61

web server 203

wheel group 66

which 58

Whitfield Diffie 105

Windows

    Disk Management tool 23

    writing ISO to USB drive 10

Windows partition

    filesystem access 28

    reclaiming 31

    resizing 23

    unmounting 31

Windows PowerShell 109

Windows SMB 133

Windows system partition 32

wipefs 231

X

X11 Forwarding 127

    compressed 128

    trusted 128

XFS file system 221

xfs_growfs 232

Y

yum.repos.d directory 72

Made in the USA
Columbia, SC
27 June 2020